The
BEST
of
Vietnamese
& Thai
Cooking

thai bird
chilies

ground
chili paste

fish
sauce

red curry
paste

thai eggplant

tamarind
pulp

egg
noodles

bean threads

wide
rice sticks

rice sticks

rice
vermicelli

clockwise from left:
rice paper, tapioca strands, and tapioca pearls

lemon grass

mung beans

fermented
soybeans

cilantro with root

tree ear
mushrooms

thai basil

clockwise from top:
star anise,
ground tumeric,
white peppercorns,
and dried chilies

black
mushrooms

saw-leaf herb

rice
paddy
herb

kaffir lime
leaves

galanga

purple
basil

mint

lemon grass

clockwise from left:
chicken satay with peanut sauce and cucumber salad;
vegetarian pad thai;
rice paper–wrapped salad rolls with vietnamese
   dipping sauce and hoisin–peanut sauce;
ginger clams and shrimp with basil;
sticky rice with fresh mango

The
BEST
of
VietNameSe
& THAI
Cooking

Favorite Recipes *from* Lemon Grass Restaurant *and* Cafes

MAI
PHAM

PRIMA PUBLISHING

PRIMA PUBLISHING and colophon are trademarks of Prima Communications, Inc.

Lemon Grass is a registered trademark of World of Good Tastes, Inc.

Cover design by Lindy Dunlavey, The Dunlavey Studio
Cover and interior photographs © 1995 by Kent Lacin

Library of Congress Cataloging-in-Publication Data

Pham, Mai.
    The best of Vietnamese & Thai cooking: favorite recipes from Lemon Grass Restaurant and Cafes / Mai Pham.
        p.   cm.
    Includes index.
    ISBN 0-7615-0016-2 (pbk.)
    1. Cookery, Vietnamese. 2. Cookery, Thai. 3. Lemon Grass Restaurant (Sacramento, Calif.) 4. Lemon Grass Cafes (Sacramento, Calif.) I. Title. II. Title: Best of Vietnamese and Thai cooking.
    TX724.5.V5P53 1995
    641.59597—dc20   95-5281
                                                       CIP

01 02 03 04 AA 10 9 8 7
Printed in the United States of America

How to Order
Single copies may be ordered from Prima Publishing, 3000 Lava Ridge Court, Roseville, CA 95661; telephone (800) 632-8676. Quantity discounts are also available. On your letterhead, include information concerning the intended use of the books and the number of books you wish to purchase.

Visit us online at www.primapublishing.com

*To my father, Xuan Pham,
and my mother, Thom Vo*

ME TOI (My Mother)

the day I was born
she adorned her tiny wrist
with a jade bracelet
she wore it proudly, solemnly
never telling anyone why or how
she was even able to
save up for something
so precious

years passed
I grew up
not knowing then
but certainly now
that she existed
to make my life
so complete and fulfilled
it would be dismal
to miss even a single day

the bracelet
she explained decades later
was a celebration of my birth
a gift of love
a symbol of endurance
a promise of commitment

today I proudly wear this bracelet
for it will always remind me
of her giving nature
her fighting spirit
and her love
she's very special all right
she's Me Toi
she's my mother

contents

IF I COULD

introduction ix

1. **HOW MOM COOKED**

   practicality, equipment, and technique 3

2. **THE QUINTESSENTIAL**

   sauces, marinades, and basic ingredients 19

3. **TWO SISTERS**

   appetizers and small dishes 57

4. **WHAT ABOUT LEMON GRASS**

   the herb and refreshing salads 81

5. **A LITTLE BIT OF HOME**

   pho bo and other soups 107

6. A TALL, KIND WOMAN

   poultry and meat dishes   125

7. THOSE FOUR DAYS

   vegetables   155

8. NEVER TASTE THE SAME

   rice and noodles   177

9. PERFECT BLACK SKIN

   fish and shellfish   201

10. DREAM ON

   desserts   231

   Glossary   253

   Index   267

acknowledgments

Several years ago, the thought of writing a cookbook while trying to run two busy restaurants was an impossible idea. It's hard enough to do just the latter. But today, thanks to the support of my family, friends, and customers, this book is finally a reality.

My gratitude goes to Prima Publishing's Jennifer Basye Sander, who first suggested this book more than seven years ago, and Ben Dominitz, for believing in it. I am thankful for their confidence and enthusiasm. To Steven Martin and the entire editorial staff, for their hard work and help in guiding me through the tedious yet rewarding experience of cookbook writing.

To Lindy Dunlavey, for her creative design touches throughout this book. I always know I'm in good hands when Lindy and her husband, Michael, are working on one of our projects, be it designing a book or a new restaurant.

I am deeply and forever grateful to all the staff at Lemon Grass Restaurant and Lemon Grass Cafes, especially Kate Griffin, Quyen Ha, Tang Nguyen, Steve Edwards, Jon O'Campo, Tony Van Reese, and Tampa Santi, for always graciously taking care of our customers while I was glued to the computer screen at home. I am lucky to have such a caring and hardworking management staff.

To the memory of Eugene Elston, who opened the first restaurant with us and worked tirelessly, even to his last day. Throughout his life, Gene always wanted to give a helping hand, even with this book. I wish he could have seen it.

To Tom and Ae Glasheen, Ed Marlow, Audre Cenedella, and Helen Burns, who spent weeks, sometimes longer, testing and retesting the recipes. I am thankful for their generous assistance as well as their patience and meticulousness.

I am grateful for the support, enthusiasm, interest, and encouragement of the thousands of loyal Lemon Grass customers. Without them I would not be cooking as long as I have.

And finally, to my husband, Trong Nguyen, the biggest cheerleader behind this and almost every major project I have encountered. Without his unconditional support and love, this book would have remained a dream.

If I Could

introduction

In 1975, when I first set foot in America after a horrifying escape from the last days of the Vietnam War, I never would have believed it if someone told me I was coming to this country to become a chef. In fact, no one in our family knew anything about what the future might hold. One minute we were in the comfort of our home in Saigon, and the next, we were fleeing our country with just the clothes on our backs.

It took a few years and some odd jobs to get over that shock. But once I decided to end my refugee predicament, I worked fast. I tore through school, trying to make up for lost time. After completing college in three years, I pursued a career in broadcast journalism, hoping to build on my earlier experiences in Saigon which, in retrospect, was rather incredible. At sixteen, I hosted a radio show for American GIs. At eighteen, I had managed to talk ABC News into giving me my first break as a television reporter. To this day I don't know how I did it. Maybe it was because I was bi-lingual. Or maybe I was at the right place at the right time. After all it was war time. But never mind that. I was beginning to feel even then that greater things were looming over the horizon.

Greater things did happen after coming to the United States. While many of my fellow Vietnamese immigrants struggled to assimilate into a new society, I was lucky enough to be working in an exciting field. In 1983, I landed a reporting job as the first Vietnamese-born television journalist in the United States. This gave me the rare opportunity to learn very much, very quickly about my newly adopted country. Just a few years before, I had been living in a refugee's quagmire. Now, I was on television every night gathering and delivering information to an audience I had just learned about. Then, after several years of reporting, I went on to work in public relations and then in government as a speech writer for the governor of California. It seems quite coincidental that

wherever I worked, I always had some kind of message to deliver. Maybe I was destined to be a messenger.

When I met my husband Trong, my life again changed dramatically. A scientist-turned-entrepreneur who had founded the successful La Bou bakery/cafe chain in Sacramento, California, Trong convinced me to open a restaurant with him. He talked about the incredible excitement and satisfaction of taking a simple idea and turning it into a successful business. Inspired by his success and encouraged by his infectious enthusiasm, I decided to give it a try. In 1988, with practically no industry experience, a do-or-die kind of commitment, and a strong belief in our unique concept, we opened Lemon Grass Restaurant. Vowing to share with Sacramento the best of Vietnamese and Thai foods, I worked night and day to adapt to a restaurant setting the recipes handed down from my mother and grandmother. I made changes here and there, seeking culinary challenge while hoping to appeal to our customers.

After the first uncertain year, Lemon Grass became a very special place. Our customers were wonderful. They came in often and knew the names of all of the staff. Appreciative of our cooking, they brought friends who in turn brought more people. Soon our clientele included regular out-of-state customers. We were ecstactic as business boomed and Lemon Grass became known as one of the best restaurants in town. I was beginning to understand what Trong said earlier about excitement.

In retrospect, there was a reason for my encounter with the restaurant. I might have stumbled into it but I was destined to do so. Even though I had been formally trained in an entirely different field, my subconscious connection to food always had been strong, even as a child.

Born in Vietnam and raised in Thailand for ten years, I was brought up with food as the center of family and universe. If feeding and nourishing is the work of love, then I grew up with incredible affection. My grandmother, who visited us every few months, would show up at the doorstep with baskets filled with live chickens, fresh mushrooms, and vegetables harvested from her garden. They were her precious gifts of love. Then my mother, sister, and I would spend the following days cutting and cooking all the foods Grandmother had brought.

When I think of my dear mother, I think of the food she prepared for us. She worked in the kitchen, from sunup to sundown, communicating her message of love in the only way she thought mattered. She cooked with joy, and when she was done, she would sit down and watch us eat.

I remember that when we all got back from work or school in the evenings, we would gather around the table to begin our nightly feast. Oftentimes my sister Denise's favorite dish—*bun thit nuong,* or grilled lemon grass beef with rice paper—was served. In the center of the table was a large plate of sliced beef. And as always there was *rau song,* or table salad—a platter filled with lettuce, mint, cucumbers, and bean sprouts. Everyone had a bowl of dipping sauce. We cooked the meat right at the table in a dome-shaped pan set on top of a portable gas stove. To savor the delicacy, we wrapped the beef, along with fresh herbs and vegetables, in rice paper before dipping it in the wonderful *nuoc mam* sauce that Denise made.

As usual during dinner, I did most of the talking and joking. Sometimes the stories were so funny that Denise couldn't stop laughing. But usually, the really great stories were saved until later, to be shared by only the two sisters at dishwashing time.

In *The Best of Vietnamese and Thai Cooking,* I have included recipes and stories that bring to life the foods I was raised with and the spirit in which they were shared. In opening Lemon Grass Restaurant, I wanted to take the best of what I learned from my mother and grandmother and blend it with my affection and appreciation for fresh, local ingredients. I wanted to share the wonderful, lively flavors of my native Vietnamese and Thai cooking, and at the same time be free to create, improvise, and build upon on what I had learned from all the years of eating and cooking. This book is a compilation of those lessons, big and small.

Some of our recipes are centuries old, some are adaptations, and others are my own creations developed on the cook line. Though created in a restaurant, all of our recipes—which take into consideration the modern demands for fresh-ness, flavors, and healthful eating—are intended for the home cook. In addition to helping you prepare tasty dishes, I hope the stories, insights, and tidbits of information nestled among the recipes will inspire you to start your own culinary adventure and see for yourself the magical powers of great food.

If I could, for a moment, believe that my recipes and stories can help liven up your table and foster the same tenderness and warmth that I remember in my own home many years ago, then I feel I have earned my biggest reward.

Thank you for letting me share my message.

—MAI PHAM

The
BEST
of
VietNameSe
& Thai
Cooking

Chapter one

How Mom Cooked

practicality, equipment, and technique

Years ago, when I was asked to develop a cooking class topic based on the inherent healthfulness of Vietnamese and Thai cuisine, I was apprehensive. I did not know if I had any substantive material or even the background to support such an undertaking. But as I got deep into the research and as I reflected upon my own experiences, I became convinced that Vietnamese- and Thai-style cooking indeed could be a healthful alternative to a modern Western diet. The typical Asian diet consists mainly of carbohydrates, vegetables, fish, and very little red meat. To stay full, we eat large portions of inexpensive foods such as rice and noodles and lots of greens, many of which grow in the wild. Meat is served only in garnish-size portions.

Consider how my mom cooked, for example. In a room no larger than 6 feet by 12 feet, her kitchen was basic and unadorned. It contained a simple little stove, a wire-screened free-standing cupboard, a one-drain sink, and a small dining table. The stove had no hood; an open space on one wall was all that allowed the occasional breeze to relieve the sometimes thick, smoky air. There was no refrigerator, freezer, oven, or dishwasher—yet the meals that came out of this traditional Vietnamese kitchen were often no less than incredible.

Every morning, usually right after the children had gone to school, but before it got too hot, my mother would walk to the nearby open-air market to fetch all the fresh ingredients for the day. For lunch, she might prepare *bun bo,* or Warm Beef on Cool Noodles as we call it at Lemon Grass. A typical meal-in-one dish, it is made with rice noodles, lettuce, mint, and cucumbers. Come lunch time, Mother would quickly stir-fry the meat and top each bowl of noodles with some. Just before eating, we would drizzle on some fish dipping sauce and then sprinkle on chopped roasted peanuts. (Both garnishes were always available in our pantry.) This incredible lunch took less than 15 minutes to prepare.

Bun bo is characteristic of Vietnamese cuisine, with its contrasting flavors and textures and herbaceous overtones. Due to history and geography Vietnamese cookery is influenced by Chinese, Indian, French, and Thai cooking. What distinguishes Vietnamese cuisine is the delicateness of its execution. For example, a Vietnamese curry is not as pungent and hot as a Thai curry, a Vietnamese stir-fry is less greasy than a Chinese stir-fry, and our bouillabaisse is generally lighter than what you would find in France. But no matter what a Vietnamese cook is creating, chances are that every dish will contain *nuoc mam,* or fish sauce. Used instead of salt or soy sauce, this seasoning staple enhances flavors and sets Vietnamese food apart from others.

Another important characteristic of Vietnamese cooking is its variety of dipping sauces. At our table, poached meats and vegetables are commonly served side by side with several dipping sauces and *rau song,* or table salad—a platter filled with lettuce, cucumbers, mint, and bean sprouts. Foods are often wrapped in lettuce or rice paper, dipped in sauce, and eaten with one's hands. Rice is served with every type of dish—soups, stews, stir-fries, and even noodle dishes.

In contrast to Vietnamese cusine, Thai food seems more homogeneously bold. While the Chinese, Malaysian, and Indian overtones are evident, the Thai repertoire is characterized by extreme flavors—fiery hot, puckeringly sour, and syrupy sweet. Curries are laced with coconut milk and are accented with chilies. Soups are perfumed by shredded kaffir lime leaves, lime juice, and fish sauce. Satays are marinated in coriander, turmeric, and lemon grass, and stir-fries are seasoned with chilies and basil almost by the cupsful.

Traditional Asian preparation and cooking techniques are dictated not only by eating habits but also by geography and economics. Meats and fish, which are generally expensive, are cut small to stretch meals. Smaller pieces of meat

also cook faster and so help conserve scarce fuel. In the hot, humid climate of the tropics where most homes have only windows to cool off the rooms, it makes sense to serve lots of salad-type dishes and foods that require little or no cooking. My grandmother would scream if she saw me roasting a leg of lamb and then turning on the air conditioner to cool down the hot kitchen.

Asian cuisine is also relatively inexpensive to prepare. With the exception of exotic elements such as shark fins, most basic ingredients are cheap and increasingly available. While no supermarkets in the West can compare to the festive atmosphere of Asia's open-air markets—where live chickens, duck, and fish are haggled over—many large grocery stores now carry basic ingredients such as fish sauce and rice noodles. Unfortunately, many lesser known items such as those listed in this chapter can be found only at Asian grocery stores.

useful tips

In preparing to cook Vietnamese and Thai food, keep a few useful tips in mind. The first step in cooking most dishes is to focus on the aromatics. Invest in a mortar and pestle to smash the aromatics—garlic, chilies, spices, lemon grass—before browning them in a little oil. This technique releases essential oils and gives food a real kick.

Be aware that heat is critical to flavor, especially with stir-fry dishes or dishes that require browning. Prawns that have been sautéed over moderate heat taste different from those cooked over a very hot fire. Make sure to heat the pan or wok thoroughly before cooking. The pan is ready when a drop of water cast on the surface sizzles and evaporates immediately.

Fresh ingredients are another requirement for great cooking. In some instances, a dried or canned ingredient will do, but main ingredients such as meat, fish, or vegetables must be of the highest and freshest quality. There can be no compromises here. At Lemon Grass, for example, I have no qualms about using commercial peanut butter to make peanut sauce, but I search far and wide to purchase the best possible lamb loin chops to go with it. Learn to think like chefs and cook with seasonal ingredients. Experiment with alternative shopping—visit ethnic grocery stores, farmers' markets, co-ops, and specialty stores.

Because vegetables and noodles play a significant role in our cuisine, be mindful of the little nuances that make a big difference. For example, many recipes in this book call for vegetables to be blanched before being added to the pan. This is an important step because some vegetables take longer to cook than other ingredients. Except in certain cases where simmering is required, stir-fry dishes should be cooked in minutes. Blanched vegetables allow you to cook quickly, before the aromatics are cooked out of the sauce, and before other ingredients have a chance to become watery. Noodles, especially rice-based ones, are fragile and must be handled with care. Take note of special precautions listed in the following chapters.

Organization is another key factor. Read the recipes thoroughly *first* and have all the ingredients ready before you begin cooking. Arrange the ingredients on a tray in the order they will be used. Most of our recipes take less than 30 minutes to cook, so you have to be organized! Before starting, envision how you want the meal to come together; before serving, have all your plates and platters warmed.

And, last, to be successful at any new cuisine, develop a thorough understanding of its basic ingredients and techniques. Arm yourself with curiosity and

actively seek knowledge through observing and doing (that's how I trained myself to be a chef). Pick a recipe you think you would enjoy and cook it several times until you have mastered it. As with learning a new language, once you have mastered a few basic rules, the rest becomes more natural.

So, with a little knowledge about the basics and a little ingenuity, curiosity, and enthusiasm, you can cook up some great Vietnamese and Thai food right in your own home!

tools and equipment

Southeast Asian cooking calls for only simple utensils—several sauté or stir-fry pans, soup/stock pots, and a couple of saucepans. In other words, you probably already own all the utensils you need to cook the recipes in this book. There are, however, a few specialized tools that I would highly recommend.

MORTAR AND PESTLE

To put it succinctly, it's impossible to create authentic Southeast Asian flavors without a mortar and pestle. When recipes call for the garlic, chilies, and spices to be pounded and smashed in a mortar, the resulting flavor will be intense and highly aromatic because the oils are released directly into the food. The flavor is far superior to that of recipes in which the aromatic ingredients are merely sliced or chopped. When purchasing a mortar, choose one at least 6 inches in diameter. To smash ingredients, pound hard and let the weight of the pestle do the work. The louder the thump, the better the flavor. Wash the mortar and pestle with mild soap, rinse, and pat dry.

RICE COOKER

Make life simple and buy a rice cooker, preferably a 12-cup version. Any brand will do, although ones with insulated inserts keep rice warm longer. To protect the special coating on the insert, always use a rubber spatula or wooden spoon. This versatile piece of equipment can also double as a steamer. Simply put a round rack on the bottom of the insert and fill with water to just below the rack. Place the food to be steamed in a shallow dish and rest it on top of the rack. For easier cleaning, always soak the insert in water to loosen any stuck rice.

WOK

Some cooks use a wok as a pan, pot, steamer, and deep-fryer all-in-one! If you're interested in serious wokking, consider purchasing one at least 14 inches in diameter, preferably made of spun steel or cast iron. A new wok should be treated or "seasoned" before using. Heat the wok and then rub oil over its surface, using a paper towel. Wipe off any excess oil. Repeat until a nice black patina has developed. To wash the wok, use very mild soap and avoid abrasive cleaning materials.

You may also want to consider purchasing a nonstick wok. Because stoves designed for home use rarely generate the level of heat necessary for cast-iron woks, a teflon-coated one may be more convenient since it requires less energy. If you have an electric stove, a flat-bottom wok is preferred since it can stand upright without a ring holder and direct contact with the heating element heats the wok faster.

FOOD PROCESSOR

Let me admit right off that at Lemon Grass, food processors are our number one friends and work horses. Life would be horrible without them. We use food

processors for the jobs we dread but must do—slicing, grinding, and chopping hundreds of pounds of lemon grass, onions, and garlic. We also use food processors to blend all of our dressings. One time our main machine broke down just as we were about to grind 200 pounds of lemon grass for the week. The kitchen staff panicked; there was talk of desertion. Luckily, I was able to run out and buy not one, but three, machines and several sets of blades. Two of them immediately went to the kitchen and the third spare sat in the back wine room, ready to jump into action if needed. Today, we also arm the kitchen with an industrial-strength food processor. You would be well served with just one good-quality food processor.

KNIVES

Cooking requires lots of chopping and cutting, and the success of these steps depends on good, sharp knives. A good knife has an even balance of weight and a firm grip. Choose one according to your personal preference—see how it feels and cuts. There are many techniques for sharpening knives, but here is one approach I find works well: Using a steel, hold the blade of the knife at about a 20-degree angle and slide it across the steel starting at the top and moving toward the covered handle. Lift and repeat, in a uniform direction and pace, five or six times on each side. Rinse the knife in water and wipe dry.

basic techniques

The most common remark I get from students is that Southeast Asian cooking is really very simple. That's true, for the most part. Once all the ingredients have been prepared and cut, the actual cooking time for most Vietnamese

and Thai dishes is 15 to 30 minutes. The distinctive flavors and colors of our cuisine result predominantly from two practices: use of interesting herbs and spices, which are added toward the very beginning and end for optimum flavor, and fast cooking, which maintains the ingredients' true character.

BRAISING/SIMMERING

Probably my favorite way of cooking, braising and simmering should start with an aromatic base. Thai curries, stews, and soups generally use this technique. With a little oil in a hot pan, add garlic and spices and stir until they sizzle and give off a wonderful aroma. Next, add the meat and sauté it in the seasonings before adding the vegetables and liquid. (Unlike stir-frying, braising requires the addition of broth or water.) Thai Green Curry with Chicken is prepared using this method and takes less than 15 minutes to cook. Braised meats are juicy and succulent and the resulting sauce is wonderful with rice and noodles.

STIR-FRYING

Stir-frying requires a wok or a good-size fry pan with high walls so that food will not spill out when the ingredients are swooshed around. The number one rule for great stir-frying is to be organized. Do what we do at Lemon Grass: Have all your ingredients and seasonings prepared, measured, and laid out on a tray in the order they are to be cooked. Have all your tools—spatulas, chop sticks, wooden spoons—ready to be used. The number two rule is to wait for the pan to get very hot before you start cooking. Cook the aromatics first by sautéing the garlic and seasonings. Then, add the remaining ingredients and quickly stir-fry. The high heat, coupled with steam produced from the vegetables, will cook the food in minutes. If the pan should get too hot, lift the wok or pan off the stove

for a few seconds. Don't reduce the heat—it may take a while for the pan to return to its original temperature, causing some of the ingredients to overcook.

STEAMING

The Chinese are partial to bamboo steamers, but the Vietnamese like the stainless steel or aluminum ones. I remember my mother occasionally used a steamer to cook fish and meatloaf-type dishes, but most of the time she used it to cook desserts. Though not as widely practiced in the Western world as in Asia, steaming is a practical cooking method since it generally uses less energy than baking, and requires no special equipment. (In fact, to save time and energy, my mother used to steam cabbage in a bowl placed directly on top of a pot of rice that was being cooked.) Although a stackable bamboo steamer set is nice to have, a wok or big soup pot will do the trick. Simply place chopsticks or a rack on the bottom of the pot over water. Place the dish with food to be steamed on the rack, and cover the pot tightly. Make sure the water doesn't boil away during cooking. Always let the steamer cool down a bit before removing the dish. Be careful as hot steam can cause painful burns!

POACHING

Poaching food may not sound exciting or impressive, but it is very practical. Because Vietnamese cuisine uses many dipping sauces, what better way to prepare meats and vegetables for those wonderful condiments than to bring out their pure character through poaching? For subtle flavor, try using an herb and/or spice-infused poaching liquid such as a chili and lemon grass–infused broth or a white wine–tomato broth, for example.

GRILLING

In Western culture, barbecuing and grilling usually take place in the summer when the weather is nice and friends and family gather to eat outdoors. But in Southeast Asia, grilling is a necessity, especially for homes that have no indoor kitchens or the luxury of kerosene-fueled stoves. I remember that when days were too hot to cook indoors, my sister and I would set up a small hibachi-style barbecue in our yard to grill small pieces of meat, fish, or prawns. The smoke had the neighbors salivating and everyone knew what we were having for dinner. Consider grilling your food, even if the weather isn't so nice and no one is coming over. Grilling requires little oil and imparts great flavor.

PAN FRYING

Halfway between deep-frying and stir-frying, pan frying is generally used to cook whole fish or larger pieces of meat. This method produces a wonderful, crispy exterior. Use a deep-fry pan and just enough oil to barely cover the items to be cooked. The oil should be hot, about 350 degrees, before placing the food in the pan. Otherwise, the food may get soggy and greasy.

DEEP-FRYING

If you follow some basic rules, deep frying also can produce wonderful, crispy foods without being overly greasy. Use only a flat-bottom wok or a heavy, deep saucepan when deep frying. (Both are stable and have large cooking surfaces.) Work at a well-ventilated stove and have a splatter screen on hand to avoid burns caused by sputtering oil. Use any good-quality oil such as vegetable, peanut, canola, safflower, or corn oil. Avoid olive oil because its fruitiness can overwhelm the natural flavor of foods. Before deep frying, always preheat your wok or pan, and allow the oil to slowly heat up to about 375 degrees before cooking. To test the temperature, snip off a piece of the ingredient to cook and drop it into the oil. If it sizzles and floats to the surface immediately, the oil is hot enough. Bring foods to room temperature before deep-frying and do not overcrowd the pan. Have utensils ready such as slotted spoons, tongs, and chopsticks. Set out paper towels for draining the fried food.

an com ngon

BON APPÉTIT

If there is one ingredient on which the cuisines of Vietnam and Thailand are built, it is rice. Not only is rice at the heart of our cooking, but it seems to symbolize powers beyond food. I remember my uncles and aunts who were rice farmers talking about their fortunes in terms of good or bad rice harvests. In our home town, My Tho, the local economy centered on rice harvests. If it was a good year for rice, commodity prices were stable and the economy saw a boost. But if a bad monsoon struck or war activities depressed the production of rice, the economy would suffer and commodity prices would skyrocket.

As a child I was taught that rice symbolizes life and well-being. Nourishing and healing, rice gives strength. If you are sick and weak, you eat rice to get better. Admittedly, at a young age, I had learned to respect this notion through a scary fable. I was always told by my mother that for every grain of rice

I threw away, I would have to eat as many worms in hell to make up for my sins. Believing that, I never left a grain of rice in my bowl until, of course, when I got a little older.

Eating rice is also part of sharing and partying. In fact, all one has to say to affectionately extend a dinner invitation is *"an com!"* in Vietnamese or *"kin kao"* in Thai. "Eat rice" says it all.

So how does this relate to planning a meal? Simple. Do what my family does and plan all meals around rice. Even when noodles are served, rice is offered since a meal is not considered complete without it. To Asians, a good, simple, and balanced meal consists of lots of rice and at least three dishes that offer striking yet harmonizing flavors such as salty, sweet, sour, spicy, and bitter. A good example of a meal incorporating such different tastes would be a grilled dish such as Lemon Grass Beef with Rice Paper. Pieces of beef, lettuce, mint, and an assortment of vegetables are wrapped in rice paper, then dipped in *nuoc cham,* or Vietnamese fish dipping sauce. The wrapping, the dipping sauce, and the ever-present *rau song,* or table salad, are the essence of Vietnamese cooking. Another example would be the slightly salty and spicy Mom's Catfish in Claypot balanced with the fragrantly sweet and sour Vietnamese Fisherman's Soup and accompanied by a mild but delicious Su Co's Delight. Planning a meal requires some thought. Too much of the same taste is not balanced. For example, if the main entrée is garlicky, perhaps the other dishes should not be. If one dish is very spicy, the accompanying dishes should be neutral and soothing.

For a traditional treat, serve all dishes at the same time and place the serving platters in the center of the table so diners can help themselves. (The recipes in this book are designed to be served with one to two or three other dishes.) Make sure every guest has his or her own bowl of dipping sauce. For a more Western and formal approach, present food on individual, "composed" plates. Since Vietnamese cuisine is quite delicate and Thai cooking is bold, I have found them to be complementary. So feel free to serve a Vietnamese appetizer followed by a Thai meal and vice versa. It's quite delightful.

As for beverages, the Vietnamese typically drink tea and beer during meals. In traditional Asian dining, the notion of pairing wine with a particular dish is quite frankly not an issue. Since no grape wines are produced locally and alcohol consumption is limited to festive occassions, the interest in blending wine with food is practically non-existent. The pleasure of dining is in the overall experience—the variety of dishes and the juxtaposition of the different textures, flavors, and colors. Identifying a single wine that would complement a family-style meal in which three to five dishes are served simultaneously—or a banquet in which a dozen or more dishes are offered—would be difficult, to say the least.

Am I saying forget wine? Absolutely not. Having experienced the pleasure of sipping wine, I must admit that there is definitely a place for this Western beverage at the Thai or Vietnamese table. Though it becomes difficult to select one wine appropriate for a meal with multiple courses, it is possible if the pairings are made to complement the main dishes only. At Lemon Grass, most dishes are served as separate courses, so the wine selection becomes rather simple. Our grilled lamb chops with peanut sauce are frequently ordered with merlot or cabernet sauvignon, and fish is served with light-bodied chardonnays as well as fumé and sauvignon blancs.

In the summer, the malty, full-bodied Asian beers such as Singha, Tsingtao, and Saigon seem to fly out of the bar alongside orders of rice-paper

wrapped salad rolls or chicken satays. Champagnes, gewürztraminers, and Rieslings also complement the foods we serve at Lemon Grass. The traditional method of pairing wines with food—reds for red meats and whites for white meats—seems safe until you get to the spicy, highly flavored sauces that may accompany them. In that case, it might be wiser to try to pair the wine with the sauce.

But the enjoyment of wine with food is really just a matter of personal taste. Drink whatever pleases your palate, and remember, the overall experience is what's important. *An com ngon,* or, *bon appétit!*

Chapter two

The Quintessential

sauces, marinades, and basic ingredients

To understand a cuisine, it is imperative to understand the various sauces that make it unique. In Vietnamese and Thai cooking, no sauce is as important and as quintessential as fish sauce. Called *nuoc mam* in Vietnamese and *nam pla* in Thai (literal translation: fish water), fish sauce has no substitute. Made from fish and salt, it is used much like soy sauce is. With a sprinkle here and there, fish sauce gives Vietnamese and Thai cuisine a complexity found in no other cuisine. Once available only at Asian grocery stores, the sauce is now on the shelves of many supermarkets.

Although the recipe varies from one manufacturer to another, fish sauce generally is produced by drying anchovies in the sun for a few hours, then layering the fish alternately with salt in earthenware vats. After that fermentation process, the liquid is siphoned and transferred into ceramic urns to sit for several months to allow the flavor to develop. When it is ready for bottling, water and, in some cases, caramel are added. The first siphoning is highly prized and is reserved for dipping sauces. The second pressing is used for cooking. The art of making fish sauce is treated almost like national security, and the debate is endless over such questions as the superiority of certain brands, the season in which the anchovies have richer oils, and even the types of urns used for the most full-bodied flavor.

I remember my mother sending me to the store for a liter of Phu Quoc fish sauce made by a famous manufacturer on an island southwest of Vietnam. I would take a clean glass bottle and ask our neighborhood shopkeeper to fill it up. Using a ladle made from a bamboo stick attached to a hollowed-out coconut shell half, she lowered it into a crusty urn filled with fish sauce. Then, she carefully ladled the sauce through a funnel into the bottle. On days when she was in a good mood, she poured in a little extra. Excited about the freebie, I grabbed the bottle and ran home, eager to break the news to my mother.

Today fish sauce is no longer stored in urns, at least not the ones imported to this country. Bottled in glass and plastic containers (the former is generally better), fish sauce has two main uses—to season food during cooking and to make dipping sauces. But there are two golden rules to remember: One, never, *ever*, serve fish sauce straight from the bottle—you must dilute it to make a dipping sauce. Two, never add fish sauce to a hot, dry pan while cooking. Sprinkle it only into foods that have liquids; otherwise, the smell will be overpowering and your friends will leave before dinner is ready.

Since dipping sauces made from fish sauce are critical to Vietnamese and Thai cooking, it is important to know there are three main styles—light, heavy, and flavored. *Nuoc cham*, the Vietnamese dipping sauce, is a typical, light version consisting of fish sauce that has been diluted with water and accented with garlic, chilies, lime juice, and sugar. (You can make a dipping sauce from soy sauce the same way.) *Nam pla prik*, a Thai dipping sauce, is a heavier, more pungent, undiluted version made with lime juice, garlic, and lots of hot chilies. The flavored sauces give a twist to the dipping sauce repertoire. In the Ginger-Lime Dipping Sauce, the freshly grated ginger adds a wonderful, refreshing spiciness and aroma. Use a flavored dipping sauce to enhance the overall balance of a dish, especially one in which the main meat or vegetables are not overly seasoned. The amount of fish sauce to use depends entirely upon personal taste. As with salt, always start with a sprinkling or two, and add more if necessary.

Besides *nuoc mam,* a number of other basic ingredients, sauces, and marinades are necessary for Vietnamese and Thai cooking. Instead of making multiple trips to the store, consider stocking your pantry with the essential ingredients. That way, you will be more inclined to undertake Thai and Vietnamese cooking.

The asterisked items listed below are ingredients that you *must* have to recreate the authentic flavors of Southeast Asia. Note that more common items such as fish sauce and rice noodles often can be found at any large supermarket.

Bean sauce Made from fermented soy beans, water, and salt, this sauce comes as whole beans or a purée. I prefer the whole beans sold in jars marketed under Koon Chun. Bean sauce is salty, so use sparingly. It's wonderful when used to jazz up Thai noodle stir-fry dishes.

Chicken stock Though not an exotic item, this one ingredient distinguishes restaurant cooking from home cooking. Chicken stock is used as a base for soups and is added to sauté and stir-fry dishes that need a little liquid to help cook the ingredients. Many recipes in this book call for unsalted chicken stock. If you don't have fresh stock, canned low-sodium chicken stock works well too. At Lemon Grass, we make stock out of just chicken bones and water and nothing else. To make stock, remove the skin and all visible fat from chicken bones. Place in a large soup pot, cover with water, and simmer for 1 hour. Skim the surface often to remove impurities. Strain before using. If you would rather not make stock, always have canned low-sodium chicken stock on hand. Chicken bouillon is not a good substitute. If you must use bouillon, make sure to reduce the salt or fish sauce called for in the recipe.

Coconut milk* In Southeast Asia and other parts of the tropics where cows' milk and other dairy products are practically non-existent, *nuoc dua* (Vietnamese) or *nam gati* (Thai), or coconut milk, becomes the obvious substitute. Made from grated coconut meat and water, it enriches soups, curries, stews, roasts, beverages, and desserts. In Thailand, coconut milk is especially important in curries, imparting a richness and sweetness that complement the spiciness. In Vietnam, its use in savory dishes is less frequent, although its role is significant in desserts and puddings. In Asia, one buys freshly grated coconut meat at the market and then squeezes the milk from it at home. Of course, no coconut milk is as good as that made fresh, but several acceptable canned versions are available. The Chaokoh or Chef's Choice brand, sold in 14-ounce or 7-ounce cans, is consistently good. In many traditional curry recipes, the thick, creamy part of the coconut milk is scooped off the top and used as an oil for stir-frying spices. Keep in mind that the coconut milk called for in Thai recipes refers to the unsweetened kind, not the sweetened one used in piña coladas. If coconut milk is not available, substitute cows' milk.

Fish sauce* Discussed extensively above, *nuoc mam,* or fish sauce, is the most important ingredient in this cuisine. Like soy sauce, this salty fish extract is used to season food or make dipping sauces. Purchase fish sauce packed in glass bottles. Brands such as Squid and Viet Huong are consistently good. Wipe the opening of the bottle clean after each use and store in the refrigerator or the cool part of a cupboard. Fish sauce will last up to two to three years with no noticeable change. If you see pieces resembling crushed glass at the bottom of your bottle, don't panic. Fish sauce that has been sitting around tends to develop salt crystals.

Five-spice powder This fine brown powder is made from a blend of star anise, fennel, cinnamon, ginger, and orange peel. Lending a licorice, woodsy fragrance, this spice combination is great in marinades, especially for roast ducks, stews, and vegetarian dishes. This powder, which can vary from one brand to another, is sold in cellophane bags.

Galanga* Called *kha,* and also known as Thai ginger, galanga is a cousin of ginger. Its unique, earthy, gingery flavor is used in soups, curries, and stir-fries. Available fresh, frozen, or dried (don't bother with the latter), galanga is easy to use. Without peeling, just cut off thin slices and add to the pan. The flavor of galanga is best captured when added at the last minute of cooking.

Since galanga is available only at Asian grocery stores, buy it fresh or frozen, and store it in your freezer.

Ginger At Lemon Grass Restaurant, *gung,* or ginger, is used almost as extensively as garlic. Sharp and pungent, ginger adds extraordinary flavor and zing to food, from savory dishes to desserts. We normally peel the ginger, then finely grate it, and add as we would minced garlic. When you throw garlic, ginger, and chilies into a very hot pan, what follows is almost guaranteed to be wonderful.

Green curry paste* If you like Thai curries as much as I do, the good news is they are quite easy to make if you keep green curry paste on hand. Although nothing compares to a curry made from freshly roasted spices and herbs, store-bought *gaeng keow wan* or green curry paste is quite excellent. (Note that Thai cooks rarely make their own curry pastes.) Made with green chilies, lemon grass, garlic, galanga, shallots, and shrimp paste, green curry paste greatly enhances meat, fish, or vegetables. Though they are among the mildest pastes, green curries are generally embellished with fresh green chilies. Use curry paste sparingly, however. Buy small 8-ounce tubs since you rarely need more than 2 tablespoons at a time. For better flavor, refrigerate the paste after opening. If you're going to stock only one kind of Thai curry paste, buy this one.

Ground chili paste* Made from ground red chilies, garlic, and vinegar, this ingredient is a must. Although you can substitute dried or fresh chilies, a little jar of chili paste will go a long way when you need to cook up something spicy in a pinch. A stir-fry that starts with oil, chili paste, and garlic is on solid ground. Sold in small plastic jars, chili paste will keep almost indefinitely.

Hoisin sauce* Made from soybean purée, sugar, and caramel sauce, hoisin sauce is used primarily in dipping sauces, marinades, and stir-fries. When mixed with onions, garlic, chilies, vinegar, and crushed peanuts, this sauce is incredibly delicious. Never serve hoisin sauce straight from the can, not even with moo-shoo pork! Break away from that tradition and you will see that this sauce was never meant to be eaten out of the can! Hoisin sauce (try Koon Chun) is available in a can or glass jar.

Jasmine rice* Although there are countless varieties, all rice can be categorized as either long-grain or short-grain. In Southeast Asian cooking, *gao thom*, the aromatic long-grain "jasmine" rice, is preferred. Similar in texture and fragrance to basmati rice, jasmine rice sold in the United States is imported primarily from Thailand and Vietnam. Depending on the batch and the season in which it was harvested, jasmine rice ranges from very fragrant to not very distinguishable. There are no strict rules to cooking rice, but I have found the 1-to-1½ rice/water ratio works best. However, the more rice used, the less water is needed. Our Vietnamese cooks once taught an American sous chef to put in enough water to just touch the first knuckle joint of his finger. Well, the rice got a bit too soggy—his Western finger was too long—and we decided from then on to measure all rice and water before cooking. We've never had a problem since then. For instructions on cooking jasmine rice, please refer to pages 50–51.

Fortunately, jasmine rice is now available at large supermarkets. Not too long ago, it was sold only at Asian grocery stores in 10-, 25-, or 50-pound bags and was available in twenty different brands—the ideal amounts and choices for Asian families. Remember what I said about rice earlier?

Kaffir lime leaves* These jade-green citrus leaves impart a heavenly, lemony aroma that is positively addicting. Used extensively to flavor and liven up curries, soups, and stir-fries, *bai makrut*, or kaffir lime leaves, are picked off wild lime trees. The leaf resembes a figure 8. In Thailand, they are chopped and put into soups and curries or cut into thin slivers and added to stir-fries or fish cakes. Kaffir lime leaves are somewhat difficult to find, especially in communities with small Asian populations, but they are well worth the effort. (In fact, I like them so much I brought some seeds back from Thailand one year and started my own little kaffir lime orchard in our greenhouse.) Look for frozen or dried leaves, which are usually packed in small plastic bags. If you are lucky enough to find them frozen, buy a few bags to throw in your freezer. The dried leaves must be soaked in hot water before using. If not available, substitute lime zest.

Lemon grass* Known as *xa* in Vietnamese and *takrai* in Thai, lemon grass is a common herb used for two main purposes—to infuse a sauce, soup, or curry and to marinate meats and fish. Its lemony and gingery aroma enhances and complements the flavor of almost every ingredient it touches. For an extensive discussion on this herb and its methods of handling and preparation, please see pages 83–84.

Oyster sauce* Made from oyster extract, caramel sauce, and soy sauce, this thick, brown sweet-salty sauce is used to enhance stir-fries, especially those with beef. Its velvety texture is particularly useful in marinades because the gentle coating seals in flavor and keeps the meat moist and supple after cooking. Packaged in bottles and tins, oyster sauce is now available in a vegetarian version. Look for brands that are MSG-free. I have found products made by Lee Kum Kee and Panda to be consistently good.

Peanuts As a child, I loved to snack on boiled or roasted *dau phong*, or peanuts. When roasted and pounded into a coarse meal, peanuts make a delicious garnish for both savory dishes and desserts. The Thais use them in curries, salads, and satays. Keep roasted peanuts on hand to grind in a spice mill when needed for garnishes. If you want to roast the peanuts yourself, buy the shelled, skinless ones at an Asian grocery store and either bake or dry roast in a pan over low heat. Many recipes in this book call for a garnish of chopped peanuts.

Red curry paste Available in plastic tubs or cans, red curry paste is made like green curry paste, except that roasted dried red chilies are substituted for green chilies. The smoky flavor of roasted dried red chilies stands up particularly well against red meats such as beef or lamb. The Mae Ploy brand is quite good.

Rice noodles* The most important noodles in our cuisine are those made from rice flour, called *banh pho* in Vietnamese or *sen* in Thai. Categorized as either flat or round, these noodles, which are also called rice sticks, are available fresh or dried. (For practical purposes, I prefer dried.) Most popular are the dried, flat, fettucine-like noodles made from rice flour, water, and salt. Flat rice noodles are distinguished by width— small, medium, or large. The first two sizes are used primarily in soups, and the widest noodles are used in stir-fries such as *rad na*. The round variety, also called rice vermicelli, is known as *bun* in Vietnamese or *sen mee* in Thai. Round noodles are used in salad-style dishes and in soups.

Traditionally, rice noodles are soaked in water before using. I prefer blanching them, which removes the sometimes strong rice flour odor.

Rice paper* No other cuisine uses the paper-thin *banh trang* wrapper quite like the Vietnamese. Made from rice flour, water, and salt, rice paper wrappers are used to make spring rolls and to wrap small pieces of meat and fish to be eaten with the hands. To use, rice paper must be soaked in warm water to become pliable. Packaged and sold in 6-inch, 10-inch, and 12-inch rounds, rice paper is particularly desirable when you want a wrapper that does not compete with the taste or texture of your filling. Rice paper will keep for months if the package is resealed tightly. Look for a nice whitish color, an even thickness, and no broken pieces (a sign of brittleness). I prefer the Elephant or Butterfly brand.

Sesame oil Made from roasted sesame seeds, this rich, nutty oil is not used for cooking but instead to flavor salads, stir-fries, soups, rice, and dumplings. Sesame oil is graded similarly to olive oil (it has first and second pressings, for example). I prefer Japanese-style sesame oil, either Kadoya or Marukan brand, to Chinese-style.

Shallots In a Vietnamese or Thai kitchen, shallots—not onions—are considered one of the most important ingredients. Considered more aromatic than its common onion cousin, shallots are roasted then pounded in a mortar along with lemon grass, chilies, and other spices to make curry pastes or marinades. In addition, a favorite Vietnamese garnish is fried shallot rings. If you don't have shallots, substitute onions.

Soy sauce* No soy sauce is created equal. My soy sauce collection runs the gamut: all-purpose Japanese Kikkoman; light Thai-style Golden Mountain brand; sweet soy sauce (dark soy and caramel sauce) for rich, dark color; Chinese-style dark soy sauce containing molasses; and varied soy sauces that are generally mushroom- or onion-based. Buy soy sauce in small glass containers, and make sure the mouth of the bottle is wiped clean after each use.

Spring roll wrappers Also used for *lumpia* (the Filipino version of spring rolls), these wrappers are thin cream-colored sheets made with wheat flour. Although the traditional spring roll recipe calls for rice paper, these wrappers are easier to work with and create a less greasy product when fried. Sold in 1-pound packages, these 8-inch square sheets can be found in the frozen food department of any Asian grocery store.

Star anise As beautiful as it is fragrant, this six- to eight-pointed star spice (also known as *hoi* in Vietnamese) imparts a flavor resembling cinnamon and cloves. Used to flavor soups (especially Vietnamese beef noodle) and stews, this spice is sold in clear cellophane bags. I always transfer the spice to a beautiful glass jar to show it off in the kitchen.

Tamarind Called *me* in Vietnamese, this sour fruit is used to flavor soups and salads. Tamarind usually is sold in a syrupy liquid form or in dried blocks. To make tamarind juice, mix about 3 ounces of tamarind pulp with $1/2$ cup hot water and let sit for 30 minutes. Push mixture through a sieve and discard the pulp. Tamarind may be substituted with lemon or lime juice mixed with a dash of brown sugar.

Vietnamese-style curry powder Vietnamese curry powder is similar to Madras-style curry powder. Sold in plastic jars or small 5-ounce bags (and sometimes mixed with curry or bay leaves), this curry powder is used not only for curries, but to spice up stir-fries and soups.

Yellow curry paste The "Indian" version of Thai curry, yellow curry paste is the mildest of all, and in my opinion, has many uses. Made with ingredients similar to green and red curry pastes, yellow curry paste includes turmeric, which gives it a beautiful golden color. Yellow curry greatly enhances fish, chicken, or vegetarian dishes. In addition to curries and stews, curry pastes also can be used to make sauces for topping grilled meats and fish.

vietnamese dipping sauce

MAKES 1½ CUPS

If you know only one thing about Vietnamese cuisine, know that nuoc cham *is the single most important table sauce. Slightly sweet and sour, this fish dipping sauce is served with almost every dish.*

According to my sister Denise, a self-proclaimed fish dipping sauce master, the difference between mediocrity and greatness is in the lime pulp. Every time she made nuoc cham, *Denise not only would squeeze every drop of juice from the limes, but she also would scrape out every bit of pulp. Even though everyone has his or her secret method, the truth is, the proportion of ingredients is what distinguishes one recipe from another. In the northern part of Vietnam, or so Southern gossip has it, the dipping sauce is rather bland—just a little water has been added to the fish sauce. As you come down to the Central region, a few chilies have been added. Then, as you approach the gastronomic South, the least you can expect is a lively concoction of fresh chilies, smashed garlic, sugar, lime juice, and lime pulp—all garnished with fine slivers of carrots and thinly sliced chili peppers. This is Denise's recipe (yes, it's the Southern version). It will keep for 1 month if refrigerated.*

2 SMALL CLOVES GARLIC, SLICED

1 TEASPOON GROUND CHILI PASTE

1 FRESH THAI BIRD CHILI, CHOPPED (OPTIONAL)

¼ CUP FISH SAUCE

⅔ CUP HOT WATER

2 TABLESPOONS FRESH LIME JUICE WITH PULP

¼ CUP SUGAR

2 TABLESPOONS SHREDDED CARROTS FOR GARNISH

Place garlic, chili paste, and chili in a mortar. With a pestle, pound into a paste. If you do not have a mortar and pestle, finely mince the garlic and chili.

Combine the garlic mixture with the remaining ingredients in a small mixing bowl. Stir until the sugar has dissolved. Ladle sauce into serving bowls and float the carrot slivers on top.

> Every Vietnamese mother (and sister) makes this sauce differently. I insist that mine is made with fresh, smashed Thai bird chilies, definitely with lime pulp, not too diluted with water, and a little sweet.

thai chili dipping sauce

MAKES ABOUT 1/2 CUP

Nam pla prik, *the Thai version of Vietnamese dipping sauce, is much more potent, pungent, and hot. There are dozens of versions—if not more—but this basic recipe goes well with everything.*

6 TO 8 FRESH THAI BIRD CHILIES, OR 4 JALAPEÑOS, CHOPPED
1 CLOVE GARLIC, FINELY MINCED
2 TABLESPOONS FRESH SQUEEZED LIME JUICE
1/4 CUP FISH SAUCE

Combine all ingredients in a sauce bowl. Serve as a dipping sauce or an accompaniment to noodle or rice dishes. Sauce will keep up to 3 weeks if refrigerated in an airtight container.

My favorite season to make nam pla prik *is the summer, when Thai bird chilies are abundant, inexpensive, and, better yet, available in yellow, green, and red. To me, the best part of this sauce is the marinated chilies.*

ginger-lime dipping sauce

MAKES 2/3 CUP

Some of our very best customers say this is the best sauce they've ever tasted. Tangy, spicy, and cleanly flavored, this sauce is great with steamed chicken or duck, or with pan-fried fish and grilled meats.

2 CLOVES GARLIC, SLICED
2 FRESH THAI BIRD OR ANY CHILIES, CHOPPED AND/OR
1 TEASPOON GROUND CHILI PASTE
2 TABLESPOONS VERY FINELY MINCED FRESH GINGER
1/4 CUP FISH SAUCE
2 TABLESPOONS FRESH LIME JUICE, PREFERABLY WITH PULP
1/4 CUP WATER
4 TABLESPOONS SUGAR

Place the garlic, chilies, chili paste, and ginger in a mortar and pound into a paste. Transfer to a mixing bowl and add the remaining ingredients and mix until well blended. Transfer to a glass jar and cover with a tight lid. If refrigerated sauce will keep up to 3 weeks.

My mother would make this sauce whenever she could buy fresh oc gao, or periwinkles. My sister and I would get excited because we got to climb the guava tree to pick the leaves for steaming the periwinkles. To eat, we carefully poked the meat with a toothpick, pulled it out while turning the shell, and dipped it in the sauce. I remember the meat being sweet and crunchy and the sauce being absolutely wonderful.

hoisin-peanut sauce

MAKES 2 CUPS

Probably one of the most versatile sauces in the Lemon Grass repertoire, this sauce is served with our signature, Rice Paper–wrapped Salad Rolls. When mixed with garlic, chilies, and ginger, it's spectacular on grilled fish, chicken, or beef. It's also wonderful as a marinade!

1 CUP HOISIN SAUCE

1/2 CUP WATER

1/4 CUP RICE WINE VINEGAR

1/3 CUP PURÉED OR FINELY MINCED YELLOW ONION

1 TABLESPOON GROUND CHILI PASTE, OR TO TASTE

1 TABLESPOON CHOPPED ROASTED PEANUTS FOR GARNISH (PAGE 55)

Put first four ingredients into a small saucepan and bring to a boil. Reduce heat and let simmer for 5 to 7 minutes. Add a little water if too thick. Set aside to cool. Transfer mixture to a sauce dish and garnish with chili paste and chopped peanuts.

In the ancient imperial capital of Hue, located in the central region of Vietnam, this sauce is sometimes made with coconut milk and chopped pineapples. The taste is obviously richer, but the tartness of the pineapple balances it quite well. I prefer this version with Grilled Shrimp Paste on Sugar Cane (pages 214–215).

cilantro-lime soy sauce

MAKES ABOUT ⅔ CUP

Using soy sauce as the base, the smashed ginger, chilies, garlic, and lime juice make this sauce remarkably memorable. Use as a dipping sauce for roast duck, soft-shell crab, and steaks, or drizzle it over rice.

1 CLOVE GARLIC

2 FRESH THAI BIRD CHILIES AND/OR

1 TEASPOON GROUND CHILI PASTE, OR TO TASTE

1 (1-INCH) PIECE FRESH GINGER, PEELED AND THINLY SLICED

2 TABLESPOONS FINELY CHOPPED FRESH CILANTRO

¼ CUP SOY SAUCE

2 TABLESPOONS FRESH LIME JUICE WITH PULP

3 TABLESPOONS WATER

2 TABLESPOONS SUGAR

Place the garlic, chilies, chili paste, and ginger in a mortar and pound into a paste. Transfer paste into a glass jar with a tight-fitting lid and add the remaining ingredients. Mix well until sugar is dissolved. To serve, pour into small ramekins. Sauce may be stored in the refrigerator up to 2 weeks.

basic curry sauce

MAKES 2 CUPS

This recipe works with either Thai- or Indian-style curry pastes. I have used red, green, and yellow curry pastes, and they are all excellent. I prefer yellow or green, which complement most meats, especially seafood and chicken. Use this sauce as a base for curry stews, or use to top grilled dishes.

1 TABLESPOON VEGETABLE OIL
1 SHALLOT, MINCED
1 CLOVE GARLIC, MINCED
1 TABLESPOON YELLOW CURRY PASTE
1 CUP UNSWEETENED COCONUT MILK
1 CUP CHICKEN STOCK OR WATER
2 TABLESPOONS FISH SAUCE
2 TABLESPOONS SUGAR
PINCH GROUND TURMERIC

Heat the oil in a small saucepan over moderate heat. Add the shallot, garlic, and curry paste and allow to sizzle for 15 to 20 seconds. Stir in about 3 tablespoons of the coconut milk. Allow to bubble for 1 minute, and add the remaining coconut milk, stock, fish sauce, sugar, and turmeric. Stir again and let simmer for 5 minutes. Remove from heat and set aside until ready to use.

If sauce is too thick, add a little water. If too thin, add a little cornstarch and water. To prepare this thickener, mix 2 tablespoons cornstarch to ⅓ cup water. Drizzle just enough thickener into sauce, stirring constantly, until it thickens slightly.

green curry paste

MAKES ABOUT 1 CUP

Sometimes when the rain keeps me indoors and I feel like cooking, I make Thai curries from scratch. Although store-bought pastes work well too, homemade curries are highly aromatic, especially if made with fresh coconut milk. Once you have made the paste, divide it into 2-tablespoon portions and freeze for later use. You rarely need more than that amount at a time. A mortar and pestle is necessary to make this paste.

1 TEASPOON CUMIN SEEDS

1 TABLESPOON CORIANDER SEEDS

3 WHITE PEPPERCORNS, OR 1 TEASPOON GROUND WHITE PEPPER

1 MODERATELY HOT FRESH GREEN CHILI (SUCH AS PASILLA OR HATCH), QUARTERED

6 FRESH GREEN CHILIES (ANY KIND), CHOPPED

4 CLOVES GARLIC, SLICED

4 SHALLOTS, SLICED

1/4 CUP MINCED LEMON GRASS

1 TABLESPOON THINLY SLICED GALANGA

1/4 CUP CHOPPED FRESH CILANTRO, INCLUDING STEMS, LEAVES, AND ROOTS

1 TEASPOON FRESH LIME ZEST

1 TEASPOON SHRIMP PASTE (OPTIONAL)

2 TEASPOONS SALT

1 TABLESPOON VEGETABLE OIL

Place a small sauté pan over low heat and add the cumin and coriander seeds. Shake and brown the seeds until lightly toasted, about 2 to 4 minutes. Transfer to a small bowl. In the same pan, roast the peppercorns in the same manner. Add the roasted peppercorns to the bowl with the seeds. Place the quartered green chilies in the pan and roast lightly until dark spots begin to appear. (Do not let them blacken.) Set aside. Roast the chopped chilies, garlic, and shallots (one item at a time) in the same manner. Set aside.

Using a mortar and pestle or spice mill, grind the roasted cumin, coriander, and peppercorns and set aside. In the mortar, place the roasted chilies and the remaining ingredients except for oil and pound into a fine paste. Combine the paste with the ground roasted spices and oil and mix until smooth. If not kept in the freezer, paste will last for about 2 weeks in the refrigerator.

yellow curry paste

MAKES ABOUT 1 CUP

In this recipe, almost every ingredient is the same as in green curry paste, but roasted red chilies are substituted for green and turmeric is added.

1 TEASPOON CUMIN SEEDS

1 TABLESPOON CORIANDER SEEDS

3 WHITE PEPPERCORNS, OR 1 TEASPOON GROUND WHITE PEPPER

1/4 CUP SMALL DRIED RED CHILIES, SPLIT AND SEEDED

4 CLOVES GARLIC, SLICED

4 SHALLOTS, SLICED

1 TABLESPOON GROUND TURMERIC

1 TABLESPOON GALANGA, THINLY SLICED

1/4 CUP MINCED LEMON GRASS

1 TEASPOON FRESH LIME ZEST

1 TEASPOON SHRIMP PASTE (OPTIONAL)

1 TEASPOON SALT

1 TABLESPOON VEGETABLE OIL

Place a small sauté pan over low heat and add the cumin and coriander seeds. Shake and brown the seeds until lightly toasted, about 2 to 4 minutes. Transfer to a small bowl. Place the peppercorns in the same pan and roast in the same manner. Remove the peppercorns and add to the small bowl. Then place the red chilies in the pan and roast very lightly until dark spots begin to appear. (Do not let them blacken.) Remove from heat and set aside. Roast the garlic and shallots (one item at a time) in the same manner and set aside.

Using a mortar and pestle or spice mill, grind the roasted cumin, coriander, and peppercorns and set aside. Place the roasted chilies in the mortar and pound until fine. Add the remaining ingredients except for oil and pound into a fine paste. Combine the paste with the ground roasted spices and oil, and blend together until smooth. Paste is now ready for use. To store, divide into 2-tablespoon portions and place inside sealable plastic bags and freeze. Paste will keep up to 3 months.

red curry paste

MAKES ABOUT 1 CUP

The roasted red chilies add richness and complexity to this paste. Red curry is especially good with beef and lamb.

1 TEASPOON CUMIN SEEDS

1 TABLESPOON CORIANDER SEEDS

3 WHITE PEPPERCORNS, OR 1 TEASPOON GROUND WHITE PEPPER

1/2 CUP SMALL DRIED RED CHILIES, SPLIT AND SEEDED

4 CLOVES GARLIC, SLICED

4 SHALLOTS, SLICED

2 TABLESPOONS PAPRIKA

1 TABLESPOON GALANGA, THINLY SLICED

3 TABLESPOONS LEMON GRASS

1 TEASPOON FRESH LIME ZEST

1 TEASPOON SHRIMP PASTE (OPTIONAL)

1 TEASPOON SALT

1 TABLESPOON VEGETABLE OIL

Place a small sauté pan over low heat and add the cumin and coriander seeds. Shake and brown the seeds until lightly toasted, about 2 to 4 minutes. Transfer to a small bowl. Place the peppercorns in the pan and roast in the same manner. Remove and add to the roasted seeds. Place the red chilies in the same pan and roast very lightly until dark spots begin to appear. (Do not let them blacken.) Remove from heat and set aside. Roast the garlic and shallots (one item at a time) in the same manner. Set aside.

Using a mortar and pestle or spice mill, grind the roasted cumin, coriander, and peppercorns and set aside. Place the roasted chilies in the mortar and pound until fine. Add the remaining ingredients except for the oil and pound into a fine paste. Combine the paste with the ground roasted spices and oil, and blend together until smooth. Paste is now ready for use. To store, divide into 2-tablespoon portions and place inside sealable plastic bags and freeze. Paste will last up to 3 months.

sweet thai chili sauce

MAKES ABOUT 2 CUPS

A wonderful dipping sauce for fried or grilled dishes. In Thailand, it's generally served with chicken wings, barbecued chicken, or ribs. I find this condiment equally delicious with tempura shrimp and onion rings. (Maybe an alternative to ketchup?)

3 TABLESPOONS GROUND CHILI PASTE
2 TEASPOONS MINCED GARLIC
$1/2$ CUP RICE WINE VINEGAR
$2/3$ CUP WATER
$2/3$ CUP SUGAR
1 TEASPOON SALT
4 TEASPOONS CORNSTARCH
4 TABLESPOONS CHOPPED FRESH CILANTRO

In a small saucepan, but without any heat, whisk together the chili paste, garlic, vinegar, water, sugar, salt, and cornstarch until well blended. Stirring often, bring mixture to a boil. Reduce heat and let simmer for about 5 minutes. When cooled, stir in the cilantro and serve. Sauce should be sweet and sour and slightly thickened. Sauce will keep for 2 weeks in refrigerator.

roasted tomato-chili sauce

MAKES 1½ CUPS

This is the Thai version of salsa. Traditionally made with cherry or red tomatoes, it's great with grilled fish or meats. I find a more interesting combination consists of small yellow, red, and green-striped tomatoes.

2 TABLESPOONS DRIED CHILI FLAKES

4 SHALLOTS, SLICED

4 CLOVES GARLIC, SLICED

2 TO 5 FRESH CHILIES, ANY KIND, CHOPPED

1 CUP *TOTAL* YELLOW PEAR, RED CHERRY, AND GREEN-STRIPED TOMATOES

2 TABLESPOONS FISH SAUCE

1 TEASPOON FRESH LIME JUICE

3 TEASPOONS BROWN SUGAR

2 TABLESPOONS CHOPPED FRESH CILANTRO

Pan-roast the dried chili flakes in a large skillet over low heat, until slightly brown, about 15 seconds. Transfer chili flakes to a mixing bowl and set aside. Place the shallots and garlic in the same skillet, and pan-roast until evenly golden, about 3 to 5 minutes. Add them to the mixing bowl. Roast the chilies in the same manner. Add to mixing bowl. Place the tomatoes in the same skillet and roast over low heat, turning them often so the skin is evenly charred. Set aside.

Place the roasted chili flakes, shallots, garlic, and chilies in a mortar and pound into a paste. (You may also mince shallots, garlic, and chilies by hand.) Transfer to a mixing bowl. Add the fish sauce, lime juice, sugar, and cilantro and mix well. Chop the tomatoes and add to the mixture. Transfer to a dipping bowl and serve.

This salsa is a great dip for vegetables and shrimp chips and is also delicious served alongside grilled steak or fish.

spicy peanut sauce

For added flavor and tex-

ture, pan-roast ¼ cup of

raw, shelled peanuts over

low heat for 20 minutes.

Smash fine in a mortar

and add to sauce.

There are many different recipes for satay sauce, including those that call for chopped roasted peanuts. I prefer to use creamy peanut butter, because it sticks to the meat but not to your teeth! Try this sauce with steaks, lamb chops, and even grilled seafood.

1 TABLESPOON VEGETABLE OIL
1 TEASPOON RED CURRY PASTE
½ TEASPOON GROUND TURMERIC
½ CUP CREAMY PEANUT BUTTER
½ CUP UNSWEETENED COCONUT MILK OR COW'S MILK
½ CUP WATER
2 TEASPOONS FISH SAUCE
1 TEASPOON FRESH LEMON JUICE
SUGAR TO TASTE

Heat the oil in a nonstick saucepan over moderate heat. Add curry paste and turmeric and stir often until mixture sizzles, about 1 minute. Add peanut butter, coconut milk, water, fish sauce, lemon juice, and sugar and reduce the heat to low. Stirring constantly with a whisk, cook for 3 minutes. When mixture begins to bubble, remove from heat, and continue to stir. If sauce is too thick, thin with water. Taste and adjust seasonings to an interesting balance of sweet, salty, and spicy flavors.

fried shallots

MAKES ABOUT 2/3 CUP

Fried shallots are a tasty garnish for soups, salads, and noodle dishes. My mother always keeps a small jar of these crunchy things on hand as part of her everyday condiments.

1 CUP VEGETABLE OIL
1 CUP THINLY SLICED SHALLOTS

Line a cookie tray with paper towels and spread the shallots on top. Let sit for 15 to 20 minutes to air dry. (This technique helps make the shallots crispy.) Heat the oil in a skillet over low heat. (The oil is ready when a piece of shallot slowly bubbles and floats to the top.) Add the shallots and, using chopsticks or a small spatula, stir the shallots so they do not tangle. Fry the shallots until golden, about 5 minutes. With a slotted spoon or skimmer, remove the shallots and drain on paper towels. Save the oil for another use. When the shallots are cool, transfer to a glass jar with a tight-fitting lid. They keep at room temperature for 2 weeks.

spicy thai cucumber salad

SERVES 4 TO 6

*Although you can serve it as a salad or appetizer, this traditional Thai dish gener-
ally is used as a relish or garnish. At Lemon Grass, we serve this with Chicken Satay and
Crispy Spring Rolls. The refreshingly sweet and tart flavors of this salad nicely complement
grilled or dried meats. This salad is also a good accompaniment to fried rice.*

DRESSING
1/4 CUP RICE WINE VINEGAR
1/4 CUP SUGAR
1/2 TEASPOON SALT
3 TABLESPOONS WATER

SALAD
2 CUCUMBERS, PREFERABLY ENGLISH OR HOTHOUSE,
   HALVED LENGTHWISE AND THINLY SLICED
1/2 SMALL YELLOW ONION, FINELY CHOPPED
10 FRESH MINT LEAVES, CHOPPED
1 FRESH CHILI, PREFERABLY RED, THINLY SLICED,
   OR 1 TEASPOON GROUND CHILI PASTE
6 FREH CILANTRO SPRIGS, CHOPPED
2 TABLESPOONS CHOPPED ROASTED PEANUTS FOR GARNISH (PAGE 55)
1 TABLESPOON FRIED SHALLOTS (OPTIONAL, PAGE 45)

To turn this salad into a relish, quarter the cucumber lengthwise and thinly slice, and mince the onion.

To enhance the salad, add grilled sausage or chicken. In Thailand, a typical cucumber salad is often jazzed up with thin slices of grilled Chinese sausage.

Combine the rice wine vinegar, sugar, salt, and water in a mixing bowl until well blended.

Add the cucumbers, onion, mint, chili, and cilantro and toss well. Let sit for 15 minutes.

Garnish with chopped peanuts and serve.

scallion oil

MAKES ABOUT ²/₃ CUP

In Vietnam, this popular seasoned oil is brushed on fresh rice noodles and grilled meats and used as a topping for rice dishes. Depending on your whim, you may want to jazz up the oil by doing what we do at Lemon Grass Restaurant—embellish it with ginger, chilies, garlic, and kosher salt—it is exquisite!

¹/₂ CUP VEGETABLE OIL
5 SCALLIONS, CHOPPED

Heat the oil in a small saucepan over moderate heat. Add the scallions and as soon as they bloom in the hot oil, remove from the heat. Transfer to a bowl and let cool. Scallion oil can be made in advance and stored at room temperature for 3 days, or in the refrigerator for 2 weeks. If refrigerated, bring to room temperature before serving.

When buying scallions, choose smaller, thinner ones as they are more aromatic than the larger ones.

vietnamese sweet and sour sauce

MAKES ABOUT 2 CUPS

This typical sweet and sour sauce complements any pan-fried or grilled dish. For an interesting twist, try adding fresh pineapples.

2 TABLESPOONS VEGETABLE OIL
2 SHALLOTS, MINCED
2 CLOVES GARLIC, MINCED
1 TEASPOON GROUND CHILI PASTE
2 TABLESPOONS KETCHUP
1 TABLESPOON FISH SAUCE
1 TABLESPOON SUGAR
4 RED RIPE TOMATOES, CUBED
$1/2$ CUP CHICKEN STOCK
2 TABLESPOONS CORNSTARCH
$1/3$ CUP WATER
$1/2$ TEASPOON FRESH LEMON JUICE

Heat the oil in a medium saucepan over moderate heat. Sauté the shallots and garlic until nicely golden and fragrant, about 1 minute. Add the chili paste, ketchup, fish sauce, and sugar and stir for 1 minute. Add the tomatoes and chicken stock and cook over low heat until slightly reduced, about 3 to 5 minutes. If sauce is too thin, combine the cornstarch and water in a separate bowl and stir into the sauce 1 teaspoon at a time. Sauce should be only slightly thickened, just enough to coat a spoon. Stir the lemon juice into the sauce and remove from heat.

steamed jasmine rice

MAKES ABOUT 5 CUPS

Sometimes the best part of the day at Lemon Grass is when the lights of our multiple rice pots go off, signaling that the rice is done. Gradually a perfumy, nutty fragrance fills the air. If the smell is rather intense, I know the rice must have been from a 'new crop' and so may be a tad mushy. I run to the back and ask Albert, our grill cook who oversees the rice cooking, to see if he had reduced the water a bit. You see, if the rice happens to be from the current year's harvest, it has a higher moisture content. To compensate for that, the water must be reduced or the rice will become mushy.

2 CUPS THAI JASMINE RICE
3 CUPS WATER

Pick through the rice and remove any hulls or stones.

Place the rice and water in a pot and bring to a rolling boil. Using a wooden spoon or chopsticks, stir to loosen the rice. Let boil for 2 minutes then reduce heat to very low. Cover with a tight-fitting lid and steam for 20 to 30 minutes. Remove from heat, uncover, and fluff rice with a fork. Keep covered and warm until needed. (If your rice happens to be "new crop," reduce the water by 1/4 to 1/3 cup.)

If you wish to wash rice as some Asian cooks do, try this method: Place the rice in a strainer. Under running water, wash the rice, using your hand to stir the grains around. Personally, I think this step is unnecessary and may remove some of the fragrance of jasmine rice.

sticky jasmine rice

MAKES 4 CUPS

In Vietnam and Thailand, not only is sticky rice used for desserts, but it is also a popular substitute for regular rice. This is especially true with farm workers, who must keep their bellies full during a long, hard day. The secret to making fluffy sticky rice is to soak it overnight. If you don't have time, soak it in hot water for 3 hours before cooking. As with regular rice, sticky rice can be embellished to include just about anything you desire. A traditional garnish for sticky rice is fried shallots and chopped roasted peanuts.

2 CUPS STICKY RICE, PREFERABLY LONG GRAIN

Place the rice in a mixing bowl and add enough water to cover it. With your hands rub the rice vigorously. Drain off the milky water. Add more water and repeat until water runs clear. Soak rice in clean water overnight.

Before cooking, drain the rice and place on a steamer lined with cheesecloth. Fill pan with water, making sure it doesn't touch the rice. Steam for 30 to 40 minutes, occasionally fluffing with a fork. If rice seems dry, sprinkle with hot water and toss slightly. Put the lid back on and continue steaming for another 2 to 3 minutes. Let rice stand, covered, 10 minutes before serving.

caramel sauce

MAKES ABOUT 2/3 CUP

Somewhere along the way, the forefathers and foremothers of Vietnamese cuisine decided that a bottle of fish sauce and a jar of caramel sauce were indispensable in the kitchen. Caramel sauce is indeed handy. A little spoonful gives our stews, ragouts, and even grilled dishes a nice color, as well as adding a slightly nutty sweetness. Consider setting aside a small jar for spotaneous use. Molasses and other store-bought versions are not good substitutes.

1 CUP SUGAR
3/4 CUP WATER
1 CUP BOILING WATER

Combine the sugar and the 3/4 cup water in a small saucepan and bring to a boil. Reduce the heat and simmer for 12 to 15 minutes. Stir continuously with a spoon or wire whisk. Have the 1 cup boiling water ready on a back burner. When the caramel sauce begins to bubble and turn very dark brown, move the pan to a cool burner. Stirring continuously, drizzle in only enough boiling water to slightly thin out the syrup 1 to 2 tablespoons. (This will ensure that the sauce doesn't become too thick later.) Let the sauce cool before transferring to a jar with a tight-fitting lid.

table salad

SERVES 4

This platter usually consists of whole-leaf lettuce, mint, cucumbers, beans sprouts, other greens, and soaked rice paper. Often it accompanies dishes in which little pieces of meat and seafood need to be wrapped and eaten with the hands. A nice table salad usually includes several different kinds of herbs, such as mint, basil, purple basil, and cilantro.

2 HEADS RED LEAF LETTUCE, LEAVES SEPARATED AND WASHED

1/2 CUCUMBER, JULIENNED

2 CUPS BEAN SPROUTS

6 FRESH MINT SPRIGS

6 FRESH THAI BASIL SPRIGS

6 FRESH PURPLE BASIL SPRIGS (OPTIONAL)

10 FRESH CILANTRO SPRIGS

20 (6-INCH) ROUND RICE PAPERS (OPTIONAL)

VIETNAMESE DIPPING SAUCE (PAGE 32)

Arrange all the ingredients in attractive rows on a large platter. To eat, tear off a piece of lettuce large enough to wrap and top with some cucumber, bean sprouts, and herbs. Add a piece of meat or whatever you are serving and roll into a small cylinder. Dip in sauce and enjoy.

If serving rice paper, immerse in warm water (about 100 degrees) and then fill with above ingredients and accompanying meats.

cilantro-curry mayonnaise

MAKES 1 CUP

As a child, I loved mayonnaise. Every time American friends went shopping at the military commissary, they would bring us a large jar of "American bean paste," as we called it. We used it on sandwiches and to make vegetable dips and sauces for dishes such as crab cakes. Curry powder gives the mayonnaise a nice color.

1 CUP GOOD-QUALITY MAYONNAISE
1 TO 2 TABLESPOONS CURRY POWDER
1/2 TABLESPOON VERY FINELY MINCED FRESH CILANTRO
1/2 TEASPOON FRESH LEMON JUICE

Combine all the ingredients in a mixing bowl. Let sit for 20 minutes to develop the flavors. Transfer to a sauce bowl and serve.

roasted peanuts

MAKES 1 CUP

A very popular garnish, chopped roasted peanuts are used to top Pad Thai *and other noodle dishes, barbecued meats, stews, salads, and even desserts. At Lemon Grass, much like at our parents' homes, we always keep a jar of freshly roasted peanuts nearby just in case we need this handy garnish.*

1 CUP RAW, SHELLED PEANUTS

Roast the peanuts in a nonstick pan over very low heat until lightly toasted, about 7 to 10 minutes. Let cool. Put in a spice mill and grind. Transfer to a glass jar and cover with a tight-fitting lid. If you prefer to use a mortar, pound the peanuts until crushed to a coarse meal.

If raw peanuts are unavailable, use commercially roasted peanuts and grind in a spice mill.

Chapter three

Two Sisters

appetizers and small dishes

My sister Denise was a mischievous thing. When she turned 18, she got a Honda motorcycle for her birthday. Powered by a small 50cc engine, it was scooter-style and perfect for girls. The windshield kept our hair from messing up, while the bottom guard protected our skirts and pants from the wind.

One day Denise suggested that we go to a popular restaurant in Bien Hoa, just north of the outskirts of Saigon, to eat some of the best *cha gio*, or spring rolls, one could find. I asked if it was the same place I had heard about that dipped their spring rolls in beer or coconut juice before frying. I could never figure out which one, even to this day, but I was excited. You see, every time Denise went out on a date I had to go along because it was the only way Mother would let her go.

Dressed in a new ruffly shirt and bell bottoms, I hopped on Denise's scooter. But the moment she stepped on the gas pedal, I knew it was a mistake. In a city where streets were cluttered with bicycles, cars, buses, *cyclos* (or pedi-cabs), and motorcycles carrying families of five, Denise drove her motorcycle with no fear. Revving up the engine, she rode the scooter full-speed, cutting off traffic, weaving in and out, and sometimes even racing with military trucks. She was having fun, but I was terrified.

But maybe it was all worth it. By the time we got to the restaurant, her friend was already there waiting. Taking a table underneath a coconut tree, we all sat down and began a little feast of appetizers. Soon a platter of the famous *cha gio* arrived—golden, translucent, crispy, and hot. Trying to appear somewhat ladylike and graceful, I gently reached over for some lettuce leaves and mint and began to wrap the precious morsels. The spring rolls were truly the best I had ever had. And just as I was savoring the last piece, another sumptuous meal emerged from the kitchen. It was *bo bay mon,* or beef cooked in seven ways. I was beginning to really like Denise's date.

The *bo bay mon* dishes were wonderful, especially the one in which the beef was cooked in a lemon grass–infused broth and then wrapped in rice paper. In another dish, the beef was marinated in garlic and whisky, wrapped in beef caul, and grilled. All of the dishes arrived on small plates, and almost every one of them had to be eaten by hand except, of course, for the beef rice soup served at the end.

Nowadays, every time I dine at a Vietnamese restaurant specializing in *bo bay mon,* I always think about the two sisters and the mischievous, yet tender, moments they shared as kids. It's hard to believe how long it has been since those motorcycle days. To me it seems as if it was only yesterday.

crispy spring rolls

MAKES ABOUT 25 PIECES

Cha gio are considered culinary treasures, delighting everyone who's tried them. Light and crispy, spring rolls are traditionally wrapped with rice paper. At Lemon Grass, however, we use a more durable type of spring roll wrapper made from wheat flour. Also used for Filipino-style lumpias, they are marketed under the Menlo brand and stocked in the frozen food department of Asian grocery stores. These 8 × 8-inch wrappers seal the filling so well that no oil can seep through during frying; this is not the case with rice paper.

FILLING

1 OUNCE DRIED BEAN THREAD NOODLES, SOAKED IN HOT WATER FOR 30
    MINUTES, DRAINED, AND CUT INTO 1/2-INCH PIECES WITH A SCISSORS
    (ABOUT 2/3 CUP)

1 TABLESPOON DRIED TREE EAR MUSHROOMS, SOAKED IN HOT WATER FOR
    30 MINUTES, DRAINED, AND STEMS TRIMMED AND CHOPPED WITH A
    SCISSORS

2/3 CUP FINELY MINCED YELLOW ONION

2 CARROTS, GRATED

3 GREEN ONIONS, THINLY SLICED

2 EGGS

2 TABLESPOONS FISH SAUCE

1/2 TABLESPOON MINCED GARLIC

1/4 TEASPOON SALT

2 TEASPOONS SUGAR

1/2 TEASPOON GROUND BLACK PEPPER

1/2 POUND GROUND CHICKEN

1/2 POUND GROUND PORK

ASSEMBLING AND FRYING

2 TABLESPOONS CORNSTARCH

1/3 CUP WATER

15 *THIN* SPRING ROLL WRAPPERS SUCH AS MENLO BRAND

OIL FOR FRYING

To enjoy a spring roll the Vietnamese way, always put it on a lettuce leaf, top with cucumber and mint, and wrap it up. Then dip in Vietnamese dipping sauce. Customers who have eaten them this way are fans for life.

Like dough, spring roll filling should not be over-mixed or it will become too dense. Use your hands or a fork to gently mix the ingredients together.

If you're entertaining, just

cook the spring rolls

halfway and bake at 250°

for 20 to 25 minutes. The

skin stays nicely crisped.

To serve as hors

d'oeuvres, cut the rolls in

half diagonally. To freeze,

cook halfway, then cool

before freezing. To use,

thaw and bake until thor-

oughly hot and crispy.

Spring rolls will keep in

the freezer for up

to 1 month.

ACCOMPANIMENTS
TABLE SALAD (PAGE 53)
VIETNAMESE DIPPING SAUCE (PAGE 32)

Combine the bean thread noodles, mushrooms, onion, carrots, and green onions in a mixing bowl. Set aside.

Beat the eggs in a large bowl. Mix in the fish sauce, garlic, salt, sugar, and black pepper. Add the chicken and pork and using a fork, break up the meat, so it is thoroughly mixed with the seasonings. Add the noodle mixture and mix well. Set aside.

Combine the cornstarch and water in a small saucepan. Bring to a boil over low heat and stir often to prevent sticking. If mixture seems too thick, add more water. This will be the "glue" to seal the edges of the wrapper.

Cut the wrappers in half diagonally. You will have two equal triangles. Starting with the longest side toward you, place about 2 tablespoons of filling on the bottom area of

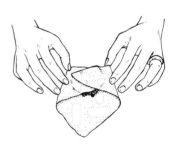

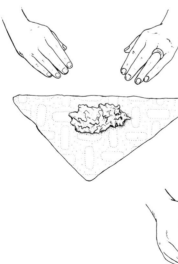

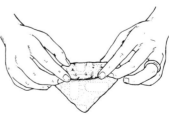

the triangle. Using your fingers, mold the filling into a cyclinder 2 inches long and 1 inch wide. Fold the two pointed ends of the wrapper in and roll to enclose. Dab a little corn-starch mixture along the edges (do not use too much "glue") and seal the roll. Set aside while you finish making the remaining rolls. Do not stack them.

To fry, preheat a large wok or fry pan. When hot, pour enough oil in to completely cover the spring rolls. Heat to about 325 degrees. Carefully place the rolls into the oil. Do not crowd the pan or place the rolls on top of each other. Fry the spring rolls until filling is cooked, about 5 to 6 minutes on each side, turning often until they are nicely brown and crisp. If they brown too quickly, reduce the heat as the oil is too hot. Remove the cooked spring rolls from the pan and drain on paper towels. Serve immediately with dipping sauce and table salad.

rice paper-wrapped salad rolls

SERVES 6 TO 8

No single dish better represents the delicateness of Vietnamese cuisine than this one. Traditionally filled with juicy shrimp and pork, they also can be stuffed with grilled chicken, salmon, or just about anything, such as leftover turkey from Thanksgiving.

1/3 POUND PORK SHOULDER

12 MEDIUM-SIZE RAW SHRIMP WITH SHELLS

8 (12-INCH) ROUND RICE PAPERS (KEEP EXTRA ON HAND JUST IN CASE YOU TEAR SOME)

1 SMALL HEAD RED LEAF LETTUCE, LEAVES SEPARATED AND WASHED

1/4 POUND RICE VERMICELLI, COOKED IN BOILING WATER 4 TO 5 MINUTES, RINSED, AND DRAINED

1 CUP BEAN SPROUTS

1/2 CUP FRESH MINT LEAVES

ACCOMPANIMENTS

1 CUP HOISIN-PEANUT SAUCE (PAGE 35) OR VIETNAMESE DIPPING SAUCE (PAGE 32)

1/4 CUP CHOPPED ROASTED PEANUTS FOR GARNISH

2 TABLESPOONS GROUND CHILI PASTE FOR GARNISH

Cook the pork in boiling salted water until just tender, about 30 minutes. Set aside to cool and then slice into 1 × 2 1/2-inch pieces. Cook the shrimp in boiling salted water until just done, about 3 minutes. Shell, devein, and cut in half lengthwise. Refresh in cold water and set aside.

Just before making the rolls, set up a salad roll "station." Fill a large mixing bowl with hot water. If necessary, keep some boiling water handy to add to the bowl if the temperature drops below 110 degrees. Choose an open area on the counter and arrange the following items in the order used: the rice paper, the hot water, a damp cheesecloth, and a platter holding all the stuffing ingredients.

(recipe continues)

Working with only 2 rice paper sheets at a time, dip 1 sheet, edge first, in the hot water and turn it to wet completely, about 10 seconds. Lay the sheet down on the cheesecloth and stretch the sheet slightly to remove any wrinkles. Wet the other rice paper the same way and place it alongside the first.

Line the bottom third of the wet pliable rice sheet with 3 shrimp halves, cut side up, and top with two slices of pork. Make sure the ingredients are neatly placed in a straight row as in the diagram. Fold a piece of lettuce into a thin rectangle about 5 inches long and place it on top. (You may need to use only half of a leaf.) Next, top with about 1 tablespoon of vermicelli, 1 tablespoon bean sprouts, and 4 to 5 mint leaves. Make sure the ingredients are not clumped together in the center, but evenly distributed from one end to

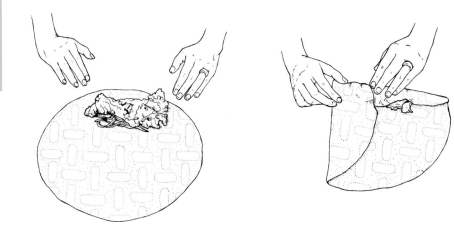

the other. Using your second, third, and fourth fingers, press down on the ingredients while you use the other hand to fold over both sides of the rice paper. (Pressing down on the ingredients is particularly important because it tightens the roll.) With fingers still pressing down, use two thumbs to fold the bottom edge over the filling and roll into a cyclinder about 1 1/2 inches wide by 5 inches long. Finish making all the remaining rolls.

To serve, cut the rolls into two or four equal pieces and place the cut rolls upright on an appetizer plate. Serve with hoisin-peanut sauce or Vietnamese dipping sauce on the side. Top sauce of choice with chopped peanuts and chili paste. If you like, garnish the rolls with mint or cilantro sprigs.

chicken satay with spicy peanut sauce

SERVES 4 TO 5

The Thais have a knack for barbecues. As a child, I was always impressed by how street vendors carefully threaded the chicken onto skewers made of coconut leaves. It was cleverly engineered—the skewer had a small handle made out of a trimmed leaf. The fragrance of coconut milk and curry powder sizzling over a hot grill was mouthwatering.

1 TEASPOON FISH SAUCE
1 TEASPOON SUGAR
1 TEASPOON CURRY POWDER
1/2 TEASPOON GROUND TURMERIC
1 TEASPOON MINCED GARLIC
PINCH OF GROUND CORIANDER
PINCH OF GROUND CUMIN
PINCH OF SALT
2 TABLESPOONS COCONUT MILK
2 TABLESPOONS VEGETABLE OIL
1 1/2 POUNDS SKINLESS, BONELESS CHICKEN BREASTS
20 (6-INCH) BAMBOO SKEWERS, SOAKED IN HOT WATER FOR 30 MINUTES TO
    PREVENT BURNING

ACCOMPANIMENTS
SPICY PEANUT SAUCE (PAGE 44)
SPICY THAI CUCUMBER SALAD (PAGES 46–47)

Whisk together all the ingredients except the chicken in a bowl.

Slice the chicken breasts diagonally against the grain into 1-inch wide strips. Add the chicken to the bowl and marinate for 15 minutes.

Preheat grill to medium heat.

Thread the chicken on to the bamboo skewers.

Grill the meat until just done, about 2 to 3 minutes on each side. To serve, ladle some peanut sauce, about 2 to 3 tablespoons, in the center of an appetizer dish. Top with chicken skewers and garnish with cucumber salad.

When barbecuing, make sure the fire is medium to low. The most common mistake with home barbecues is the high heat, which causes meats to brown quickly on the outside before they are actually cooked inside.

If you do not have a grill or barbecue, simply omit the skewering and pan-sear the chicken strips in a nonstick pan. You can also broil them.

vietnamese beef carpaccio

SERVES 4 TO 6

As a child, I was never a great fan of this raw beef dish. Prepared similarly to the French beef tartar, it had a chewy texture and was unappealing to my young palate. However, once I learned how to slice the meat paper-thin, like the way the Italians prepare carpaccio, I began to adore this dish. The flavors are lively and refreshing. Allow 3 to 5 slices per person.

SAUCE
1/2 CUP GINGER-LIME DIPPING SAUCE (PAGE 34)
JUICE OF 1/2 LIME

BEEF
1/2 POUND BEEF ROUND
10 FRESH MINT LEAVES
10 FRESH BASIL LEAVES
5 FRESH CILANTRO SPRIGS, STEMMED
2 TABLESPOONS FINELY MINCED YELLOW ONION
1 TEASPOON DRIED RED CHILI FLAKES
2 TABLESPOONS CHOPPED ROASTED PEANUTS
3 TABLESPOONS FRIED SHALLOTS (OPTIONAL, PAGE 45)

Prepare the ginger-lime dipping sauce and stir in the additional lime juice. Set aside. Wrap the beef round in plastic wrap and freeze until hardened, about 1 hour.

Stack the mint, basil, and cilantro leaves on top of each other. Press down gently with your hand and cut into very thin slivers.

Using a very sharp knife, cut the partially frozen beef into paper-thin slices. Lay the beef rounds in a circular pattern on a large platter, with each piece overlapping the other slightly. Cover the entire platter with the beef slices but do not stack them. (Beef carpaccio should be served only in small portions, so reserve any leftovers for another use.)

Just before serving, drizzle the sauce over the beef and tilt the plate so it completely soaks the meat. Sprinkle with the herbs, minced onion, chili flakes, roasted peanuts, and fried shallots.

To enjoy this delicacy, use a small seafood fork to pick up the meat. Roll the meat around the fork so the garnishes are wrapped inside. Toasted bruschettas or crackers make wonderful accompaniments.

Thinly sliced ahi tuna also can be used in this recipe.

firecracker prawns

SERVES 4

This dish draws inspiration from a very simple, yet highly effective, Asian technique. The prawns, with the shells left on to lock in their natural sweetness, are pan-seared over high heat so the shells 'crackle' with each bite. (Yes, you can eat the brittle shells, especially if the prawns are small.) In Chinese restaurants, versions of these delicacies are simply called salt-baked prawns (though it's actually pan-fried). A great way to serve this dish is with a side dish of cucumber salad and a glass of cold beer!

1/2 POUND MEDIUM-SIZE RAW PRAWNS WITH SHELLS
3 TABLESPOONS MINCED SHALLOT
3 TABLESPOONS CORNSTARCH
1 1/2 TABLESPOONS KOSHER SALT
1 TEASPOON COARSELY CRACKED BLACK PEPPER
3 TABLESPOONS VEGETABLE OIL
2 SHALLOTS, THINLY SLICED
1/4 CUP THINLY JULIENNED RED BELL PEPPER
2 GREEN ONIONS, DIAGONALLY SLICED INTO 1/2-INCH PIECES
1 FRESH JALAPEÑO, THINLY SLICED (OPTIONAL)
FRESH CILANTRO SPRIGS FOR GARNISH
SPICY THAI CUCUMBER SALAD (PAGES 46–47)
GINGER-LIME DIPPING SAUCE (PAGE 34)

Rinse the prawns. Using a sharp serrated knife and laying the prawns down flat on the cutting board, carefully cut through the shell along the back. Make a shallow slit into the body of the prawns, about 1 inch long. (Do not cut too deep as prawns will shrink when cooked.) Remove the dark vein, rinse, drain, and pat dry with paper towels.

Rub the minced shallot into the open slit making sure to tuck some underneath the shells. Set aside.

Truly fresh crustacean is a rarity in this country, except in certain coastal cities. That's rather sad, especially for someone who remembers how fun it was to scoop up live shrimp from the river. Most prawns you see at the grocery store today are frozen "black tigers" farmed in Thailand and other parts of Asia. With blueish-green and dark striped shells, they turn bright pink when cooked. For the most part, the quality is good, although their meat is not as sweet and tender as the white shrimp.

Combine the cornstarch, salt, and pepper in a bowl and mix well. Dredge the prawns in the cornstarch mixture. Spread the prawns in a single layer on a tray.

Heat the oil over high heat in a nonstick pan large enough to hold all the prawns. Add the prawns and toss quickly until they turn opaque, about 2 minutes. Add the red bell pepper, green onions, and jalapeño and stir-fry for 1 more minute. Remove from heat. Garnish with cilantro. Serve with ginger-lime dipping sauce and Thai cucumber salad.

The best place to buy shrimp is at Asian markets or specialty food stores. They are available in thawed form and in 4- to 5-pound frozen blocks. Check for freshness by smelling the shrimp. If it looks dried out and has a strong odor, it probably has sat around too long after thawing. The jumbo-size prawns are usually not as easily available; the price is quite prohibitive, and only specialty restaurants will use them.

sizzling saigon crepes

MAKES 4 LARGE CREPES

Resembling an oversized omelet, banh xeo, *or sizzling crepe, is a favorite dish served at street corners in Saigon. It's traditionally made with shrimp and pork, but any meat combination would be equally delicious.*

BATTER
2 CUPS RICE FLOUR
1/4 CUP ALL-PURPOSE FLOUR
1 CUP UNSWEETENED COCONUT MILK
2 CUPS WATER
3 GREEN ONIONS, THINLY SLICED
1/2 TEASPOON SALT
1 TEASPOON SUGAR
2 TEASPOONS CURRY POWDER
1 TEASPOON GROUND TURMERIC

FILLING
4 TABLESPOONS VEGETABLE OIL
1 YELLOW ONION, VERY THINLY SLICED
1/2 POUND BONELESS, SKINLESS CHICKEN BREAST, THINLY SLICED AND
     THEN CUBED
12 MEDIUM-SIZE RAW SHRIMP, PEELED, DEVEINED, AND HALVED
     LENGTHWISE
4 CUPS BEAN SPROUTS
2 CUPS WHITE MUSHROOMS, THINLY SLICED

ACCOMPANIMENTS
1 CUP VIETNAMESE DIPPING SAUCE (PAGE 32)
TABLE SALAD (PAGE 53)

For smaller crepes, use a smaller pan. Remember to use less batter as a thick crepe will be chewy.

My mother's recipe calls for sprinkling cooked mung beans on the crepe before the bean sprouts are added. At Lemon Grass, we have omitted this ingredient because the mung beans do not seem to have much fla-vor, although the texture is nice. Sorry, Mom.

Whisk together all the batter ingredients in a mixing bowl. Set aside.

In a 10-inch nonstick fry or omelet pan, heat 1 tablespoon of the oil over high heat. Add about 1 tablespoon of the onion, 2 tablespoons of the chicken, and 6 of the shrimp halves and toss in pan until the shrimp turns opaque, about 20 seconds. Whisk the batter well, then ladle about 2/3 cup into the pan, tilting it so the batter completely covers the surface. Immediately return pan to stove. Reduce heat to moderate. Neatly pile about 1 cup bean sprouts and 1/2 cup mushrooms on one side of the crepe, closer to the center than the edge. Immediately reduce heat to low. Cover the pan with a lid and let cook for another 3 minutes, making sure the bottom doesn't burn. Remove lid and let crepe cook for 2 more minutes to dry out the batter. To remove the crepe, lift the side without the bean sprouts and fold over. Using a spatula, gently slide the crepe onto a large plate. Wipe the pan clean and cook the remaining 3 crepes. Serve crepes with table salad and Vietnamese dipping sauce. To enjoy this dish the traditional way, tear off a bite-size piece of crepe and wrap it with lettuce and mint. Dip in the sauce, and then eat.

chili clams

SERVES 4 TO 6

Being a great fan of clams, especially those prepared in a simple fashion—steamed in a little garlic, wine, and chicken stock—I decided that our restaurant should have a clam appetizer, but prepared with a Thai flair.

1 TABLESPOON VEGETABLE OIL

1 TEASPOON MINCED GARLIC

2 TEASPOONS GROUND CHILI PASTE, OR TO TASTE

1 TEASPOON DRIED RED CHILI FLAKES

$1/2$ TABLESPOON MINCED LEMON GRASS

1 STALK FRESH LEMON GRASS, CUT INTO 3-INCH PIECES (OPTIONAL)

2 CUPS UNSWEETENED COCONUT MILK

$1 1/2$ TABLESPOONS FISH SAUCE

$1/2$ TEASPOON FRESH LIME JUICE

4 DOZEN FRESH MANILLA CLAMS, SCRUBBED CLEAN

10 FRESH CILANTRO SPRIGS FOR GARNISH

Heat the oil, garlic, chili paste, and chili flakes in a wok or sauté pan over moderate heat. Add the minced lemon grass and stir until mixture is nicely fragrant, about 1 minute. Reduce heat, and add the lemon grass stalk, coconut milk, fish sauce, and lime juice and bring to a slow boil. (The gentle boil will help extract the flavor from the lemon grass.) Add the clams, then cover with a lid. Let clams cook until they open, about 3 to 4 minutes. Remove from heat and serve the clams with the broth immediately. Garnish with cilantro sprigs.

grilled eggplant canapés with ginger and scallion

MAKES ABOUT 3 DOZEN PIECES

My mother often served steamed eggplant as a side dish. In this recipe, I have turned it into a wonderful appetizer—delicate and dainty looking, these little morsels are full of flavor. They are best served at room temperature when all the flavors are fully developed.

3 JAPANESE EGGPLANTS, SLICED 1/4 INCH THICK LENGTHWISE, BRUSHED
      WITH OLIVE OIL, AND GRILLED UNTIL SOFT (ABOUT 3 TO 4 MINUTES) OR
      BAKED UNTIL JUST SLIGHTLY SOFT
2 TABLESPOONS VEGETABLE OIL
1/4 CUP MINCED YELLOW ONION
4 SCALLIONS, SLICED THIN DIAGONALLY
2 TEASPOONS MINCED FRESH GINGER
1/2 TEASPOON GROUND CHILI PASTE, OR TO TASTE
1 TEASPOON FISH SAUCE
1/4 TEASPOON SALT
1 TEASPOON FRESH LIME JUICE
1 RED RIPE TOMATO, SEEDED AND MINCED
2 TABLESPOONS MINCED RED BELL PEPPER
1/3 CUP MAYONNAISE
1 CUP ARUGULA OR MIXED BABY GREENS
TOASTED BAGUETTE SLICES OR CRACKERS

To turn this dish into a salad, leave the eggplant in large pieces and marinate with the green onion mixture. Serve on an attractive platter, lined with arugula or mixed baby greens, and top with the eggplant.

Cut cooked eggplant into 1 1/2-inch-long pieces and set aside.

Heat the oil in a small saucepan until hot. Add the onions, scallions, ginger, and chili paste and sautée until onions are slightly wilted, about 2 minutes. Remove from heat and add the fish sauce, salt, lime juice, tomato, and red bell pepper.

To assemble, dab a little mayonnaise on baguette slices (this helps the food stick to the bread) and top with a piece of arugula. Add a slice of the eggplant, then top with a tiny dollop of the onion mixture. Finish making the remaining canapés.

spicy salmon cakes

MAKES 10 TO 12 CAKES

Inspired by the Thai tod mun pla, a chewy cake made with white fish, this fun dish calls for salmon, curry paste, and lime leaves. The cakes can be made in advance and sautéed just before serving.

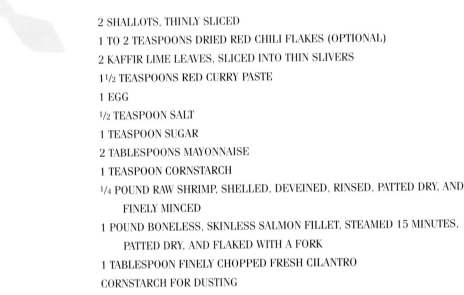

2 SHALLOTS, THINLY SLICED

1 TO 2 TEASPOONS DRIED RED CHILI FLAKES (OPTIONAL)

2 KAFFIR LIME LEAVES, SLICED INTO THIN SLIVERS

1½ TEASPOONS RED CURRY PASTE

1 EGG

½ TEASPOON SALT

1 TEASPOON SUGAR

2 TABLESPOONS MAYONNAISE

1 TEASPOON CORNSTARCH

¼ POUND RAW SHRIMP, SHELLED, DEVEINED, RINSED, PATTED DRY, AND
     FINELY MINCED

1 POUND BONELESS, SKINLESS SALMON FILLET, STEAMED 15 MINUTES,
     PATTED DRY, AND FLAKED WITH A FORK

1 TABLESPOON FINELY CHOPPED FRESH CILANTRO

CORNSTARCH FOR DUSTING

OIL FOR PAN-FRYING

ACCOMPANIMENTS

SWEET THAI CHILI SAUCE (PAGE 42)

3 CUPS MIXED BABY GREENS

Blend the shallots, chili flakes, lime leaves, curry paste, egg, salt, sugar, mayonnaise, cornstarch, and shrimp in a food processor until just smooth. (Alternatively, mix ingredients by hand.) Transfer to a mixing bowl and fold in the salmon and cilantro. Using wet hands, shape into patties about 3 inches in diameter and $1/2$ inch thick. Dust with cornstarch on both sides and set aside.

Fill a nonstick pan with about $1/3$ inch oil and heat until moderately hot. Gently place the patties into the oil and pan-fry each side until just done and golden brown, about 2 to 3 minutes. Remove patties from pan and drain on paper towels. To serve, place baby greens on a plate and top with salmon cakes. Drizzle sweet Thai chili sauce on top.

spicy crab cake delights

I call this a delight because it is! When our friends Tom and Ae Glasheen tested this recipe, they brought over the most gorgeous looking crab cakes I had seen in a long time. First thing I asked was, were there more? No amount of crab cake is enough for me. If you ever find good ones at a restaurant (which will be rare as crab is much too expensive), do what I do and order them before they are all gone!

1 EGG
1 SMALL ONION, MINCED
1 SCALLION, MINCED
1/2 TEASPOON MINCED GARLIC
1/2 TEASPOON CURRY POWDER
1/2 TEASPOON FISH SAUCE
1 TEASPOON FRESHLY CRACKED BLACK PEPPER
2 TABLESPOONS MAYONNAISE
1/2 TEASPOON DRIED RED CHILI FLAKES (OPTIONAL)
1 OUNCE CELLOPHANE NOODLES, SOAKED IN HOT WATER FOR 30 MINUTES,
    DRAINED, AND CHOPPED INTO 1/4-INCH PIECES (2/3 CUP)
2/3 POUND CRABMEAT, PREFERABLY DUNGENESS OR BLUE CRAB
1/2 PLUS 1 CUP JAPANESE-STYLE BREAD CRUMBS, PREFERABLY
    PANKO BRAND
1/2 CUP VEGETABLE OIL
4 CUPS BABY GREENS
1 CUP CILANTRO-CURRY MAYONNAISE (PAGE 54)

The best crabmeat to use is freshly picked Dungeness crab or blue crab. The latter, which is more affordable, is actually quite good, but picking out the meat from this small crab can be a chore. If you can't talk your butcher into picking it fresh for you, buy a small tub of crabmeat. It's not as good, but it will be delicious just the same.

Combine the first ten ingredients in a mixing bowl and mix well. Then add the crabmeat and the $^1/_2$ cup bread crumbs and gently fold into the sauce, making sure the crabmeat remains in big pieces. (To me, a great crab cake should be lumpy.) Using wet hands, form the crabmeat mixture into balls and gently press down the centers to make patties about 3 inches in diameter and $^1/_2$ inch thick. Dredge the patties in the 1 cup bread crumbs and set aside.

Heat the oil over moderate heat in a large fry pan. Cook the cakes until nicely brown, about 3 minutes on each side.

To serve, place about 1 cup of baby greens on a plate and top with two cakes. Serve the curry-mayonnaise sauce on the side.

five-spice quail

SERVES 4

In Vietnam, a favorite pastime is to savor and nibble on these birds, and wash down with large cold bottles of lager. This ritual, which can take place on any sidewalk, but definitely underneath a shady tree, usually lasts as long as it takes to scrape every bit of meat and cartilage from the tiny quails—but certainly finishes no sooner than when the last drop of beer is emptied.

This dish was on the Lemon Grass menu when we first opened. Called "flaming bird" because we flambéed it tableside, it was a hit among the few who dared order it. Apparently, many customers did not want to go through the hassle of eating the quails with their fingers, which, by the way, is a prerequisite. No fingers, no quail!

2 SHALLOTS, THINLY SLICED
2 CLOVES GARLIC, THINLY SLICED
1 TABLESPOON OYSTER SAUCE
1/2 TEASPOON WHITE PEPPER
1/2 TEASPOON FISH SAUCE
1 1/2 TEASPOONS FIVE-SPICE POWDER
1 TABLESPOON VEGETABLE OIL
4 QUAILS, WASHED, PATTED DRY, AND FLATTENED
1 TABLESPOON KOSHER SALT
1 TEASPOON SZECHUAN PEPPERCORNS, LIGHTLY SMASHED
MOM'S CABBAGE SALAD (OPTIONAL, PAGE 96)
1/2 LIME, CUT INTO 4 PIECES

Place the shallots and garlic in a mortar and pound into a paste. Transfer to a mixing bowl. Add the oyster sauce, white pepper, fish sauce, five-spice powder, and oil and mix well. Add the quail and let marinate for 30 minutes.

Meanwhile, prepare the salt mixture. In a small sauté pan over low heat, dry roast the salt and peppercorns until fragrant, about 2 to 3 minutes. Divide salt mixture into small ramekins.

Preheat oven to broil. Place quail, skin side up, on a baking sheet and place under the broiler on the top rack. Cook to desired doneness, about 10 to 15 minutes. If barbecueing, preheat grill to moderate heat. Cook each side about 3 to 5 minutes. Serve on a bed of cabbage salad with the salt mixture on the side. Squeeze lime juice into the salt mixture before dipping pieces of quail in it.

grilled prawns with spicy peanut sauce

MAKES 4 SERVINGS

When we were planning our wedding reception, Trong and I wanted something that would really excite people. We chose this dish because it was delicious, attractive, and great for cooking outdoors. We were right, because throughout the reception, a big crowd constantly gathered around the grill. In fact, some people found the prawns infinitely more interesting than the wedding toast or any other events going on. Later, as we were watching the wedding video, we couldn't stop giggling at how some guests devoured a dozen or so prawns at a time. That's okay, though. Everyone enjoyed it . . . the food, that is!

1 1/2 TABLESPOONS MINCED LEMON GRASS
1 TEASPOON MINCED GARLIC
1/2 TEASPOON GROUND CHILI PASTE
1/4 TEASPOON SALT
1/2 TEASPOON SUGAR
2 TABLESPOONS VEGETABLE OIL
16 MEDIUM-SIZE RAW PRAWNS, PEELED AND DEVEINED
8 (5-INCH) BAMBOO SKEWERS, SOAKED IN HOT WATER FOR 30 MINUTES TO
    PREVENT BURNING
SPICY PEANUT SAUCE (OPTIONAL, PAGE 44)
SPICY THAI CUCUMBER SALAD (PAGES 46–47)

Combine the lemon grass, garlic, chili paste, salt, sugar, and oil in a mixing bowl. Add the prawns and let marinate for 15 minutes.

Preheat a grill to moderate.

Pierce the pointed end of each bamboo skewer through 2 prawns lengthwise, starting from the tail end to the top section.

Just before serving, grill the prawns over medium heat until just done, about 2 to 3 minutes on each side. If serving individually, place two skewers in the center of a plate and drizzle on satay sauce. Serve with a small mound of cucumber salad on the side.

A few customers complained about this dish saying the prawns wouldn't slide off the skewer. One customer, in an attempt to loosen a prawn, sent it flying clear across the room, where it landed on another table where a diner was enjoying the same dish but without any problem. We noticed that the second diner wiggled the prawns to loosen them and then slid them right off. With that in mind, I later asked the cooks to wiggle the prawns on the skewers before cooking. Since then we haven't had any complaints.

Chapter four

What About Lemon Grass

the herb and refreshing salads

In the fall of 1987, a year before our restaurant was to open, and after months of agonizing over a name for the restaurant, Trong woke up very late one night and asked, "What about 'Lemon Grass'?" I was ecstatic. No other name could have been more appropriate and destined for the restaurant. An herb used extensively in both Vietnamese and Thai cooking, lemon grass gives the two cuisines continuity, diversity, and identity. Its citrusy aroma represents the lively, sharp flavors of our cooking and its sturdiness seems to stand up to any food combination. The name sounds Asian and implies a light cuisine. With all this in mind, we immediately registered 'Lemon Grass' as our trademark.

The use of lemon grass as an herb dates back centuries. In its tropical, humid home of Southeast Asia, lemon grass grows wildly and profusely. It is a pale green plant resembling a large woody, fibrous green onion with the upper leaves almost menacingly sharp. In our cuisine, lemon grass is used in two main ways. When finely minced, it is added to marinades, curries, and salads. Bigger pieces of lemon grass are generally used to infuse broths and soups. This includes occasionally adding it to the water used for steaming crab and fish. Today, as the appreciation of, and familiarity with, this exotic herb increases in the West, lemon grass is making its way across new frontiers, into desserts and even drinks.

In this chapter on salads, you will find that with the exception of a few cross-cultural creations, our dressings are either lime juice– or rice vinegar–based and are made with very little oil. Thai salads are very tart, and their dressings are spiked with fresh lime juice, chilies, lemon grass, and fish sauce. The Vietnamese salads are mild by comparison, with tartness often balanced by sweetness. For a new twist, consider eating salads the way I ate them as a child—with lots of rice. Although this may be an awkward idea in the West, a minty Thai chicken salad served alongside a steaming bowl of jasmine rice is a wonderful meal.

lemon grass

BUYING AND GROWING

Fresh lemon grass, especially as found at farmers' markets, is grayish-green at the stalk, with small flecks of white powder clinging to the plant. A nicely trimmed stalk is about 12 inches long, with the outside tough layers peeled off to show the more tender part of the plant. Choose those with fat bulbs—there will be more of it to use. If you want to grow lemon grass, pick stalks with healthy roots. Simply root in water and then transplant to a large pot. Lemon grass thrives in full sun and loves sandy soil. Bring the plant indoors during the winter to avoid frost. When harvesting lemon grass, use a sharp knife and cut off the stalk just above the ground level. Leave the remaining root intact and a new plant will sprout.

STORING

A rather sturdy herb, lemon grass will stay fresh for 2 to 3 weeks if stored in a plastic bag in the vegetable compartment of the refrigerator. But since its best use is in a marinade, it makes good sense to mince the lemon grass immediately, place in a sealable plastic bag, and freeze before it has a chance to dry up. Frozen lemon grass will keep up to 4 to 5 months.

PREPPING

My grandmother would cringe if she heard me say this, but considering our lifestyle today and knowing how many people just wouldn't use lemon grass if they had to chop it by hand every time they needed it, my best solution is this: pre-prep lemon grass. Buy at least 5 pounds of lemon grass and very thinly slice the bottom thirds in a food processor or by hand. If you're using a food processor, feed the bulb parts to the blade first. (Stop when you get to the green, fibrous parts of the stalk.) Cut the leftover top part of the stems into 2-inch pieces and store in sealable plastic bags in the freezer. Next, finely mince the sliced lemon

grass. Transfer to sealable plastic bags and store in the freezer. For easier handling, put only $1/2$ cup minced lemon grass per bag. To use, simply remove the bag
from the freezer and either break off or cut out a chunk of lemon grass and return
the rest to the freezer. Of course, nothing is better than freshly minced lemon
grass, but I find the advantages of having it when you need it far outweigh the
slight loss in flavor.

minty thai chicken salad

SERVES 4 TO 6

Like others in the family of Thai salads called larb, *this salad is unique because the meat is cooked directly in the dressing. When serving, invite guests to spoon a little chicken on top of a cabbage leaf and eat with their hands. The recipe also works with shrimp or beef.*

1 TABLESPOON VEGETABLE OIL
1 TABLESPOON DRIED RED CHILI FLAKES, OR TO TASTE
1/2 TEASPOON PAPRIKA
2/3 POUND SKINLESS, BONELESS CHICKEN BREAST OR THIGH, MINCED
2 TEASPOONS BROWN SUGAR
3 TABLESPOONS FISH SAUCE
1/3 CUP FRESH LIME JUICE
1/2 SMALL YELLOW ONION, MINCED
1 TABLESPOON MINCED LEMON GRASS
3 KAFFIR LIME LEAVES, CUT INTO FINE SLIVERS
2 ROMA TOMATOES, SEEDED AND CHOPPED
1/2 CUP FRESH MINT LEAVES
4 TO 6 RED LEAF LETTUCE LEAVES
12 FRESH CILANTRO SPRIGS FOR GARNISH
1/2 HEAD WHITE CABBAGE, CORED AND CUT INTO 2-INCH WIDE WEDGES

Heat the oil in a medium nonstick pan over low heat. Add the chili flakes and paprika. Stir for 5 seconds. Add the chicken, brown sugar, and fish sauce and increase the heat to medium. Cook until meat turns white, 3 to 4 minutes. Transfer chicken (but not the juices) to a mixing bowl and add the lime juice, onion, lemon grass, lime leaves, tomatoes, and mint and toss gently. To serve, line salad plates with red leaf lettuce and place a small mound of the chicken mixture on top. Garnish with cilantro and serve with a cabbage wedge.

Kaffir lime is important to ensure the intensely citrus flavor of this dish. If not available, substitute 1 teaspoon lime zest.

To turn this dish into elegant hors d'oeuvres, trim cabbage leaves (especially the cup-like smaller leaves toward the center) into small round pieces, and top with chicken and a small sprig of cilantro.

thai seafood salad

SERVES 4 TO 6

As attractive as it is delicious, this dish is one of my favorites at the restaurant. You can use whatever seafood ingredients you like, although the salmon, prawn, and scallop combination seems to work best because of the variety of textures and flavors. The tamarind, which is a sour fruit commonly used in Asian sauces, gives the dressing a complex tartness. If not available, substitute cider vinegar.

VINAIGRETTE

3 TABLESPOONS TAMARIND PULP

1/3 CUP HOT WATER

1/4 CUP VEGETABLE OIL

2 SHALLOTS, MINCED

1 TEASPOON MINCED GARLIC

2 TEASPOONS MINCED LEMON GRASS

1 TABLESPOON DRIED CHILI FLAKES, OR TO TASTE

2 TABLESPOONS SUGAR

2 TABLESPOONS RICE WINE VINEGAR

2 TABLESPOONS FISH SAUCE

SEAFOOD

1 TABLESPOON VEGETABLE OIL

1/2 POUND BONELESS, SKINLESS SALMON FILLET, CUT AGAINST THE GRAIN
INTO STRIPS ABOUT 1 INCH THICK AND 4 INCHES LONG

12 RAW MEDIUM SHRIMP, PEELED AND DEVEINED

1/3 POUND SEA SCALLOPS

SALAD

1/4 POUND MESCLUN OR MIXED GREENS, WASHED AND DRIED

1 STARFRUIT, THINLY SLICED, OR 1/2 CUP JULIENNED JICAMA

1/2 CUP RED, RIPE CHERRY TOMATOES

Combine the tamarind pulp and hot water, and let soak for 15 minutes. Using the back of a small spoon, mash the pulp until mushy. Push the juice and pulp through a sieve, scraping the pulp to extract as much flavor as possible. Set juice aside.

To make the vinaigrette, heat the 1/4 cup oil in a saucepan over moderate heat and add the shallots, garlic, lemon grass, and chili flakes and stir-fry until fragrant, about 1 minute. Remove from heat and add the sugar, rice wine vinegar, fish sauce, and the tamarind juice. Set aside.

To prepare the seafood, heat the 1 tablespoon oil in a nonstick fry pan over high heat. Brown all the salmon pieces until just cooked, 2 to 3 minutes on each side. Transfer to a plate. If pan is dry, add additional oil. Continue by cooking the shrimp then the scallops until just done, about 1 minute or so on each side.

Just before serving, toss the greens and starfruit in the vinaigrette and portion onto individual salad plates. Top each plate with a piece of salmon and a couple shrimp and scallops. Scatter a few cherry tomatoes around the edge of each plate and serve.

spaghetti-squash salad with poached shrimp and basil

SERVES 4 TO 6

    When I first saw our cooks prepare this dish for staff meals, I thought it was ingenious! Green papayas traditionally are used in this recipe, but since they can be difficult to find, spaghetti squash makes a great substitute. Besides, I find this adapted version much more attractive.

1 (2 TO 3 POUND) SPAGHETTI SQUASH

DRESSING
2 TABLESPOONS FISH SAUCE
1/4 CUP FRESH LIME JUICE
2 TABLESPOONS SUGAR
1 TEASPOON SALT
1 TEASPOON GROUND CHILI PASTE, OR TO TASTE
1 SMALL YELLOW ONION, THINLY SLICED
3 RIPE ROMA TOMATOES, SEEDED AND CUT INTO THIN WEDGES
1/3 POUND COOKED MEDIUM SHRIMP, PEELED AND DEVEINED
20 FRESH THAI BASIL LEAVES, COARSELY CHOPPED
20 FRESH MINT LEAVES, COARSELY CHOPPED

GARNISH
1/4 CUP CHOPPED ROASTED PEANUTS (PAGE 55)
1/4 CUP FRIED SHALLOTS (OPTIONAL, PAGE 45)
12 FRESH CILANTRO SPRIGS

Fill a large soup pot with enough water to cover the squash and bring to a boil. Meanwhile, cut the squash in half lengthwise and using a large spoon, scrape off the seeds and inner skin of the cavity. When the water comes to a rolling boil, drop the squash in and cook until slightly tender in the center, 3 to 5 minutes. (It's better to undercook than to overcook.) Remove from heat and rinse squash with cold water until it is cool enough to handle. Use a fork to gently scrape off the flesh starting from one side and working across the squash to the other. The flesh will break off into strands. Scrape off only one layer at a time, otherwise the strands will be too thick. (You may scrape to within $1/4$ inch of the skin.) Soak the squash strands in ice water for about 15 minutes to "crisp" them. Drain and dry in a salad spinner.

Combine the fish sauce, lime juice, sugar, salt, chili paste, and onion in a large mixing bowl. Add the spaghetti squash, tomatoes, shrimp, basil, and mint and toss gently. To serve, portion onto individual plates and garnish with the roasted peanuts, fried shallots, and cilantro sprigs.

thai caesar salad

For a more striking

presentation, use only the

smaller inner romaine

lettuce leaves and serve

them whole.

This dressing also makes

a delicious sandwich

spread.

Everyone has his or her idea about what a Caesar salad should be, and I have mine. After tasting countless versions, I decided that the following recipe is my favorite interpretation of this classic. The fried garlic lends a complex, nutty flavor, and the fish sauce enhances the flavor without adding fishiness. If you want to make mayonnaise from scratch, you may do so—although I find the commercial stuff works great.

1 CLOVE GARLIC, SLICED AND PAN-FRIED IN OIL UNTIL NICELY BROWNED,
    ABOUT 1 MINUTE
1 TEASPOON MINCED GARLIC
1 TABLESPOON FISH SAUCE
1½ CUPS MAYONNAISE
2 TEASPOONS RED WINE VINEGAR
ZEST OF 1 LEMON
JUICE OF ½ LEMON
1 TEASPOON SUGAR
1 TEASPOON FRESHLY CRACKED BLACK PEPPER
2 KAFFIR LIME LEAVES, CUT INTO THIN SLIVERS AND THEN CHOPPED
1 LARGE HEAD ROMAINE LETTUCE, WASHED, DRIED, CUT INTO BITE-SIZE
    PIECES, AND REFRIGERATED
½ CUP FRESHLY GRATED OR SHAVED GOOD-QUALITY PARMESAN CHEESE
2 CUPS READY-MADE CROUTONS

Place the pan-fried and minced garlic, fish sauce, mayonnaise, vinegar, lemon zest, lemon juice, sugar, and black pepper in a food processor. Blend until smooth and creamy, about 1 minute. Stir in the chopped lime leaves and refrigerate dressing until use.

To serve, toss the romaine with the dressing until well coated. (Add the dressing incrementally. A great Caesar salad should not be overdressed.) Sprinkle on the cheese and croutons and gently toss. Serve immediately.

ginger noodle salad

SERVES 6 TO 8

This noodle salad reminds me of a much plainer, although just as delicious, version I had as a child. The Chinese-Vietnamese love to serve this dish with freshly cooked egg noodles tossed with Chinese black vinegar, soy sauce, and green onion slivers. This recipe is much more embellished, and if served with grilled chicken or prawns, becomes a grand entrée!

1 POUND DRIED CHOW MEIN–STYLE NOODLES, COOKED UNTIL JUST DONE, RINSED, AND DRAINED

1/2 CUP SOY SAUCE, PREFERABLY DARK

3 CUPS BROCCOLI FLORETS, BLANCHED, RINSED IN COLD WATER, AND DRAINED

1/2 RED BELL PEPPER, CUT INTO THIN STRIPS

3 CUPS BEAN SPROUTS

2 GREEN ONIONS, THINLY SLICED ON THE DIAGONAL

6 FRESH CILANTRO SPRIGS FOR GARNISH

DRESSING

2 TABLESPOONS MINCED FRESH GINGER

1/3 CUP SUGAR

1/3 CUP RICE WINE VINEGAR

1 TABLESPOON DRIED CHILI FLAKES (OPTIONAL)

1/3 CUP GOOD-QUALITY DARK SESAME OIL

The noodles can be combined with the soy sauce 2 to 3 days in advance and stored in the refrigerator. Toss gently before serving.

For best results, buy the dried chow mein noodles that are white and straight like spaghetti. The dried curly noodles do not work as well.

Combine the cooked noodles with the soy sauce in a mixing bowl. Refrigerate for at least 2 hours.

To make the dressing, place all the ingredients with the exception of the sesame oil in a food processor and blend until creamy. With the motor running, slowly pour in the sesame oil and blend for about 20 seconds. (Do not overblend or the dressing will turn whitish.)

To serve, gently toss the noodles with the dressing, adding 3 to 4 tablespoons at a time. The noodles should be evenly coated but not soggy. Add the broccoli, red bell pepper, bean sprouts, and green onions and gently toss. Garnish with cilantro sprigs.

roast duck salad with watercress and mandarin orange

SERVES 4

You can buy the roast duck ready-made at any Asian grocery store with a Chinese-style deli. Or, roast the duck at home. An impressive dish, this gorgeous salad is rather simple to assemble.

DRESSING
1 TABLESPOON MINCED SHALLOT
1 TABLESPOON FRESH LIME JUICE
2 TABLESPOONS RICE WINE VINEGAR
1/4 CUP FRESH ORANGE JUICE
2 TABLESPOONS SOY SAUCE
1/4 TEASPOON SALT
2 TABLESPOONS HONEY
1/4 CUP SESAME OIL

SALAD
1/2 FIVE-SPICE ROAST DUCK, COOKED (PAGES 132–133)
3 BUNCHES WATERCRESS, WASHED, DRIED, TOUGH STEMS REMOVED, AND
 TORN INTO BITE-SIZE PIECES
1 HEAD BUTTER LEAF LETTUCE, WASHED, DRIED AND TORN INTO
 BITE-SIZE PIECES
1/2 CUP DRAINED CANNED MANDARIN ORANGE SEGMENTS

Whisk together the shallot, lime juice, vinegar, orange juice, soy sauce, salt, honey, and sesame oil until well blended. Set aside.

Using a sharp knife, cut off the leg, wing, and breast from the cooked duck. Remove the bones and any visible fat and discard. Using a bread knife to cut through the skin without tearing it, cut the meat into bite-size pieces. (If you prefer, remove the skin and shred the meat into bite-size pieces by hand.)

Just before serving, gently toss the duck, watercress, and lettuce with the dressing and transfer to individual salad plates. Garnish with the mandarin orange segments.

I must confess that I never eat chicken skin. However, when it comes to duck, especially roast duck, it's sinful to throw out the skin, especially considering all the trouble it takes to crisp it! The skin is probably one of the best parts of the roast duck. So do what I do—enjoy duck the traditional way, and eat vegetables for the next two or three days!

grilled beef salad with pineapple

SERVES 4

In Bangkok, when the sun is blazing hot around midday, sometimes the best lunch selection is just a small plate of yum nua, or spicy beef salad, and a cold glass of beer. The fresh pineapple, though not traditional, complements the spiciness and tartness of this dish.

1/4 CUP FRESH LIME JUICE

1 1/2 TABLESPOONS FISH SAUCE

2 TABLESPOONS BROWN SUGAR

2 TO 5 THAI BIRD OR SERRANO CHILIES

1 POUND NEW YORK OR FLANK STEAK, GRILLED
        AND SLICED 1/4 INCH THICK

1/2 SMALL RED ONION, THINLY SLICED

1/2 FRESH PINEAPPLE, PEELED, CORED, AND SLICED INTO
        BITE-SIZED PIECES

1/4 CUP THAI BASIL LEAVES

1/2 SMALL CUCUMBER, THINLY SLICED

1 LARGE RIPE TOMATO, CUT INTO THIN WEDGES

CILANTRO SPRIGS FOR GARNISH

Combine the lime juice, fish sauce, brown sugar, and chilies and set aside.

To assemble the salad, gently toss the dressing, steak, onion, pineapple, basil, cucumber, and tomato. Let the ingredients sit in the dressing for 2 to 3 minutes to absorb flavor before serving. If you like, serve the salad on a platter lined with lettuce. Garnish with cilantro.

green papaya salad

SERVES 4 TO 6

The papaya called for in this recipe is the larger and meatier green Asian papaya, which for now can be purchased only at Asian or Latin grocery stores. Do not use sweet papaya in this salad.

In Thailand, the papaya is shredded and then bruised. Although this method produces intense flavor, I have always thought the papaya looked too mushy. I prefer the julienne cut—it still looks great after being bruised.

One morning, while staying in Bangkok, my husband and I were wandering around in search of a more traditional Western-style breakfast, like blueberry pancakes perhaps. (We had just finished a non-stop eating spree from Taipei to Hong Kong.) We couldn't find any pancakes, but instead found a Thai breakfast buffet that featured an interesting "salad" bar. All that were present were a mortar and pestle, green papayas, chilies, garlic, and dried shrimp. Our order was made fresh before our eyes, and what we had was very close to this recipe. It's delicious, especially if the papaya, which is subtle in taste, is bruised slightly to release its flavor. Be careful, this salad can get mighty hot.

3 TO 5 FRESH THAI BIRD CHILIES OR ANY RED CHILIES, THINLY SLICED

1 CLOVE GARLIC, THINLY SLICED

1 SHALLOT, THINLY SLICED

3 DRIED SHRIMP, SOAKED IN WARM WATER FOR 5 MINUTES AND RINSED (OPTIONAL)

2 TEASPOONS BROWN SUGAR

1/2 TEASPOON SALT

1 TABLESPOON FISH SAUCE

4 TABLESPOONS FRESH LIME JUICE

1 SMALL UNRIPE GREEN PAPAYA, PEELED, JULIENNED, AND RINSED AND PATTED DRY WITH PAPER TOWELS (ABOUT 2 TO 3 CUPS)

1 LARGE CARROT, PEELED AND FINELY SHREDDED, SOAKED IN ICE WATER FOR 10 MINUTES, AND DRAINED

8 CHERRY TOMATOES, CUT IN HALF

1 SMALL HEAD RED LEAF LETTUCE, LEAVES SEPARATED AND WASHED

2 TABLESPOONS CHOPPED ROASTED PEANUTS FOR GARNISH (PAGE 55)

Combine the chilies, garlic, shallot, shrimp, and sugar in a mortar and pound into a paste. Transfer to a mixing bowl and add the salt, fish sauce, and lime juice and blend well.

Add the papaya to the mortar. Using a spoon to continuously turn the papaya, gently pound it so the fruit bruises slightly, about 1 minute. You may have to work in several small batches. Add the papaya to the spice mixture. Add the carrot and tomatoes and toss. Transfer to a serving plate lined with lettuce leaves and garnish with peanuts.

mom's cabbage salad

SERVES 4 TO 6

In Vietnam, cabbage is the salad ingredient of choice. Easily available and inexpensive, cabbage has a crunchy texture that stands up well to any dressing, and its mild taste complements any meat or fish. My mother always served this salad with slices of cooked pork and shrimp, but I have found it wonderful with just about any meat—even turkey and fish.

For more flavor and complexity, add some shredded ngo ngai, *or saw-leaf herb, to this salad.*

DRESSING
1/2 YELLOW ONION, THINLY SLICED (ABOUT 1/4 CUP)
1 OR 2 FRESH RED CHILIES, CHOPPED (OPTIONAL)
2 TEASPOONS FISH SAUCE
3 TABLESPOONS FRESH LIME JUICE
1 TEASPOON SALT
3 TABLESPOONS SUGAR
2 TABLESPOONS WATER
2 TEASPOONS WHITE VINEGAR

SALAD
1/2 SMALL HEAD WHITE CABBAGE, SHREDDED, SOAKED IN COLD WATER FOR
    15 MINUTES, DRAINED, AND DRIED
1 CUP SHREDDED CARROTS, SOAKED IN COLD WATER FOR 15 MINUTES,
    DRAINED, AND DRIED
1/2 ENGLISH OR HOTHOUSE CUCUMBER, HALVED AND THINLY SLICED
1/4 CUP FRESH MINT LEAVES, CHOPPED
5 FRESH CILANTRO SPRIGS, CHOPPED
3 TABLESPOONS FRIED SHALLOTS FOR GARNISH (OPTIONAL, PAGE 45)

Combine the dressing ingredients in a small mixing bowl and blend well. Set aside. (Dressing can be made in advance and stored in the refrigerator for up to 2 weeks.)

Toss the cabbage, carrots, cucumber, mint, and cilantro together in a large salad bowl. Add the dressing, a little bit at a time, and continue to toss gently. Garnish with fried shallots.

new york steak with baby greens and sweet nectarines

SERVES 4

This salad is one of my favorites. The bitterness of the greens and the crunchy sweetness of the nectarines are pleasantly juxtaposed against the heartiness of the beef. Prepare this dish in the summer when nectarines are full-flavored and ripe. Come to think of it, I came up with this salad while at a farmers' market.

DRESSING
1 TABLESPOON MINCED SHALLOT
3 TABLESPOONS CHAMPAGNE VINEGAR OR WHITE WINE VINEGAR
2 TABLESPOONS DIJON MUSTARD
3 TABLESPOONS OLIVE OIL
2 TABLESPOONS WATER
1 TEASPOON SUGAR
SALT AND PEPPER TO TASTE

SALAD
1 POUND NEW YORK STEAK, GRILLED OR BROILED MEDIUM-RARE
1/4 POUND BABY GREENS, WASHED AND PATTED DRY
3 RIPE BUT FIRM NECTARINES, SEEDED AND SLICED INTO THIN WEDGES
3 TABLESPOONS COARSELY CHOPPED THAI BASIL LEAVES
1/4 RED ONION, SLICED PAPER THIN

Combine all the dressing ingredients, mix well, and set aside.

Slice the cooked steak against the grain into slices about 2 1/2 inches long and 1/2 inch thick.

In a salad bowl, toss the baby greens, nectarines (reserve a few wedges for garnish), basil, onion, and steak with the dressing. To serve, neatly place a mound of salad in the middle of a plate and garnish with nectarine wedges.

curried rice salad

SERVES 6 TO 8

I always like to make this colorful salad for parties because the bright yellow rice laced with green cucumbers, red bell peppers, and purple grapes looks festive and beautiful. It's also a great dish for potlucks because it seems to go with everything.

RICE
2 CUPS LONG GRAIN RICE
3 CUPS WATER
1/2 TABLESPOON SALT
2 TEASPOONS CURRY POWDER
1 TEASPOON GROUND TURMERIC

DRESSING
1/2 TEASPOON GROUND CUMIN
1 TABLESPOON MINCED SHALLOT
1/4 CUP RED WINE VINEGAR
1 TABLESPOON FRESH LIME JUICE
1 TABLESPOON KOSHER SALT
1/4 CUP CHOPPED FRESH CILANTRO
2 TEASPOONS DRIED CHILI FLAKES (OPTIONAL)
1 TABLESPOON SUGAR
1/3 CUP EXTRA VIRGIN OLIVE OIL

SALAD
1/2 CUP DICED RED BELL PEPPER
1 CUP DICED CUCUMBER
1/2 CUP DICED TOMATOES
1/2 CUP FINELY MINCED YELLOW ONION
2 TO 3 CUPS CHAMPAGNE GRAPES OR SMALL SEEDLESS RED OR GREEN
    GRAPES, WASHED

Place rice, water, salt, curry powder, and turmeric in a medium pot and bring to a boil. Using a wooden spoon, stir the rice so the ingredients are well blended. Let the rice boil gently for 3 minutes, then reduce heat to a very low simmer and cover with a tight-fitting lid. Cook until the water has evaporated and the rice is fluffy, 25 to 30 minutes. Do not lift the lid before then.

While the rice is cooking, make the dressing. In a food processor, blend all the ingredients together except for the olive oil. Process until a little creamy, about 1 minute, then slowly drizzle in the oil with the motor running. Set aside.

Once the rice is cooked, fluff with fork, and transfer to a large bowl. Set aside to cool. Just before serving, combine the red bell pepper, cucumber, tomatoes, onion, grapes, dressing, and rice and toss gently. Salad may be refrigerated, although it loses flavor the second day.

seafood and saffron rice salad

SERVES 6 TO 8

I have always had a fascination with Italy. When I first stepped foot there several years ago, I knew immediately why. The passion the Italians have for their food and wine is incredible. In fact, it's infectious. While walking down the narrow streets of Venice, I often stopped by restaurants to look at the wonderful window displays. Even when I had just eaten, still I would dream about the next meal. One time, I thought about how great seafood antipasto would be in a salad with saffron rice. Once home in Sacramento, I decided to give it a try.

RICE
1 TEASPOON SAFFRON THREADS

3 CUPS WATER

2 CUPS RICE, PREFERABLY JASMINE

$1/2$ TABLESPOON SALT

1 TEASPOON GROUND TURMERIC

DRESSING
3 TABLESPOONS MINCED SHALLOTS

$1/4$ CUP BALSAMIC VINEGAR

$1/2$ CUP EXTRA VIRGIN OLIVE OIL

1 TABLESPOON KOSHER SALT

SALAD
2 TABLESPOONS OLIVE OIL

3 CLOVES GARLIC, THINLY SLICED

1 TABLESPOON CHILI FLAKES

1 TEASPOON KOSHER SALT

1 POUND BLACK MUSSELS, SCRUBBED CLEAN

$1/2$ CUP DRY WHITE WINE

$1/3$ POUND RAW MEDIUM PRAWNS, PEELED AND DEVEINED

$1/3$ POUND FRESH SCALLOPS

$1/3$ POUND WHITE MUSHROOMS, HALVED

$1/2$ CUP DICED RED BELL PEPPER

¼ CUP COARSELY CHOPPED FRESH SWEET BASIL
1 CUP YELLOW OR RED CHERRY TOMATOES, HALVED
6 SPRIGS FRESH PARSLEY FOR GARNISH

Place the saffron threads and water in a medium pot and bring to a boil. Let boil for 3 to 4 minutes, then add the rice, salt, and turmeric. Using a wooden spoon, stir the rice often so that it doesn't stick to the bottom of the pot. Let rice boil for 2 minutes, then reduce heat to a very low simmer and cover with a tight-fitting lid. Cook until the water has evaporated and rice is fluffy, about 20 minutes. Do not lift the lid before then.

While the rice is cooking, make the dressing. Blend all the dressing ingredients together and set aside.

Once the rice is cooked, fluff with fork and transfer to a tray to let it cool.

In a large skillet or fry pan, heat the 2 tablespoons olive oil over high heat. Add the garlic and stir until fragrant, about 30 seconds. Add the chili flakes, salt, and mussels and toss around in the pan until the mussels begin to open, about 2 to 3 minutes. Add the wine, prawns, scallops, and mushrooms and cook until all ingredients are done, another 2 to 3 minutes.

Transfer the seafood to a mixing bowl. Set aside to cool to room temerature, then refrigerate for at least 1 hour.

Just before serving, add the dressing to the seafood mixture along with the red bell pepper, basil, and tomatoes. Fold the cooled rice into the seafood mixture and toss gently. Tranfer to a large platter and garnish with sprigs of flat-leaf parsley.

nutty chinese chicken salad

SERVES 6 TO 8

My Chinese friends tell me they don't know how this dish ever came about since it's not part of the traditional Chinese repertoire. In any case, I suppose there's a desire in the Western world to indulge in a salad that ties together the things we love—chicken, soy sauce, and lettuce. Here's my version.

DRESSING

1 (1-INCH) PIECE FRESH GINGER, PEELED AND THINLY SLICED

2 CLOVES GARLIC, SLICED

1 TEASPOON DRIED CHILI FLAKES

1/3 CUP RICE WINE VINEGAR

3 TABLESPOONS WATER

1 TABLESPOON MOLASSES

2 TABLESPOONS HONEY

3 TABLESPOONS SOY SAUCE

1/2 CUP GOOD-QUALITY DARK SESAME OIL

SALAD

2 CUPS COOKED CHICKEN, SLICED INTO STRIPS 2 INCHES LONG AND
    1/4 INCH WIDE

1 SMALL HEAD ICEBERG LETTUCE, SHREDDED

1/2 SMALL HEAD ROMAINE LETTUCE, SHREDDED, CRISPED IN COLD WATER,
    AND DRIED

1 CARROT, PEELED AND SHREDDED, CRISPED IN COLD WATER, AND DRIED

3 STALKS CELERY, THINLY SLICED

1/2 RED ONION, THINLY SLICED

1/2 CUP ROASTED WHOLE PEANUTS

2 TABLESPOONS CHOPPED FRESH CILANTRO

1 OUNCE FLAT RICE NOODLES, FRIED IN HOT OIL FOR 5 SECONDS (NOODLES
    SHOULD PUFF UP) AND DRAINED, FOR GARNISH

To make this salad more attractive, try cutting the carrots into "ribbons." Using a peeler, slice the carrots into thin shavings and soak in ice water for 15 minutes.

Combine all dressing ingredients in a food processor and blend until the ginger and garlic are finely minced. With the motor running, slowly drizzle in the sesame oil.

Place half of the dressing in a large mixing bowl and add the chicken. Let sit for 5 minutes, so the chicken absorbs the flavor of the dressing.

Add the iceberg and romaine lettuces, carrot, celery, onion, peanuts, and cilantro and toss gently, adding more dressing if necessary. Garnish with rice noodle puffs.

thai calamari salad

SERVES 4 TO 6

If you've been to Bangkok and didn't get to taste this, you definitely should go back and do so. To me, no salad is as Thai as yum pla muk. *It's so sour it makes my mouth pucker and so hot I must have a glass of beer nearby. Fresh calamari or squid is a bit diffi-cult to find outside Asian markets and fish markets. But if you like calamari, it's well worth the effort. If you don't, substitute shrimp.*

2 TABLESPOONS VEGETABLE OIL

2 TABLESPOONS MINCED SHALLOT

1/2 TABLESPOON MINCED GARLIC

1 TABLESPOON DRIED CHILI FLAKES, OR MORE TO TASTE

2 TABLESPOONS SUGAR

1/4 CUP FRESH LIME JUICE

3 TABLESPOONS FISH SAUCE

2 POUNDS FRESH OR FROZEN CALAMARI WITH OR WITHOUT TENTACLES,
      CLEANED AND CENTER TUBES CUT INTO 1-INCH RINGS

1/2 CUCUMBER, PREFERABLY ENGLISH OR HOTHOUSE, HALVED LENGTHWISE,
      SEEDED, AND SLICED 1/4 INCH THICK ON THE DIAGONAL

1/4 CUP FRESH MINT LEAVES, COARSELY CHOPPED

1 TABLESPOON MINCED LEMON GRASS

1/2 YELLOW ONION, THINLY SLICED

2 KAFFIR LIME LEAVES, CUT INTO THIN SLIVERS

2 TOMATOES, PREFERABLY ROMA, SEEDED AND CUT INTO THIN WEDGES

2 CUPS SHREDDED ICEBERG LETTUCE OR WHITE CABBAGE

10 FRESH CILANTRO SPRIGS FOR GARNISH

Heat the oil in a wok or a medium stir-fry pan over moderate heat. Add the shallot, garlic, and chili flakes and stir until fragrant, about 20 seconds. Add the sugar and lime juice and stir for another 20 seconds. Remove from heat and add the fish sauce. Transfer to a mixing bowl.

Bring water to a rolling boil in small soup pot. Place the calamari in a strainer with a handle. Lower into the pot and blanch the calamari until it turns almost white, about 10 to 20 seconds. Do not overcook or the calamari gets very tough. Remove from boiling water and rinse under cold running water. Drain and set aside.

Just before serving, add the calamari to the dressing. Toss until well coated. Add the cucumber, mint, lemon grass, onion, lime leaves, and tomatoes. To serve, line a platter with shredded lettuce and top with salad. Garnish with cilantro.

Chapter five

A Little Bit of Home

pho bo and other soups

In my old neighborhood in Saigon, mornings and *pho bo,* or beef noodle soup, went hand in hand. Every morning, a crowd would gather at a noodle soup shop about a block from where we lived. Although two competitors were right across the street, this particular shop was always the most popular.

At seven in the morning, all the small wooden tables and chairs—some spilling out onto the sidewalk and street—already were taken. With his face sweating and eyes squinting behind the billowing soup pot, Uncle Hai, the owner, was intent on feeding everyone quickly. His makeshift kitchen, located directly in front of the store, consisted of only a counter and one stove for the large soup pot in the middle. The large pot had a divider separating the beef stock from the boiling water. First, Uncle Hai heated large serving bowls by ladling boiling water in them and then emptying it back into the pot. Then, he grabbed a handful of noodles and placed them inside a wire basket. After blanching them for a few seconds, he lifted the basket and banged it against the edge of the pot a few times, fearing that even one excess drop of water would dilute and spoil his broth. Working in an almost panicky rhythm, he transferred the noodles to a bowl and topped them with chopped onions, cilantro, and a few slices of rare beef along with some cooked meat. To finish assembling the soup, Uncle Hai then carefully poured the broth against the inside edge of the bowl so that all the toppings would stay intact. Each time he ladled the broth, a wonderful beefy, gingery aroma filled the air. Mesmerized by his movements and teased by the aroma of his soup, I became more eager for my own bowl. When it finally arrived, I realized it was well worth the wait. I glanced across the room and knew I was not alone in thinking that. By then a larger crowd had gathered, all waiting for the next available seat.

In the seventies, when Trong returned to Saigon after six years of study in the United States, his top priority was not to lay the groundwork for a job after graduation but to seek out the best *pho* recipe. Back then, it was nearly impossible to find a restaurant in Sacramento serving *pho bo*. Although his goal seemed rather odd (especially for a technically minded person striving to become Vietnam's first American-trained geneticist), Trong had a plan of a different sort all along. With a great *pho* recipe, he would be able to recreate what every Vietnamese expatriate longed for—a little bit of home and a sense of familiarity—all with just a large, steaming bowl of soup. Sounds deep, but that is the power of *pho*.

And powerful it was. After persuading a family friend and the proprietor of one of Saigon's most popular restaurants to share her trade secrets, on the condition they would never be disclosed, Trong was able to secure the recipe along with a bag of "secret" spices.

A few months after returning to Sacramento, Trong put this recipe to great use. A onetime student activist, Trong orchestrated a university fundraising event that centered on this beloved dish of the Vietnamese. Trong served what was reportedly (I was still ducking artillery fire in Saigon at the time) the first authentic *pho* in Sacramento. It was an astounding success, with hundreds of Vietnamese and American students queueing up from one end of the hall to another for a steaming bowl of beef noodle soup. Today, even after two decades, I still hear about this great event and how wonderful and aromatic the soup was— even from those who came late and had their soup diluted with water because Trong ran out of broth.

With more than one million Vietnamese in the United States, restaurants specializing in *pho* are now rather common. But not all of our soups fall into this meal-in-itself category. The non-noodle soups, which are usually clear, are frequently prepared at home and treated not so much as a first course, but as a companion dish to enhance a great meal.

vietnamese beef noodle soup

SERVES 6 TO 10

In Vietnam, beef knuckle bones are used to make the broth. However, because they are quite awkward for home use, I have modified the recipe to include items that are easily available and handled. By the way, this soup really cannot be made in small quantities—it won't taste as good, trust me. So invite some friends over or save the leftovers for the following day. The secret to great pho is to serve it in very large, heated soup bowls with lots of broth.

BROTH

4 POUNDS BEEF CHUCK, TRIMMED OF VISIBLE FAT AND CUT INTO 3 TO 4 PIECES

6 QUARTS WATER

3 TABLESPOONS SALT

2 (5-INCH) PIECES FRESH GINGER, UNPEELED

2 YELLOW ONIONS, PEELED

10 WHOLE STAR ANISE

8 WHOLE CLOVES

1/4 CUP FISH SAUCE

5 TABLESPOONS SUGAR

NOODLES

1 POUND DRIED SMALL RICE STICKS, SOAKED IN HOT WATER 20 MINUTES
    THEN DRAINED

ACCOMPANIMENTS

1/4 POUND TOP SIRLOIN (OPTIONAL)

1 YELLOW ONION, SLICED PAPER-THIN

3 GREEN ONIONS, CHOPPED

1/2 BUNCH FRESH CILANTRO, CHOPPED

1 POUND BEAN SPROUTS

24 FRESH THAI BASIL SPRIGS

1 DOZEN SPRIGS FRESH SAW-LEAF HERB (OPTIONAL)

2 LIMES, CUT INTO WEDGES

3 FRESH RED OR GREEN CHILIES, SLICED

FISH SAUCE

Fill a very large stockpot with water and bring to a boil. Add the beef chuck pieces and boil for 5 minutes. Remove from heat and drain off the water to discard impurities. Return the beef to the pot and fill with the 6 quarts of fresh water. Add salt and bring to a boil. Reduce heat to simmer and skim the surface ocassionally to remove impurities.

While the stock is cooking, dry-roast the ginger and 2 onions by placing them in a fry pan over high heat. Turn so the skins are evenly charred but not cooked, about 2 to 3 minutes on each side. Remove from heat and add to the soup stock. Then add the star anise, cloves, fish sauce, and sugar and continue to simmer until the meat is tender, about 1 1/2 hours. Remove 1 piece of chuck from the pot and set it aside to cool. Continue to simmer the other 2 or 3 pieces to create a rich beef broth, about 30 minutes more. (Don't be alarmed if the broth seems salty. Once the noodles and condiments are added, the seasonings will balance.)

Meanwhile, arrange the accompaniments on a platter and set aside. Cut the reserved piece of chuck roast into thin slices. If using the rare beef topping, slice the sirloin into very thin strips and arrange on platter.

You may continue to let the broth simmer, but remove the spices and onions from the broth. The ginger can remain. (Cooking the spices too long will make the broth dark and too pungent.) If the meat looks like it's going to fall apart in the broth, remove it and discard, or save for another use.

Just before serving, bring a large pot of water to a boil. Place a handful of noodles in a sieve with a handle and lower into the boiling water. Using a fork or chop sticks, stir the noodles often and cook until just done, about 2 minutes. Remove the sieve and shake a bit to drain well. You may cook 2 to 3 portions of noodles at a time. Transfer noodles to *large* warmed soup bowls.

To serve, place a few slices of chuck roast and sirloin on the noodles. Top with about a tablespoon each of sliced yellow onions, green onions, and cilantro. Ladle a generous amount of boiling beef broth on top. (To enjoy *pho* correctly, it is critical that the bowl be large enough to hold about 1 part noodles and 4 parts soup.) Serve with the accompaniments, allowing each guest to top the soup with bean sprouts, herbs, chilies, a squeeze of lime, and more fish sauce if desired.

yummy hot and sour shrimp soup

SERVES 4

If I could have just one thing in Bangkok, it would be this soup. Called tom yum goong, it's as characteristically Thai as you can get. Using freshwater shrimp with the tails and heads intact, the Thais make this soup very hot and very sour. It's so memorable that it can be an "entrée."

2 CLOVES GARLIC, SLICED

1 SHALLOT, SLICED

1 TEASPOON GROUND CHILI PASTE

1 FRESH RED CHILI, ANY KIND (OPTIONAL)

1 TABLESPOON CHOPPED FRESH CILANTRO

1 TEASPOON WHOLE BLACK PEPPERCORNS

2 TABLESPOONS VEGETABLE OIL

$1/3$ POUND RAW MEDIUM SHRIMP, PEELED AND DEVEINED (RESERVE
THE SHELLS)

5 CUPS HOMEMADE UNSALTED OR CANNED LOW-SODIUM CHICKEN STOCK

1 STALK LEMON GRASS, CUT INTO 1-INCH PIECES AND BRUISED WITH THE
BACK OF A KNIFE

3 THIN SLICES GALANGA

3 KAFFIR LIME LEAVES, CUT INTO THIRDS

3 TABLESPOONS FISH SAUCE

1 TABLESPOON BROWN SUGAR

$1/2$ CUP DRAINED CANNED STRAW MUSHROOMS OR SLICED WHITE
MUSHROOMS

2 RED RIPE TOMATOES, CUT INTO THIN WEDGES

$1/3$ CUP FRESH LIME JUICE

10 FRESH THAI BASIL LEAVES

5 FRESH CILANTRO SPRIGS, CHOPPED

To fully enjoy this dish, you must serve it piping hot. In Thailand, this soup comes to the table in a hot pot with charcoals stacked in the middle chimney. When the lid is opened, the table is filled with the wonderful fragrance of chilies, lime leaves, and galanga. To replicate this effect at home—and I would recommend it—warm your soup tureen and bowls before using. To keep the soup hot during the meal, keep the lid on the tureen.

Place the garlic, shallot, chili paste, chili, cilantro, and peppercorns into a mortar and pound into a paste.

Heat the oil in a soup pot over moderate heat. Add the shrimp shells and brown until fragrant, about 2 minutes. Add the spice mixture to the pot and stir until fragrant, about 20 seconds. Add the chicken stock and let simmer for 5 minutes. Using a slotted spoon, remove the shells and discard. Add the lemon grass, galanga, lime leaves, fish sauce, brown sugar, mushrooms, and tomatoes and bring to a boil. Add the shrimp and cook until almost done, about 2 minutes. (Shrimp will continue to cook in the hot broth.) Remove from heat and add the lime juice, basil, and cilantro. Serve piping hot.

vietnamese fisherman's soup

SERVES 6

Nothing can be more Vietnamese than serving canh chua *with Mom's Catfish in Claypot (page 227) and rice. A staple soup in our home, this dish my mother used to pre-pare at least twice a week, sometimes with shrimp, sometimes with catfish. In this dish, both tamarind (which imparts more flavor and body) and lime juice are used. If tamarind is unavailable, substitute equal amounts of lime juice. It's important to serve this soup imme-diately after cooking because the vegetables get soft quickly.*

Second to pho bo, *or beef noodle soup, this* canh chua *is the most popular soup in Vietnam. The veg-etables and seafood can vary but the broth must always be spicy, sour, and a little sweet. Also, don't add the herbs until you are really ready to eat!*

1/4 POUND RAW MEDIUM SHRIMP, PEELED AND DEVEINED

1/3 POUND BONELESS, SKINLESS SALMON, CUT INTO BITE-SIZE PIECES

1/4 POUND SCALLOPS

1 TABLESPOON VEGETABLE OIL

1 TEASPOON GROUND CHILI PASTE

1 TEASPOON MINCED GARLIC

5 CUPS HOMEMADE UNSALTED OR CANNED LOW-SODIUM CHICKEN STOCK

2 MEDIUM TOMATOES, CUT INTO THIN WEDGES

2 CUPS FRESHLY CUT PINEAPPLE CUBES

1/2 MEDIUM ONION, CUT INTO THIN WEDGES

2 TABLESPOONS FISH SAUCE

3 TABLESPOONS SUGAR

1/4 TEASPOON SALT

2 TABLESPOONS TAMARIND PULP, SOAKED IN 1/3 CUP HOT WATER AND
    PUSHED THROUGH A SIEVE

4 TABLESPOONS FRESH LIME JUICE

2 CUPS BEAN SPROUTS

1 HEAPING TABLESPOON CHOPPED FRESH RICE-PADDY HERB OR
    SAW-LEAF HERB

1 HEAPING TABLESPOON CHOPPED FRESH THAI BASIL

2 TABLESPOONS FRIED SHALLOTS FOR GARNISH (PAGE 45)

Bring water to a boil in a medium pot. Using a strainer with a handle, blanch all seafood for about 10 to 20 seconds. (This removes impurities and keeps the chicken stock clear when you add the seafood later.) Set aside.

Discard water and wipe the pot dry. Add the oil and heat over moderate heat. Add the chili paste and garlic and allow to sizzle until fragrant, about 10 seconds. Add chicken stock and bring to a boil. Then add the seafood, tomatoes, pineapple, onion, fish sauce, sugar, salt, tamarind, and lime juice. Cook until seafood is just done, about 3 to 5 minutes. Remove from heat, and add bean sprouts and herbs. Garnish with fried shallots and serve piping hot.

thai chicken soup with coconut milk and galanga

SERVES 4

Few soups can top the delicateness and uniqueness of this Thai chicken soup. The secret is the galanga—whether it's fresh or frozen, remember to give it a few whacks with a knife before adding it to the broth. Otherwise, you'll be missing the aroma of this exotic root.

1 TABLESPOON VEGETABLE OIL

1 SHALLOT, THINLY SLICED

1/2 TEASPOON MINCED GARLIC

1 TABLESPOON MINCED LEMON GRASS

1 TEASPOON DRIED RED CHILI FLAKES, OR TO TASTE

1 TEASPOON GROUND CHILI PASTE, OR TO TASTE

1 (1-INCH) SECTION FROZEN OR FRESH GALANGA, THINLY SLICED AND
    BRUISED WITH THE BACK OF A KNIFE

3 CUPS HOMEMADE UNSALTED OR CANNED LOW-SODIUM CHICKEN STOCK

2 TABLESPOONS FISH SAUCE, OR TO TASTE

1 TEASPOON SUGAR

2 CUPS UNSWEETENED COCONUT MILK

1/3 POUND CHICKEN BREASTS OR THIGHS, SKINNED, BONED, AND CUT INTO
    1/2 INCH CUBES

1 CUP STRAW OR WHITE MUSHROOMS

1 CUP CUBED RED RIPE TOMATO

1/2 TABLESPOON FRESH LIME JUICE

2 KAFFIR LIME LEAVES, CUT IN HALF

6 FRESH CILANTRO SPRIGS, CHOPPED, FOR GARNISH

Heat the oil in a saucepan over medium heat until moderately hot. Add the shallot, garlic, lemon grass, chili flakes, and chili paste and brown slightly, about 30 seconds. Working quickly and without burning the spices, add the galanga, chicken stock, fish sauce, sugar, and coconut milk. Bring to a boil and add the chicken, mushrooms, and tomato. As soon as it comes to a second boil, turn off the heat and add the lime juice and lime leaves and serve immediately. Garnish with the cilantro.

For a richer broth, increase the proportion of coconut milk to chicken stock. For a thinner broth, reduce the ratio of coconut milk to chicken stock. Or, substitute regular, lowfat, or nonfat cows' milk for the coconut milk.

Advise guests not to eat the galanga and lime leaves—they are for flavoring only.

chicken and bean thread noodle soup

SERVES 4 TO 6

As a child, I loved this soup because it was fun trying to eat the long, chewy noodles and drink the broth at the same time. (Hint: use a spoon and chopsticks.) I have added a pinch of ground turmeric to this clean-tasting, clear broth soup so that the transparent noodles show up better.

2 TABLESPOONS VEGETABLE OIL

1 CLOVE GARLIC, THINLY SLICED

2 SHALLOTS, THINLY SLICED

5 CUPS HOMEMADE UNSALTED OR CANNED LOW-SODIUM CHICKEN STOCK

1/3 POUND WHOLE BONELESS, SKINLESS CHICKEN BREASTS, CHOPPED

1 CUP DRIED BEAN THREAD NOODLES, SEPARATED AND SOAKED IN WARM
     WATER FOR 30 MINUTES, DRAINED, AND CUT INTO 4-INCH STRANDS WITH
     A SCISSORS

2 TABLESPOONS DRIED TREE EAR MUSHROOMS SOAKED IN HOT WATER 30
     MINUTES AND CHOPPED IF LARGE

1/4 TEASPOON GROUND TURMERIC

2 TABLESPOONS FISH SAUCE

2 TEASPOONS SUGAR

1 CUP CHOPPED BABY BOK CHOY OR FRESH SPINACH

3 GREEN ONIONS, THINLY SLICED ON THE DIAGONAL

10 FRESH CILANTRO SPRIGS, CHOPPED FOR GARNISH

Heat the oil in a small soup pot over moderate heat until hot. Add the garlic and shallots and stir until fragrant. Add chicken stock and bring to a boil. Add the chicken, bean thread noodles, mushrooms, and turmeric and cook until chicken turns white, about 5 to 7 minutes. Add the remaining ingredients except the cilantro and cook until vegetables are wilted, another 2 minutes. Garnish with cilantro and serve.

Also called wood ears or cloud ears, tree ears are commonly used in Chinese and other Asian cooking. Sold in dried form ranging in color from very black to brown to gray, these mushrooms have little flavor and are mainly used to add texture. I prefer the tiny charcoal-black variety as they are more tender and crunchy. These days, tree ear mushrooms also come conveniently presliced. Just soak in water for 30 minutes before using.

stuffed-cucumber soup

SERVES 6

If you haven't tasted cooked cucumbers, you're missing out on a great thing. Cucumbers are one of those vegetables that taste wonderfully different once cooked. This recipe can be used with hollowed-out bitter melons or small, fuzzy melons. The smaller the vegetable, the more elegant this soup looks.

STUFFED CUCUMBERS

4 BLACK MUSHROOMS, SOAKED IN HOT WATER FOR 30 MINUTES, DRAINED
   AND RINSED
1 OUNCE BEAN THREAD NOODLES, SOAKED IN HOT WATER FOR 30 MINUTES
   AND DRAINED
2 SMALL CUCUMBERS
$1/3$ POUND GROUND LEAN PORK
1 EGG
$1/2$ TEASPOON FISH SAUCE

SOUP

1 TABLESPOON VEGETABLE OIL
2 SHALLOTS, THINLY SLICED
5 CUPS UNSALTED HOMEMADE OR CANNED LOW-SODIUM CHICKEN STOCK
$1/4$ TEASPOON SALT
1 TEASPOON FISH SAUCE
1 TEASPOON SOY SAUCE
1 GREEN ONION, THINLY SLICED ON THE DIAGONAL, FOR GARNISH

Wrap the mushrooms and bean thread noodles with a damp cheesecloth and squeeze to remove excess water. Mince the mushrooms, then chop the bean thread noodles.

Peel the cucumbers lengthwise, leaving strips of peel intact. Cut into $1^1/2$-inch pieces. Using a small spoon, remove the seeds from the center.

Combine the mushrooms, noodles, pork, egg, and fish sauce until mixture starts to stick together. Stuff mixture into the hollowed-out cucumber pieces, using your hands to mold the filling so it is rounded on the ends.

Heat the oil in a soup pot over moderate heat. Add the shallots and sauté until fragrant, about 1 minute. Add the chicken stock and bring to a boil. Add the stuffed cucumbers, salt, fish sauce, and soy sauce. Reduce heat and simmer for 15 minutes.

To serve, place 2 to 3 stuffed cucumbers in the center of each shallow serving bowl, then ladle the broth on top. Garnish with green onion.

thai clam chowder with asian pumpkin

SERVES 6 TO 8

If you like clam chowder, this version with a Thai twist is great and easy to pre-
pare. You may use canned or frozen clam meat. When I prepare this dish for guests, I jazz
up the presentation a bit and put a few whole clams into each bowl.

4 POUNDS FRESH CLAMS, PREFERABLY MANILLA, SCRUBBED CLEAN
3 CUPS WATER
2 TABLESPOONS BUTTER
1 TABLESPOON VEGETABLE OIL
1 YELLOW ONION, CUBED
2 TEASPOONS DRIED RED CHILI FLAKES, OR TO TASTE
1 1/2 POUNDS RED POTATOES, PEELED AND CUBED
2 POUNDS ASIAN PUMPKIN, PREFERABLY KABOCHA, PEELED,
    SEEDED, AND CUBED
1/2 CUP CHOPPED LEEKS
3 CUPS HALF-AND-HALF
1 TABLESPOON FISH SAUCE
1/4 TEASPOON SALT
2 GREEN ONIONS, CHOPPED
FRESHLY GROUND BLACK PEPPER

Put the clams and water in a wok or deep saucepan and cover. Bring to a boil.
Cook just long enough to open the shells, 3 to 5 minutes. Remove from heat. Using tongs or
a strainer with a handle, remove the open clams from the broth. Discard any that did not
open. Keep the broth in the pan. Pick out about a dozen cooked clams and set aside.
Remove the meat from the remaining clams, making sure the juices are saved and returned
to the pan. Set the clam meat aside.

When buying clams, look for those that are tightly shut. If they are open, touch them, and if they don't quickly clam up, pass them by. Avoid the bigger, thicker-shelled clams, as they have little meat and seem to take forever to open when cooked. Fresh clams should be cooked the day you bring them home. They can be stored, at most, for 2 days.

Heat the butter and vegetable oil in a soup pot until hot, then add the onion and chili flakes. Sautée until onion is wilted and fragrant, about 2 minutes. Carefully and slowly, pour the clam broth into the soup pot, leaving any sandy broth in the pan. Bring broth to a boil, then add the potatoes. Cook for 10 minutes, then add the pumpkin. Reduce heat to low, add leeks, and simmer until vegetables are tender, about 10 minutes more.

Meanwhile, chop the clam meat and set aside.

Stir the half-and-half, fish sauce, and salt into the broth and bring to a simmer. Add the clam meat and the reserved whole clams and cook until thoroughly hot, about 1 minute. To serve, place a couple whole clams in each bowl of chowder and sprinkle with green onions and ground pepper.

velvety chicken rice soup with ginger

SERVES 6

This soup is simple, delicious, and wonderful even when you're not sick—and very convenient when you're writing a cookbook! I'm one of those chefs who do not cook at home (I do it enough at the restaurant), and our refrigerator stores only juices and fruits. While writing this book, I was often homebound with little to munch on. The kitchen staff often would send lunch and dinner, and many times, this soup was part of the package.

2 TABLESPOONS VEGETABLE OIL
1 TEASPOON MINCED GARLIC
1/2 CUP RICE, PREFERABLY JASMINE
6 CUPS HOMEMADE UNSALTED OR CANNED LOW-SODIUM CHICKEN STOCK
1/3 POUND SKINLESS, BONELESS CHICKEN BREAST, CUBED
1/2 TEASPOON SALT
1 TABLESPOON FRESH GINGER, THINLY SLICED
2 SCALLIONS, THINLY SLICED ON THE DIAGONAL, FOR GARNISH
10 FRESH CILANTRO SPRIGS, CHOPPED, FOR GARNISH
GROUND WHITE PEPPER FOR GARNISH

Heat the oil and garlic in a small soup pot over moderate heat. Add the rice and toss around in the pot until rice turns white and opaque, about 3 minutes. Add the chicken stock and bring to gentle boil. Reduce heat and simmer until rice has expanded and soup is velvety, about 20 minutes. Add the chicken, salt, and ginger and simmer for another 8 to 10 minutes. Remove from heat. Transfer to individual serving bowls and garnish with scallions, cilantro, and white pepper.

Unlike Vietnamese cooks who prefer a grainy rice soup, the Chinese like theirs porridge-style. To make the Chinese version, omit browning the rice, and substitute half the chicken stock with water. Add the rice directly to the stock and slowly simmer for 1 hour, beating frequently with a wire whisk.

Heat 1/3 cup of the coconut milk in a nonstick stir-fry pan over moderate heat until bubbly and hot. Add the curry paste and lemon grass, and stir until fragrant, about 1 minute. Add the chicken stock, fish sauce, sugar, turmeric, and lime leaves. Bring to a boil. Add the chicken and cook until it turns white, 3 to 5 minutes. Reduce the heat to low. Add the remaining coconut milk, bamboo shoots, peas, and tomatoes. Continue to simmer until vegetables are thoroughly hot, about 3 minutes. Do not allow coconut milk to boil vigorously, as it will separate. Remove from heat and add the basil. Garnish with cilantro. Serve immediately with steamed jasmine rice.

In Thailand and Vietnam, a popular way to eat curry is with fresh white noodle "nests" called kanom jeen *in Thai or* bun tuoi *in Vietnamese. If you want to add noodles, increase the amount of coconut milk or stock— noodles tend to need more sauce.*

five-spice roast duck

SERVES 4

Peking-style ducks, which have meaty breasts, can be purchased at Asian grocery stores with a good meat selection. If using a frozen duck, lower the temperature by 30 degrees and increase the cooking time since the meat is not as tender.

For an even crispier skin, quarter the duck and quickly pan-sear it in a large skillet over high heat, skin-side down.

To my mind, no one does this dish better than the Chinese, who traditionally use bicycle pumps to separate the skin of the duck from the flesh so that it becomes crisp and brittle after cooking. After the marinade juices are sewn up in the cavity, the duck is slowly roasted in an upright, closet-like oven, resulting in a Chinese roast duck that is crispy, tender, and juicy. Though it's impossible to replicate this at home, the following recipe renders a tasty product without the traditional fuss. Ed Marlow, a friend and regular customer of the restaurant, tested this recipe (he used a hair-dryer to blow-dry the duck) and reported his bird turned out great.

1 FRESH ROASTING DUCK, PREFERABLY PEKING-STYLE
  (ABOUT 3 TO 4 POUNDS)
2 CUPS WHITE VINEGAR
2 TABLESPOONS KOSHER SALT
1 TABLESPOON FIVE-SPICE POWDER
3 ($1/4$-INCH-THICK) SLICES FRESH GINGER
3 TABLESPOONS RICE WINE OR DRY SHERRY
2 TABLESPOONS SUGAR
3 TABLESPOONS SOY SAUCE
$1/4$ CUP HOISIN SAUCE
$1/3$ CUP WATER
6 WHOLE STAR ANISE
3 GREEN ONIONS, CUT INTO 1-INCH PIECES
2 YELLOW ONIONS, HALVED
1 CUP CILANTRO-LIME SOY SAUCE (PAGE 36)

Remove any visible fat from the duck, including the large skin flap at the neck and in the cavity area. Remove the wing tips. Using a sharp fork or skewer, pierce holes in the skin of the entire duck about $1/2$ inch deep.

Roast duck makes a great topping for canapés. Dab a little mayonnaise on a lightly toasted piece of bread, line with a sprig of watercress, top with hand-shredded duck meat, and dot with Hoisin-Peanut Sauce (page 35).

Fill a 12-quart stockpot with water and add the white vinegar. Bring to a rolling boil. With a sieve or skimmer, carefully lower the duck into the water and blanch it for 30 seconds. Remove the duck from the water, wait for the water to reboil, and blanch the duck again. Pat the duck dry with a dish towel. Rub the salt and five-spice powder all over the bird and inside the cavity. Hang duck overnight in a cold, drafty place or place on a rack and refrigerate. (Duck can be refrigerated at this stage for 2 days.)

The next morning, combine the ginger, rice wine, sugar, soy sauce, hoisin sauce, water, and star anise. Place duck on a rack on a roasting pan and brush evenly with the marinade. Reserve remaining marinade for later use. Using an upright turkey roasting stand, place the duck directly in front of a fan and let it air-dry for 2 hours, turning frequently. (You may also use a hair dryer to blow-dry the bird. This usually takes about 30 minutes.)

Preheat oven to 400 degrees.

Place the remaining marinade (including the ginger slices and star anise) and the green onions and yellow onions into the cavity of the duck. With a metal or wooden skewer, thread the cavity shut. Place the pan on the lower rack of the oven. Roast the duck, uncovered, breast side up for 30 minutes. Reduce heat to 350 degrees, turn the duck over, and roast 30 minutes. Turn the duck over again and roast breast side up until juices run clear and meat is tender, another 30 to 40 minutes. If necessary, cover the legs and wings with foil to prevent burning. Serve with cilantro-lime soy sauce.

grilled lemon grass chicken

SERVES 4

Very simple and delicious, this dish takes minutes to make. It's especially superb if the lemon grass is freshly picked, when its citrusy aroma is rather intense. If cooked just right, the chicken stays moist and is delicious even when served cold.

2 TABLESPOONS VERY FINELY MINCED FRESH LEMON GRASS
1 TEASPOON FISH SAUCE
2 TEASPOONS SOY SAUCE
2 TEASPOONS SUGAR
2 TEASPOONS MINCED GARLIC
JUICE OF 1/4 LEMON
2 TABLESPOONS VEGETABLE OIL
2 WHOLE BONELESS, SKINLESS CHICKEN BREASTS, SEPARATED (ABOUT 2
    POUNDS)

Combine all the ingredients except the chicken in a mixing bowl. Add the chicken and marinate 20 minutes.

Meanwhile, preheat the broiler or grill to moderate.

Grill or broil the chicken breasts until their centers turn white but are still juicy, 3 to 5 minutes on each side. Serve immediately with stir-fried vegetables and rice.

stir-fried chicken with thai basil

SERVES 4

This recipe uses the basic Thai stir-fry method and is a classic example of how the Thais use herbs as vegetables. Whereas the Chinese prefer ginger in their stir-fries, the Thais opt for basil—and lots of it. The key to this recipe is to get the pan very hot before adding the seasonings and use lots of chilies and basil. I tell our cooks all the time that if you can't smell the spices, it's not good enough!

1/2 TABLESPOON CORNSTARCH

1/4 CUP WATER

1 POUND BONELESS, SKINLESS CHICKEN BREAST, CUT INTO SLICES 1/4-INCH THICK AND 2 INCHES LONG

2 TO 3 TABLESPOONS VEGETABLE OIL

1 SMALL YELLOW ONION, THINLY SLICED

1 TABLESPOON SLICED GARLIC

1 TO 3 TEASPOONS CHOPPED FRESH THAI, JALAPEÑO, OR SERRANO CHILI OR A COMBINATION

1 TABLESPOON FISH SAUCE OR TO TASTE

1 TABLESPOON OYSTER SAUCE

1/4 CUP HOMEMADE UNSALTED OR CANNED LOW-SODIUM CHICKEN STOCK

1/2 RED BELL PEPPER, THINLY SLICED

1 CUP FRESH THAI BASIL LEAVES

Whisk together the cornstarch and water in a mixing bowl. Add the chicken to the cornstarch mixture and toss a few times. Let chicken remain in the bowl until ready to cook.

Heat the oil over high heat in a wok or skillet. Swirl to coat the surface evenly. Wait for the oil to get hot, then add the onion, garlic, and chilies. Briskly toss in pan until fragrant, about 20 seconds, then add the chicken. Stir-fry until the chicken begins to turn white, about 3 to 4 minutes. Add the fish sauce, oyster sauce, and chicken stock. Cook until meat is done, another 3 to 5 minutes. Toss the red bell pepper and basil into the stir-fry and remove from heat. Serve immediately with steamed rice.

The Thais generally use two kinds of basil: the common anise-flavor basil called horapao and the spicier kaprao, or holy basil. The common Thai basil has purplish stems and smooth, green oval leaves. Holy basil has fuzzy green stems with matte leaves, ranging from green to greenish-purple. Kaprao sometimes can be found at farmers' markets. If you can't find either basil, substitute sweet basil. (Dried basil will not do.)

saigon chicken

SERVES 2 TO 4

Each cuisine has its own version of roast chicken. While the French like to use garlic, herbs, and lemon with chicken, the Vietnamese rub lemon grass, fish sauce, and garlic onto the bird. Traditionally, we do not roast chicken whole, as it would take too much fuel. But I like presenting an entire chicken to carve at the table. This dish is great hot or cold.

MARINADE

JUICE OF 1/2 LEMON

2 SHALLOTS, MINCED

6 CLOVES GARLIC, MINCED

1/4 CUP MINCED LEMON GRASS

2 TABLESPOONS FISH SAUCE

3 TABLESPOONS SOY SAUCE

1 TEASPOON BLACK PEPPER

1/4 CUP HONEY

1/2 CUP VEGETABLE OIL

CHICKEN

1 WHOLE CHICKEN (ABOUT 3 POUNDS)

2 YELLOW ONIONS, HALVED

1 LEMON, HALVED

ACCOMPANIMENT

GINGER-LIME DIPPING SAUCE (PAGE 34)

Rinse the chicken and pat dry with paper towels.

Combine all marinade ingredients and mix well. Rub the marinade all over the chicken, inside and out. Place any remaining marinade inside the cavity. Cover and refrigerate overnight. Bring chicken to room temperature before roasting.

Preheat oven to 350 degrees.

Place chicken on a rack in a roasting pan. Put the onions and lemon into the cavity. Using a wooden or metal skewer, thread the cavity shut. Roast breast side up for 40 minutes. Turn chicken over and roast another 30 minutes. Baste occasionally. Turn chicken over again and roast until meat is cooked and tender and juices are clear, another 20 to 30 minutes. Let chicken rest 10 minutes before carving. Serve with ginger-lime dipping sauce.

very crispy chicken

SERVES 4

In recipes that call for more than 1 teaspoon of salt, I generally use kosher salt because it is mild, clean tasting, and brings out flavor better than regular table salt. If you substitute kosher salt, use half the amount called for.

The Chinese really have a knack for cooking whole birds, and this is no exception. Inspired by a centuries-old technique, the chicken is first gently poached to seal in the juiciness and flavor and then finished off by deep-frying. If you like fried chicken, this is a delicious twist on the usual fare.

1 (3-INCH) PIECE FRESH GINGER, SLICED 1/4 INCH THICK AND BRUISED WITH
    A MALLET OR KNIFE HANDLE
1 WHOLE CHICKEN (ABOUT 3 POUNDS)
1 1/2 TABLESPOONS FIVE-SPICE POWDER
1 TABLESPOON SUGAR
2 TABLESPOONS KOSHER SALT
OIL FOR FRYING
2 BUNCHES FRESH WATERCRESS, STEMMED AND TORN BITE-SIZE (OPTIONAL)
GINGER-LIME DIPPING SAUCE (PAGE 34)

In a large stockpot, add 4 quarts salted water to cover the chicken and bring to a boil. Add the ginger and chicken and let the water come to a second boil. Turn off the heat but leave the pot on the stove. Cover pot and let the chicken sit in the hot water for 30 minutes.

Drain the chicken and set aside to cool. When it is cool enough to handle, split the chicken in half. Pat very dry and place in a large mixing bowl.

Combine the five-spice powder, sugar, and salt in a small bowl. Working with a sprinkle at a time, rub the spice mixture onto the chicken skin. Continue until all the spice is used. Refrigerate the chicken, uncovered, overnight.

An hour before serving, take the chicken out of the refrigerator and let sit at room temperature. In a wok or deep large saucepan, heat enough oil to almost cover the chicken, about 3 to 4 cups. Bring oil temperature to 325 to 350 degrees. (Chicken should sizzle upon contact with oil.) Fry the chicken until nicely brown and crisp, 3 to 5 minutes on each side. (Depending on the size of your pan, you may have to fry the chicken in separate batches.) Cover pan with a screen if oil begins to splatter. Remove chicken and drain on paper towels. Cut each chicken half into 2 to 3 pieces and place on a large platter lined with watercress. Serve with ginger-lime dipping sauce.

gooey ginger chicken

SERVES 4

If you like this dish or others that call for caramel sauce, consider making the sauce beforehand. Almost every Vietnamese pantry has a jar of caramel sauce.

2 TABLESPOONS VEGETABLE OIL

1 TABLESPOON CHOPPED SHALLOT

1 TABLESPOON MINCED GARLIC

1 TEASPOON CHOPPED FRESH CHILI (OPTIONAL)

3 TABLESPOONS CHOPPED FRESH GINGER

2 POUNDS CHICKEN THIGHS AND BREASTS, TRIMMED OF EXCESS FAT AND
    CUT INTO BITE-SIZE PIECES

4 TABLESPOONS CARAMEL SAUCE (PAGE 52)

1/4 CUP HOMEMADE UNSALTED OR CANNED LOW-SODIUM CHICKEN STOCK
    OR WATER

2 TABLESPOONS FISH SAUCE

2 GREEN ONIONS, CUT INTO 1/2-INCH PIECES ON THE DIAGONAL

6 FRESH CILANTRO SPRIGS FOR GARNISH

Heat the oil in a wok or fry pan over high heat. Working very quickly, add the shallot, garlic, chili, and ginger and stir-fry for 1 minute. Add the chicken, reduce the heat, and sauté in the seasonings for 3 to 5 minutes. Stir in the caramel sauce, chicken stock, and fish sauce. Reduce heat to low and cook until meat is tender and sauce clings to the chicken, 20 to 30 minutes. Stir in the green onions. Remove from heat and garnish with cilantro. Serve with lots of steamed rice.

ginger chicken and vegetable stir-fry

SERVES 4

    Years ago, when we first started exhibiting our cooking at the California State Fair, a number of fairground employees came to our booth for lunch every day. After the first week, they requested something with chicken. So I created a dish called "employee/vendor special" and anticipated selling about 10 to 20 orders a day. But I was wrong. Fair-goers wanted it too, and soon we found ourselves dishing up more than 150 plates a day. Today we sometimes offer this dish at the restaurant as a lunch special, modifying the sauce with rice wine and shiitake mushrooms and sometimes serving it on a crispy pan-seared noodle pillow.

1/2 TABLESPOON CORNSTARCH

1/4 CUP WATER

1 POUND SKINLESS, BONELESS CHICKEN BREAST, CUT AGAINST THE GRAIN
    INTO 1/4-INCH-THICK SLICES

3 TABLESPOONS VEGETABLE OIL

2 TABLESPOONS MINCED FRESH GINGER

1 TABLESPOON MINCED GARLIC

1 TEASPOON GROUND CHILI PASTE (OPTIONAL)

3 TABLESPOONS OYSTER SAUCE

1/4 CUP HOMEMADE UNSALTED OR CANNED LOW-SODIUM CHICKEN STOCK
    OR WATER

2 CUPS SNOW PEAS, STEMMED, BLANCHED, AND SHOCKED IN ICE WATER

2 ZUCCHINIS, HALVED LENGTHWISE AND SLICED 1/4 INCH THICK, BLANCHED,
    AND SHOCKED IN ICE WATER

1 CUP WHITE MUSHROOMS, SLICED

2 TOMATOES, CUT INTO THIN WEDGES

1/2 RED BELL PEPPER, JULIENNED

2 TABLESPOONS RICE WINE OR DRY SHERRY

One of the biggest challenges in cooking is controlling the flavor of the various ingredients in a dish. With stir-fries, I always blanch those vegetables that take long to cook. Vegetables that need to be stir-fried for more than 3 to 4 minutes tend to lose their crunch and color. Moreover, they secrete too much liquid and dilute the sauce. Blanching helps prevent those problems because you can finish a dish in less time.

Whisk the cornstarch and water together in a mixing bowl. Add the chicken and toss to coat.

Heat the oil over high heat in a wok or large fry pan. Working very quickly, add the ginger, garlic, and chili paste and stir-fry for 20 seconds. Add the chicken (not the remaining cornstarch mixture) and stir-fry with the spices until chicken begins to turn white, about 3 minutes. Add the oyster sauce and stir-fry for 1 more minute. Pour in the chicken stock. When stock begins to boil, add the snow peas, zucchini, mushrooms, tomatoes, and red bell pepper. Sauté until vegetables are thoroughly hot but not too soft, 2 to 3 minutes. Add the rice wine and serve immediately with steamed rice.

thai-style roasted chicken with sticky rice

SERVES 4

 While in Bangkok several years ago, we stayed at a hotel whose air-conditioning system had broken down the night we arrived. It was so hot, about 95 degrees at midnight, that we left the windows open. At about six in the morning, I was awakened by the heat, the noise of the tuk-tuks, or three-wheeled taxis, and the wonderful aroma of gai-yang, or barbecued chicken, roasting just outside our window. The chickens were small, almost the size of large cornish hens, and had the flavor I have not experienced even with the best free-range chicken in this country. It must be the tropical grass, grains, and whatever else they eat. This recipe is more authentic when grilled.

1 TABLESPOON THINLY SLICED FRESH OR FROZEN GALANGA

4 CLOVES GARLIC, SLICED

4 TABLESPOONS MINCED FRESH CILANTRO, PREFERABLY WITH
 STEMS AND ROOT

1 TABLESPOON YELLOW CURRY PASTE

1/2 TEASPOON GROUND TURMERIC

4 TABLESPOONS UNSWEETENED COCONUT MILK

2 TABLESPOONS SOY SAUCE

1/2 TABLESPOON FISH SAUCE

2 TABLESPOONS SUGAR

1/2 TEASPOON GROUND WHITE PEPPER

1 WHOLE CHICKEN, ABOUT 3 POUNDS, SPLIT AND CUT INTO 8 PIECES
 OR QUARTERED

ACCOMPANIMENTS
SWEET THAI CHILI SAUCE (SEE PAGE 42)
STICKY JASMINE RICE (SEE PAGE 51)

Place the galanga, garlic, and cilantro in a mortar and pound into a paste. Transfer mixture to a mixing bowl and add the curry paste, turmeric, coconut milk, soy sauce, fish sauce, sugar, and white pepper. Mix well and set aside.

Score the legs and other thick parts of the chicken for faster cooking. Add the chicken pieces to the marinade mixture and toss evenly to coat. Put chicken in the refrigerator to marinate overnight, or at least 4 hours.

Before cooking, bring the chicken to room temperature.

Meanwhile, preheat the broiler or grill to medium heat. Broil or grill chicken until just done, 10 to 15 minutes on each side. Serve with sweet Thai chili sauce and sticky jasmine rice.

vietnamese curry with cornish hens

SERVES 4

Every time we make this dish at the restaurant, a debate arises among the servers who seem to think it is better than the most popular dish at the restaurant—the Thai *chicken curry. Maybe because the hens are cooked the traditional way, with bones and skins intact, so that the broth is richer. This curry, which typically is made with chicken (we use hens for easier portioning), is especially delicious the next day when the flavors are more blended.*

2 TABLESPOONS VEGETABLE OIL

2 SHALLOTS, THINLY SLICED

3 CLOVES GARLIC, CHOPPED

1 PLUS 2 TABLESPOONS CURRY POWDER

2 CORNISH HENS, SPLIT AND TRIMMED OF EXCESS SKIN AND FAT

1 (2-INCH) PIECE FRESH GINGER, CUT INTO $1/4$-INCH-THICK SLICES

1 STALK LEMON GRASS, CUT INTO 2-INCH PIECES

2 CUPS HOMEMADE UNSALTED OR CANNED LOW-SODIUM CHICKEN STOCK

1 CUP UNSWEETENED COCONUT MILK OR COWS' MILK

3 KAFFIR LIME LEAVES OR BAY LEAVES

1 TEASPOON DRIED RED CHILI FLAKES

2 TABLESPOONS FISH SAUCE

$1/4$ TEASPOON SALT

1 TABLESPOON SUGAR

3 CARROTS, CUT INTO 1-INCH PIECES ON THE DIAGONAL

1 POUND RED POTATOES, QUARTERED

1 SMALL YELLOW ONION, CUT INTO THIN WEDGES

10 FRESH CILANTRO SPRIGS FOR GARNISH

Heat the oil over medium heat in a large Dutch oven. Add the shallots, garlic, and the 1 tablespoon curry powder. Stir until fragrant, about 20 seconds. Add the hens and brown, skin-side down, 3 to 5 minutes. Add the ginger, lemon grass, chicken stock, coconut milk, lime leaves, chili flakes, fish sauce, salt, sugar, and the 2 tablespoons curry powder. Simmer for about 20 minutes, then add the carrots. Cook for 5 minutes, then add the red potatoes and onion. Simmer until hens and vegetables are done and tender, another 15 to 20 minutes. Garnish with cilantro and serve hot with steamed rice or French bread.

Curry powder is an essential ingredient, so be sure to purchase a high-quality brand. The Japanese brands (available in the Asian section of supermarkets) are more similar to the Vietnamese-style mixes than the pungent Indian versions. The amount of curry to use depends on your personal taste, I like my curries with "umph."

pan-seared quail with oyster mushrooms

SERVES 2 TO 4

In Vietnam, quails, pigeons, and squabs are reserved for special occasions, especially for male-oriented gatherings where guests savor small snacks while drinking and partying. In the back, the women, who traditionally never partake in drinking, are busy preparing dishes such as this one. Because coconut products are easily available in Asia, the liquid called for is the clear juice that comes from the inside of the coconut. Though subtle in flavor, its sweetness tenderizes and enhances the meat. If you cannot locate coconut juice or coconut soda, try—no kidding—Sprite or Seven-Up.

3 SHALLOTS, THINLY SLICED

2 CLOVES GARLIC, SLICED

1/4 TEASPOON GROUND WHITE PEPPER

1/2 TEASPOON FIVE-SPICE POWDER

1/2 TEASPOON FISH SAUCE

1 TABLESPOON OYSTER SAUCE

4 QUAILS, SPLIT AND TRIMMED OF EXCESS SKIN AND FAT

2 TABLESPOONS VEGETABLE OIL

2 CUPS FRESH OYSTER MUSHROOMS, HALVED IF LARGE

1/2 CUP FRESH OR FROZEN COCONUT JUICE OR COCONUT SODA

Place the shallots and garlic in a mortar and pound into a paste. Scrape into a mixing bowl and add the white pepper, five-spice powder, fish sauce, and oyster sauce. Marinate the quails in this mixture at least 30 minutes, preferably 1 hour.

Heat the oil in a large wok or skillet over high heat. Add the quails, including the bits of shallot and garlic in the marinade, to the wok. Stir-fry until fragrant, 3 to 5 minutes. Add the oyster mushrooms and stir-fry for 2 minutes. Add the coconut juice and reduce heat to low. Simmer until sauce is slightly reduced, about 10 minutes. If you like, serve on a bed of watercress.

lemon grass beef with rice paper

SERVES 4

Very characteristic of Vietnamese cuisine, this dish usually is served with wet rice paper, table salad (lettuce, bean sprouts, and mint leaves) and Vietnamese dipping sauce. It is traditionally eaten with the hands. At the restaurant we give customers the option of eating the beef with rice and vegetables instead of rolling it in rice paper. Most, however, choose the traditional way, especially children, who find it fun and engaging.

MARINADE
3 TABLESPOONS MINCED LEMON GRASS
2 TEASPOONS MINCED GARLIC
1 TEASPOON FISH SAUCE
1 TEASPOON SOY SAUCE
1 TEASPOON SUGAR
2 TABLESPOONS VEGETABLE OIL

BEEF
1 1/2 POUNDS TOP SIRLOIN, CUT INTO SLICES 2 INCHES WIDE, 4 INCHES LONG,
    AND 1/4 INCH THICK

TABLE SALAD
1 HEAD RED LEAF LETTUCE, LEAVES SEPARATED, WASHED, AND DRIED
1 CUCUMBER, SEEDED AND JULIENNED
10 FRESH MINT SPRIGS
10 FRESH THAI BASIL SPRIGS (OPTIONAL)
1/3 POUND RICE VERMICELLI, COOKED IN BOILING WATER 4 TO 5 MINUTES,
    RINSED, AND DRAINED
3 CUPS BEAN SPROUTS

OTHER ACCOMPANIMENTS
1/2 POUND 6-INCH ROUND RICE PAPER SHEETS
1 CUP VIETNAMESE DIPPING SAUCE (PAGE 32)

For the best texture and taste, dip rice paper in water just before using. If you must pre-roll, cover completely with a damp cheesecloth and it will keep up to 2 hours. To store unused rice paper, return it to the original wrapper and seal with plastic wrap. If left exposed to the air, rice paper will become brittle and break easily. Wet rice paper lasts only 10 to 15 minutes, after which time it dries up and becomes chewy.

Combine all marinade ingredients. Add the beef and marinate for 15 minutes.

Assemble the table salad ingredients and place on a large platter, with each ingredient arranged in its own area.

If grilling beef, preheat grill to medium heat.

Place the rice paper on a plate. Heat water to have ready to dip the rice paper in when the beef is served.

Grill the beef, or pan-sear in an oiled skillet, until just done, about 20 seconds on each side or to desired doneness. Transfer to a serving plate.

Place the table salad, beef, rice paper, and dipping sauce on the table. Transfer the hot water to a large, stable bowl deep enough to dip the rice paper in. Place on the dining table.

Invite guests to dip the edge of the rice paper in the water and turn to wet evenly. Allow water to drain off a bit and place on a plate. Starting from the bottom third of the rice paper, lay down half a piece of lettuce, a tablespoon each of rice noodles and bean sprouts, and about 3 mint and 3 basil leaves, then top with 1 piece of beef. Fold the sides over and roll to enclose. The rolls should be no wider than 1 1/2 inches. To eat, dip in Vietnamese dipping sauce.

cognac- and garlic-marinated lamb chops with spicy peanut sauce

SERVES 4

This is unquestionably the most popular meat dish at Lemon Grass, and it receives rave reviews from every customer who's had it.

MARINADE

2 TABLESPOONS COGNAC OR BRANDY

1 TABLESPOON MINCED GARLIC

2 TABLESPOONS VEGETABLE OIL

1 TABLESPOON SOY SAUCE

2 TABLESPOONS OYSTER SAUCE

1/2 TEASPOON BLACK PEPPER

1 TABLESPOON WATER

LAMB

8 (4- TO 5-OUNCE) LAMB LOIN CHOPS

1 CUP SPICY PEANUT SAUCE (PAGE 44)

FRESH CILANTRO SPRIGS FOR GARNISH

Combine all the marinade ingredients in a mixing bowl. Add the lamb and marinate for 2 hours.

Preheat the broiler or a grill to high heat.

Broil or grill the lamb chops 4 to 5 minutes on each side for medium-rare. (Cooking time depends on the thickness of the chops.)

Warm the peanut sauce in a nonstick saucepan. To serve, pour 2 to 3 tablespoons of sauce on a dinner plate. Top with 2 lamb chops per plate and garnish with cilantro.

bangkok beef with basil

SERVES 4

If I told you the basil in Bangkok is more aromatic than its counterpart here, would you believe it? It's true. The tropical sun and dirt do something to the herb, I tell you. The last time we had this dish was at a famous outdoor restaurant in Bangkok. Accommodating at least a thousand diners, the place was quite a scene. Sitting in an open dining room with thousands of Christmas lights strung above and a fish-filled pond underneath, we were awestruck the entire night. Our service team consisted of several pretty waitresses in sarongs and a cadre of servers on roller skates. Like the atmosphere, the food was a wonderful confusion of textures, flavors, and colors. The dish I remember best was this one, made with kaprao, or holy basil. Hotter and more aromatic than its common Thai basil cousin, holy basil can sometimes be found at farmers' markets. If you can't find it, use Thai basil. It will work almost as well.

1 TEASPOON CORNSTARCH
3 TABLESPOONS WATER
1 POUND TOP SIRLOIN, CUT INTO THIN STRIPS
2 TABLESPOONS VEGETABLE OIL
3 CLOVES GARLIC, THINLY SLICED
2 TO 4 FRESH THAI BIRD CHILIES, CHOPPED
2 TABLESPOONS OYSTER SAUCE
1 TEASPOON FISH SAUCE
2 CUPS CANNED BAMBOO SHOOTS, BOILED 5 MINUTES, RINSED,
    AND DRAINED
1/2 RED BELL PEPPER, THINLY SLICED
1 CUP FRESH THAI BASIL LEAVES

Combine cornstarch and water until well blended. Add the beef to the mixture and toss to coat. Let rest for 10 minutes.

Heat the oil in a wok or skillet over high heat. Add the garlic and chilies and quickly toss until fragrant, about 20 seconds. Add the beef and give it a few stirs. Then add the oyster sauce and fish sauce, and stir-fry for about 1 minute. Add the bamboo shoots and stir-fry until beef is cooked and vegetables are thoroughly hot, 2 to 3 minutes. Add the red bell pepper and basil leaves and cook 1 more minute. Remove from heat and serve immediately.

spicy red beef curry

SERVES 4

No single ingredient is more important to Thai cusine than curry paste, known as *Krung kaeng*. Mainly found in soups, stews, dips, marinades, and stir-fries, they are made from a variety of spices that are roasted and pounded. Use sparingly—curry pastes are very pungent and spicy!

My Thai nanny, Chi Tu, made the best kaeng phet nua, *or red curry. She always knew which vendor at the market had the best red curry paste and which had the best freshly squeezed coconut milk. Every time she made this dish, I ate until my little belly hurt. If she were here today, she would be surprised to know how much I adored her cooking. You see, I never told her that.*

1 TABLESPOON VEGETABLE OIL

2 SHALLOTS, SLICED

2 TEASPOONS RED CURRY PASTE, OR TO TASTE

1/2 PLUS 1 CUP UNSWEETENED COCONUT MILK

1/2 TEASPOON GROUND CUMIN

1/2 TEASPOON GROUND CORIANDER

1 TEASPOON PAPRIKA

1 POUND TOP SIRLOIN OR ANY LEAN TENDER BEEF, CUT INTO THIN STRIPS
    ABOUT 2 INCHES LONG × 1 INCH WIDE

1/2 CUP HOMEMADE UNSALTED OR CANNED LOW-SODIUM CHICKEN STOCK

2 TABLESPOONS FISH SAUCE

2 TABLESPOONS SUGAR

3 KAFFIR LIME LEAVES, CUT INTO FINE SLIVERS

2 CUPS CANNED BAMBOO SHOOTS, BOILED 5 MINUTES, RINSED,
    AND DRAINED

1/2 RED BELL PEPPER, JULIENNED

20 FRESH THAI BASIL LEAVES, CUT IN HALF

8 FRESH CILANTRO SPRIGS FOR GARNISH

Heat the vegetable oil in a wok or skillet over medium heat. Add the shallots and curry paste and stir until fragrant, about 1 minute. Add the 1/2 cup coconut milk and stir for 2 minutes. Add the cumin, coriander, and paprika and stir to dissolve the spices. Add the beef and toss in the seasonings for 1 minute. Add the 1 cup coconut milk, chicken stock, fish sauce, sugar, lime leaves, and bamboo shoots and bring to a gentle boil. Cook uncovered until tender, 10 to 15 minutes. Add the red bell pepper and basil and remove from heat. Garnish with cilantro and serve with steamed rice.

grilled lemon grass pork chops

SERVES 4

This is a common way of preparing pork in Vietnam. In fact, on any given day in Saigon, you could walk down the streets and smell this barbecued pork being cooked in the open air.

2 SHALLOTS, SLICED
2 CLOVES GARLIC, SLICED
3 TABLESPOONS MINCED LEMON GRASS
1 TEASPOON FISH SAUCE
2 TEASPOONS SOY SAUCE
1/4 TEASPOON SALT
1 TABLESPOON SUGAR
1 TABLESPOON VEGETABLE OIL
4 PORK CHOPS WITH BONES, ABOUT 1/2 INCH THICK, TRIMMED
    OF EXCESS FAT
GINGER-LIME DIPPING SAUCE (PAGE 34)

Place the shallots and garlic in a mortar and pound into a paste. Transfer to a mixing bowl and add the lemon grass, fish sauce, soy sauce, salt, and sugar. Stir well. Add the pork chops to this mixture and marinate for 30 minutes.

Preheat a grill to medium heat.

Just before serving, grill or pan-sear the meat over medium heat until done, 5 to 7 minutes on each side. Serve with steamed rice, sautéed vegetables, and the ginger-lime dipping sauce.

For best results, bring the pork chops to room temperature just before cooking. For added flavor, pierce the chops all over with a bamboo skewer before marinating. (Marinating time may be cut to 15 minutes.)

For a more authentic flavor, omit the sugar and add 1 tablespoon Caramel Sauce (page 52) to the marinade.

carmelized pork in claypot

SERVES 4

A claypot is an Asian version of a casserole dish
with a handle. You can
cook and serve directly
from this pot. When buy-
ing a claypot, choose the
larger 1-quart size over a
smaller one. Large clay-
pots are more versatile
and easier to cook in.
They also hold more
steam for faster cooking.
Before using a claypot,
boil some water in it several times to wash out the
clay odor. If you have a
choice, pick a claypot that
is glazed inside and out,
top and bottom. I find that
type more durable.

In societies that are not as affluent as those in the West, food is commonly prepared on the salty side so that it can be stretched and served in smaller portions. In the
Mekong Delta, where my parents were raised, this dish often was prepared to feed the hungry farm workers at the end of the day. Because it was salty, the dish was eaten with lots of
rice and vegetables. But don't worry, I've cut down on the salt here.

3 TABLESPOONS VEGETABLE OIL
2 CLOVES GARLIC, MINCED
2 SHALLOTS, CHOPPED
1 POUND PORK SIRLOIN, CUT INTO BITE-SIZE PIECES
3 TABLESPOONS CARAMEL SAUCE (PAGE 52)
3 TABLESPOONS FISH SAUCE
$1/3$ CUP HOMEMADE UNSALTED OR CANNED LOW-SODIUM CHICKEN STOCK OR
      WATER
2 GREEN ONIONS, THINLY SLICED ON THE DIAGONAL, FOR GARNISH
$1/2$ TEASPOON GROUND BLACK PEPPER FOR GARNISH

Heat the vegetable oil in a 1-quart claypot or medium stir-fry pan over moderate
heat. Add the garlic and shallots. Stir-fry until fragrant, 2 to 3 minutes. Add the pork and
toss until the pork turns almost white, about 2 minutes. Add the caramel sauce and stir for
1 more minute until pork absorbs the sauce. Add the fish sauce and chicken stock and
cook over low heat until pork is tender and sauce has slightly caramelized, 12 to 15 minutes. Remove from heat and serve right out of the claypot, if using. Garnish with green
onions and black pepper.

thai cowboy steak with roasted tomato-chili sauce

SERVES 4

I don't often eat steaks, but when I do, I want them cowboy style—large! At the restaurant, we pamper customers with nothing less than 12 to 13 ounces of juicy, succulent New York steaks.

2 CLOVES GARLIC, SLICED

3 WHOLE BLACK PEPPERCORNS

3 FRESH CILANTRO SPRIGS, CHOPPED

2 TEASPOONS OYSTER SAUCE

2 TEASPOONS SOY SAUCE

1 TABLESPOON BRANDY

4 (8- TO 10-OUNCE) NEW YORK STEAKS, ABOUT 1 INCH THICK

ROASTED TOMATO–CHILI SAUCE (PAGE 43)

Place the garlic, peppercorns, and cilantro in a mortar and pound into a paste. Transfer to a mixing bowl and stir in the oyster sauce, soy sauce, and brandy. Add the steaks and marinate for about 1 hour.

Preheat the broiler or grill to medium high.

Before serving, grill or broil to desired doneness, about 3 to 5 minutes on each side for medium. (You may also pan-sear the steaks in a large skillet.) Serve steaks with roasted tomato-chili sauce.

Chapter seven

Those Four Days

vegetables

Walk into the Lemon Grass kitchen and if it happens to be the 1st, 14th, 15th, or 30th day of the lunar month, chances are you will find many of our staff eating vegetarian. By abstaining from meat on those sacred days, they are reaffirming their belief in the teachings of Buddha and rededicating their commitment to a life free of indulgence, greed, and conflict.

As a child, I looked forward to those four days because if my grandmother, a devout Buddhist, happened to be visiting, my mother would prepare a sumptuous vegetarian meal for all of us to enjoy together. We always had vegetarian spring rolls. Stuffed with jicama, bean thread noodles, tree ear mushrooms, and carrots and dipped in cilantro-lime soy sauce, vegetarian spring rolls were no less tasty than their meat counterpart. Our family's favorite sweet and sour soup, usually served with shrimp or fresh catfish, was prepared with fresh pineapple, tofu, cabbage, bean sprouts, and chopped *ngo gai,* or saw-leaf herb, which lent a distinctive taste. Actually, I always have preferred the vegetarian version.

When Lemon Grass first opened, we put only one vegetarian dish on the menu. In the following years, however, as health concerns over cholesterol and fitness increased, we began to expand our meatless offerings. At first, we added two entrée dishes; then came vegetarian salad rolls. By the time we added meatless spring rolls, we had decided to feature a separate vegetarian section on our menu.

In coming up with new dishes, I referred to the traditional Vietnamese vegetarian diet for inspiration. I find this apropos because even though my staff and family choose to eat vegetarian food for religious reasons, their desire for flavor and demand for freshness are still the same. In fact, in Vietnam, vegetarian food is highly regarded and requires great skill to prepare. Since we cannot rely on meat and fat for flavor, we must be innovative in selecting and preparing the ingredients. To enhance flavor and texture, sometimes a simple ingredient such as tofu is first fried then simmered before being added to the finished dish. Because of the skill required for this specialized cooking, temples—where the monks and nuns eat a strict meatless diet year-round—are known to have the best vegetarian food. As a child I loved going to temples knowing that a special treat always awaited me after each visit.

Although vegetarianism is observed for religious rather than health or other reasons, the general Vietnamese attitude toward meatless eating is far from somber. Vietnamese do not name vegetarian dishes by their ingredients but rather by the meat being emulated. At temples and vegetarian restaurants, cooks go to great lengths to disguise tofu products, shaping and molding them to look like beef and fish. Instead of calling a dish Vegetables in Claypot, it is known as *Ca Kho To Chay*, or Vegetarian Fish in Claypot. Instead of Vegetable Stew, the nuns at the temple are cooking *Thit Kho Chay*, or Vegetarian Meat Stew.

My conclusion is this: Even though we vow to not kill or eat flesh on certain days as a way to honor the sacrifices of Buddha and live by his path, we never said anything about giving up our desire for great taste or flavor, did we? If I am wrong on this, please, don't tell me.

vegetarian fisherman's soup

SERVES 6

A variation to the famous Vietnamese canh chua, *or sweet and sour soup, this dish calls for tamarind, a tropical fruit used as a souring agent. If you can't find tamarind, substitute cider vinegar or increase the lime juice to 3 tablespoons.*

3 HEAPING TABLESPOONS TAMARIND PULP, OR 2 TABLESPOONS
    CIDER VINEGAR
1 TABLESPOON VEGETABLE OIL
1/2 TABLESPOON GROUND CHILI PASTE
1 TEASPOON MINCED GARLIC
2 TABLESPOONS SOY SAUCE
5 CUPS WATER
2 TABLESPOONS SUGAR
1/2 TEASPOON SALT
1 TABLESPOON FRESH LIME JUICE
1 CUP FRESHLY CUT PINEAPPLE CUBES
1/2 MEDIUM ONION, CUT INTO THIN WEDGES
2 CUPS SHREDDED WHITE CABBAGE
2 CUPS BEAN SPROUTS
1/4 POUND EXTRA FIRM TOFU, CUBED (FRIED OR PLAIN)
3 MEDIUM TOMATOES, CUT INTO THIN WEDGES
2 FRESH THAI BIRD CHILIES, CHOPPED (OPTIONAL)
10 FRESH THAI BASIL LEAVES, COARSELY CHOPPED
10 FRESH RICE-PADDY HERB SPRIGS, COARSELY CHOPPED
    (OPTIONAL)
2 TABLESPOONS FRIED SHALLOTS (OPTIONAL, PAGE 45)

Tamarind is very common in Asia and is used not only in soups and curries but in candies and even drinks. You may find fresh tamarind at farmers' markets or specialty stores. To use, peel, seed, and remove the woody fibers from the pulp. Soak in hot water and handle according to recipe instructions.

Pour $1/2$ cup boiling water over the tamarind pulp and soak for 30 minutes. Push pulp through a sieve, scraping with the back of a spoon against the wire to extract as much liquid as possible. Set the juice aside.

Heat the oil in a small soup pot over moderate heat. Add the chili paste and garlic and stir until fragrant, about 20 seconds. Add soy sauce and stir for 10 seconds more. Then add the water, sugar, salt, tamarind juice, and lime juice. Bring to a boil. You may make the soup in advance up to this point.

Just before serving, and while the broth is boiling, add the pineapple, onion, cabbage, bean sprouts, tofu, and tomatoes. Cook until vegetables are thoroughly hot, about 2 minutes, then immediately remove from heat. Sprinkle on the chilies, herbs, and fried shallots. Serve piping hot. The authentic flavor of this soup is a bold balance of hot, sweet, and sour.

thai mushroom salad with cabbage leaves

SERVES 4 TO 6

This puckeringly sour and fiery hot dressing permeates every ingredient with intense flavor. At first I tried tofu as a substitute for the traditional meat used in this dish, but later I discovered that mushrooms add more flavor and character.

2 TABLESPOONS VEGETABLE OIL

1 TABLESPOON DRIED RED CHILI FLAKES

1 POUND WHITE MUSHROOMS, STEMMED AND CHOPPED

1 TABLESPOON SOY SAUCE

1/4 TEASPOON SALT

1/4 CUP FRESH LIME JUICE

2 TEASPOOONS BROWN SUGAR

1 TABLESPOON MINCED LEMON GRASS

3 KAFFIR LIME LEAVES, CUT INTO VERY THIN SLIVERS

1/2 SMALL YELLOW ONION, CHOPPED

1/2 CUP DICED CUCUMBER

1/4 CUP FRESH MINT LEAVES, CUT IN HALF

2 RED RIPE TOMATOES, SEEDED AND CUT INTO VERY THIN WEDGES

1 SMALL WHITE CABBAGE

FRESH CILANTRO SPRIGS FOR GARNISH

Heat the oil in a medium sauté pan over moderate heat. Add the chili flakes and stir quickly until fragrant, about 20 seconds. Add the mushrooms and toss around in the pan until slightly wilted, about 1 minute. Remove from heat.

Combine the soy sauce, salt, lime juice, brown sugar, lemon grass, lime leaves, and onion in a mixing bowl and stir until sugar dissolves. Add the mushrooms, cucumber, mint leaves, and tomatoes. Toss gently to blend the flavors. Set aside.

Meanwhile, halve the cabbage and save half for lining plates. (If cabbage is too big, cut the top third off. Otherwise, the leaves will be too long.) Cut into 6 wedges, about 2-inches thick. Wash and drain.

To serve, line salad plates with the leaves from reserved cabbage half. Top with mushroom mixture and garnish with cilantro. Serve with cabbage wedges. The traditional way of eating this dish is to use the cabbage leaves from the wedge as spoons to scoop up the mushrooms.

vegetarian spring rolls

MAKES ABOUT 24 SPRING ROLLS

The technique for making these spring rolls is no different from the meat version, except that the vegetable ingredients are a little harder to handle. Make sure to squeeze the excess water out of the carrots, onions, and jicama as the moisture will cause the wrapper to burst when frying. Use only spring roll wrappers such as the Menlo brand and not egg roll wrappers, which are too doughy.

2/3 CUP DRIED BEAN THREAD NOODLES, SOAKED IN HOT WATER FOR 30 MIN-
   UTES, DRAINED, AND CUT INTO 1/2-INCH PIECES WITH A SCISSORS
10 DRIED BLACK MUSHROOMS, SOAKED IN HOT WATER FOR 30 MINUTES,
   DRAINED, AND FINELY CHOPPED
1 CUP FINELY MINCED YELLOW ONION, PLACED IN A CHEESECLOTH AND
   SQUEEZED OF EXCESS WATER
2 CUPS SHREDDED CARROTS, PLACED IN A CHEESECLOTH AND SQUEEZED
   OF EXCESS WATER
3 GREEN ONIONS, THINLY SLICED
2 CUPS CHOPPED JICAMA, PLACED IN A CHEESECLOTH AND SQUEEZED OF
   EXCESS WATER
1/2 POUND EXTRA FIRM TOFU, DRAINED AND MASHED WITH THE
   BACK OF A FORK
1 TABLESPOON SOY SAUCE
1/2 TEASPOON SALT
2 TEASPOONS SUGAR
1/2 TEASPOON GROUND BLACK PEPPER
2 TABLESPOONS CORNSTARCH
12 SPRING ROLL (*NOT* EGG ROLL) WRAPPERS
2 TABLESPOONS CORNSTARCH
1/2 CUP WATER
OIL FOR FRYING

ACCOMPANIMENTS
CILANTRO-LIME SOY SAUCE (PAGE 36)
TABLE SALAD (PAGE 53)

I'm sorry, but there is only one way to eat spring rolls. Place one spring roll, along with 3 to 4 mint leaves and thinly sliced cucumbers, on top of a piece of lettuce. Wrap up and dip in sauce. Once introduced to this tradition, our customers vow never to eat spring rolls any other way.

If you're entertaining, cook the spring rolls half-way and bake at 250 degrees for 20 minutes, just before serving.

Combine the bean thread noodles, mushrooms, yellow onion, carrots, green onions, jicama, and tofu in a mixing bowl.

In another large mixing bowl, combine the soy sauce, salt, sugar, black pepper, and cornstarch and stir to blend. Add to the noodle mixture, and blend well. Set aside.

Whisk together the cornstarch and water in a small sauce pan. Bring to a boil. The mixture should be pasty and sticky. (This is the "glue" that you will use to seal the edges of the wrappers.)

Cut the wrappers into two triangles. Starting with the longest side toward you, place about 2 tablespoons of the filling in the bottom third of the triangle. Using your fingers, shape the filling into a 2-inch-long cylinder. Fold the two pointed ends of the wrapper in and roll to enclose. (Rolls should be about 1 inch thick.) Using your finger, dab the edges with a little cornstarch mixture (do not over "glue") and seal the roll. Set aside while you finish making the remaining rolls. Do not stack them.

To fry, preheat a wok or large skillet. When hot, pour enough oil in to completely cover the spring rolls, about 2 inches. Heat to about 325 degrees. Fry the rolls for 3 to 5 minutes on each side, turning them around in the oil until they are nicely browned and crisp. Do not crowd the pan. (You may have to cook them in batches.) Once cooked, remove from pan and drain on paper towels. Serve immediately with cilantro-lime soy sauce and table salad.

spicy eggplant and broccoli in ginger sauce

SERVES 4

If you like eggplant but have never tried Asian eggplant, try this recipe. Asian eggplants are more delicate and sweeter than the globe variety. Remember to cook the eggplants only until just done. Otherwise, they become mushy.

2 POUNDS JAPANESE EGGPLANT, PREFERABLY THE SMALL DARK PURPLE
    VARIETY, HALVED LENGTHWISE AND SLICED INTO 2/3-INCH-THICK
    PIECES, THEN SOAKED IN WATER TO PREVENT BLACKENING
3 TABLESPOONS VEGETABLE OIL
1 TABLESPOON MINCED GARLIC
1 TEASPOON GROUND CHILI PASTE
2 TABLESPOONS MINCED FRESH GINGER
1/2 SMALL YELLOW ONION, CUT INTO THIN WEDGES
3 CUPS BROCCOLI FLORETS, CUT INTO BITE-SIZE PIECES, BLANCHED, AND
    SHOCKED IN ICE WATER
2 TABLESPOONS SOY SAUCE
2 TABLESPOONS VEGETARIAN OYSTER SAUCE OR MUSHROOM SAUCE
1/2 CUP WATER
3 TABLESPOONS CORNSTARCH
1/2 RED BELL PEPPER, JULIENNED
1/4 CUP FRESH THAI BASIL LEAVES, HALVED
6 FRESH CILANTRO SPRIGS FOR GARNISH

Remove and drain the eggplant.

Heat the oil in a large wok or skillet over moderate heat. Add the garlic, chili paste, and ginger. Stir until fragrant, about 20 seconds. Add the eggplant and stir-fry for 3 to 4 minutes. Add the onion, broccoli, soy sauce, and oyster sauce. Toss until well blended. Reduce heat and let simmer for 3 to 5 more minutes.

Meanwhile, mix the water and cornstarch with a whisk or chopsticks until cornstarch is fully dissolved. Add the cornstarch mixture, 1 tablespoon at a time, to slightly thicken the stir-fry sauce just enough to coat a spoon. Add the red bell pepper and basil and remove from heat. Transfer to a serving dish and garnish with cilantro.

Grocery stores sell and label Japanese and Chinese eggplants almost interchangeably. They are different. I prefer the small, dark purple Japanese variety over the long, lavender Chinese one. To me, Japanese eggplant has a firmer, sweeter flesh and cooks better. The Chinese variety is a tad mushy when cooked and the skin is a little chewy. Unlike their Western cousins, Asian eggplants do not need to be salted before cooking.

thai jungle curry

A wonderful confusion of greens (thus the jungle connotation), this dish is especially delightful when the vegetables are freshly picked, as they often are at farmers' markets.

1 TABLESPOON VEGETABLE OIL

2 SHALLOTS, THINLY SLICED

1 (1/4-INCH) PIECE GALANGA, THINLY SLICED

2 1/2 TEASPOONS RED CURRY PASTE

2 CUPS UNSWEETENED COCONUT MILK

1/3 POUND TENDER GREEN BEANS, TRIMMED AND HALVED

1 CUP CANNED BAMBOO SHOOTS, BOILED 5 MINUTES, RINSED, AND DRAINED

1 CUP JULIENNED CARROTS

2 ZUCCHINIS, HALVED AND SLICED 1/2 INCH THICK ON THE DIAGONAL

1 TABLESPOON SOY SAUCE

1/2 TEASPOON SALT

2 TABLESPOONS SUGAR

3 KAFFIR LIMES LEAVES, CUT INTO SLIVERS

12 FRESH THAI BASIL LEAVES

Heat the oil in a fry pan over moderate heat. Add the shallots, galanga and red curry paste and stir until fragrant, about 1 minute. Add 2 tablespoons of the coconut milk and let the mixture bubble for 2 minutes. Add the remaining coconut milk and bring to a slow boil. Reduce the heat and add the green beans, bamboo shoots, and carrots. Cover and simmer until vegetables are just softened, about 5 minutes. Add the zucchini, soy sauce, salt, and sugar and cook until last vegetable begins to wilt. Stir in the lime leaves and basil leaves and remove from heat. Serve immediately with steamed rice.

spicy vegetable curry

SERVES 4 TO 6

For the past several years, we have worked with a group of dieticians and doctors from the University of California at Davis Medical Center in developing lowfat dishes that are suitable for patients with heart disease. This one was featured at a "Heart Smart" gala, and it was a hit!

2 TABLESPOONS CANOLA OIL

2 SHALLOTS, SLICED

$1/2$ TEASPOON MINCED GARLIC

$2 1/2$ TABLESPOONS CURRY POWDER

$1/2$ TEASPOON GROUND TURMERIC

1 TEASPOON GROUND CHILI PASTE (OPTIONAL)

2 TABLESPOONS SOY SAUCE

1 STALK LEMON GRASS, CUT INTO 1-INCH PIECES AND BRUISED
    WITH A KNIFE

1 (1-INCH) PIECE FRESH GINGER, SLICED INTO $1/4$-INCH-THICK PIECES

3 CUPS LOWFAT MILK

$1/2$ TEASPOON SALT

3 TABLESPOONS LIGHT BROWN SUGAR

2 CARROTS, PEELED AND SLICED INTO $1/2$-INCH ROUNDS

1 POUND RUSSET POTATOES, PEELED AND CUBED

$1/2$ YELLOW ONION, CUBED

$1/2$ HEAD CAULIFLOWER, CUT INTO BITE-SIZE PIECES

2 CUPS GREEN BEANS, TRIMMED AND HALVED DIAGONALLY

2 RED RIPE TOMATOES, CUT INTO THIN WEDGES

3 KAFFIR LIME LEAVES, CUT INTO SLIVERS

10 FRESH THAI BASIL LEAVES

The lowfat milk, which is a substitute for coconut milk in this recipe, may also be substituted with nonfat yogurt or nonfat buttermilk. Of course, none of these options has the same flavor as coconut milk, but they all provide the desired texture.

Heat the canola oil in a large saucepan over moderate heat. Add the shallots, garlic, curry powder, turmeric, and chili paste and stir until fragrant, about 1 minute. Add the soy sauce, lemon grass, and ginger and stir for another 30 seconds. Add the lowfat milk, salt, and brown sugar and bring to a boil. Add the carrots and potatoes. Reduce the heat and let simmer until they soften a bit, 5 to 7 minutes. Then add the onion, cauliflower, green beans, and tomatoes and cook until they begin to soften, another 3 to 5 minutes. Just before serving, stir in the lime leaves and basil leaves. Remove from heat and serve with steamed rice.

cauliflower in sweet and sour sauce

SERVES 4

When you are surrounded by all kinds of foods like I am, it can be hard to decide what to eat at the end of the day. I often resort to eating just a big bowl of vegetables. In this recipe, one of my favorite vegetables, cauliflower, is sautéed in a fresh tomato and soy sauce. It's simple but satisfying.

2 TABLESPOONS VEGETABLE OIL

2 SHALLOTS, THINLY SLICED

2 CLOVES GARLIC, MINCED

1 TEASPOON GROUND CHILI PASTE (OPTIONAL)

1 TABLESPOON SOY SAUCE

2 TEASPOONS SUGAR

1/2 TEASPOON SALT

3 RED RIPE TOMATOES, CUBED

1 LARGE HEAD CAULIFLOWER, CUT INTO BITE-SIZE PIECES

1/2 YELLOW ONION, THINLY SLICED

2/3 CUP HOMEMADE UNSALTED CHICKEN STOCK OR WATER

1/2 TEASPOON LEMON JUICE

2 GREEN ONIONS, CHOPPED INTO 1/2-INCH PIECES

5 FRESH CILANTRO SPRIGS FOR GARNISH

Heat the oil in a skillet over moderate heat. Add the shallots, garlic, and chili paste and stir until fragrant, about 1 minute. Add the soy sauce, sugar, and salt and stir for 30 more seconds. Add the tomatoes and simmer for 3 minutes. Add the cauliflower, yellow onion, chicken stock, and lemon juice and reduce heat to low. Simmer until vegetables are just cooked, 8 to 10 minutes, and add the green onions. Remove from heat. Transfer to a serving dish and garnish with cilantro.

thai stir-fried long beans

SERVES 4

Use long beans as you would string beans, although they take a bit longer to cook. Every time I buy long beans at the farmers' markets, I make it a point to ask the farmers to please pick them before they get too old and the beans inside toughen up. They agreed, but only on the condition that I pay for the beans by the bundle, not by weight.

2 TABLESPOONS VEGETABLE OIL
2 CLOVES GARLIC, THINLY SLICED
2 SHALLOTS, THINLY SLICED
1/2 TEASPOON RED CURRY PASTE, OR TO TASTE
1 1/2 POUNDS LONG BEANS, CUT INTO 3-INCH PIECES
1/2 CUP VEGETABLE BROTH OR WATER
3 TO 4 RIPE ROMA TOMATOES, SEEDED AND CUT INTO THIN WEDGES
1 TEASPOON FISH SAUCE
1 TEASPOON SOY SAUCE
1 TEASPOON SUGAR
3 KAFFIR LIME LEAVES, THINLY SLICED

Heat the oil in a wok or skillet over moderate heat. Add the garlic and shallots and stir until aromatic, about 30 seconds. Add the curry paste and continue to stir to prevent sticking. Add the long beans and sauté for 1 minute. Add the vegetable broth and reduce heat to low. Cook until beans are almost soft, 3 to 5 minutes. Add the tomatoes, fish sauce, soy sauce, sugar, and lime leaves. Cook for another 2 minutes and remove from heat.

vegetarian pad thai

SERVES 4

Those who know pad thai *know that it is either good or bad—there is no in-between. In Thailand, a plate of these noodles usually is made by a vendor who is a real expert and who cooks nothing else. Traditionally the Thais do not blanch the dried noodles before cooking them—they merely soak them. From an aesthetic point of view, I have always found the traditional presentation lacking: the noodles are all broken and oily. This recipe is a little more involved but worth the effort.*

NOODLES
1/2 POUND DRIED RICE STICK NOODLES, PREFERABLY MEDIUM WIDTH
2 TABLESPOONS VEGETABLE OIL
1/2 TABLESPOON MINCED GARLIC
2 SHALLOTS, SLICED THIN
1 TEASPOON GROUND CHILI PASTE, OR TO TASTE
6 TABLESPOONS KETCHUP
4 TABLESPOONS SUGAR
1 TABLESPOON SOY SAUCE
1/2 TEASPOON SALT
2/3 CUP WATER
3 CUPS BEAN SPROUTS
3 GREEN ONIONS, SLICED INTO 1-INCH PIECES ON THE DIAGONAL

TOPPING
1 TABLESPOON VEGETABLE OIL
1 SHALLOT, THINLY SLICED
1/2 TEASPOON MINCED GARLIC
2 CUPS SLICED WHITE CABBAGE
2 RED RIPE TOMATOES, SEEDED AND CUT INTO THIN WEDGES
2 CUPS BROCCOLI FLORETS, CUT INTO BITE-SIZE PIECES, BLANCHED,
    SHOCKED IN ICE WATER, AND DRAINED
1/2 YELLOW ONION, THINLY SLICED
1/2 CUP JULIENNED SNOW PEAS
3 TABLESPOONS WATER

GARNISH
1/4 CUP COARSELY CHOPPED ROASTED PEANUTS (OPTIONAL, PAGE 55)
10 FRESH CILANTRO SPRIGS
4 LEMON WEDGES

ACCOMPANIMENT
CILANTRO-LIME SOY SAUCE (PAGE 36)

Bring a pot of water to a rolling boil, then add the rice sticks. Stirring often to untangle the noodles, cook for 2 minutes, then rinse extremely well under cold running water. This will ensure that the noodles are clean and free of the pungent dried rice flour odor. Drain the noodles in a colander and spread them out to dry for at least 20 minutes. Noodles will stick together but don't be alarmed.

Meanwhile, heat the 2 tablespoons oil in a large wok or nonstick fry pan over moderate heat. Add the garlic, shallots, and chili paste and allow to sizzle about 30 seconds. Add the ketchup, sugar, soy sauce, salt, and 2/3 cup water and reduce heat to low, stirring frequently for about 5 minutes. Remove 3 tablespoons of the sauce in the pan and set aside.

Add the blanched rice noodles to the bubbling sauce, and using chopsticks, gently separate the rice noodles. Toss until the noodles absorb all the sauce and are cooked, 5 to 7 minutes. Remove from heat. Add the bean sprouts and green onions and fold them into the noodles. Remove pan from heat and set aside.

In another nonstick pan, heat the 1 tablespoon oil over moderate heat. Brown the shallot and garlic until aromatic, about 20 seconds. Add the cabbage, tomatoes, broccoli, and onion. Stir-fry until the vegetables soften, 2 to 3 minutes. Add the snow peas, reserved sauce, and 3 tablespoons water and toss for another 2 minutes. Remove from heat.

To serve, portion noodles onto individual dinner plates and top with the sautéed vegetables. Garnish with peanuts, cilantro, and lemon wedges. For extra flavor, serve with cilantro-lime soy sauce on the side.

su co's delight

Named in honor of the Buddhist nuns serving in Vietnamese temples, this was the first vegetarian dish on our menu. It is simple yet delightful. Here, the fresh vegetables are sautéed in a light vegetable broth and soy sauce.

2 TABLESPOONS VEGETABLE OIL
2 SHALLOTS, SLICED
2 CLOVES GARLIC, SLICED
6 DRIED BLACK MUSHROOMS, SOAKED IN HOT WATER 30 MINUTES, STEMMED
    (IF LARGE, CUT IN HALF)
1 TEASPOON GROUND CHILI PASTE (OPTIONAL)
3 TABLESPOONS SOY SAUCE
1 TABLESPOON VEGETARIAN OYSTER SAUCE OR MUSHROOM SAUCE
1/2 TABLESPOON SUGAR
1 1/2 CUPS VEGETABLE BROTH OR WATER
1 ZUCCHINI, HALVED LENGTHWISE AND SLICED INTO 1/2-INCH-THICK PIECES
2 CUPS ASPARAGUS, CUT INTO 2-INCH PIECES
2 CUPS BROCCOLI FLORETS, BLANCHED, SHOCKED IN ICE WATER,
    AND DRAINED
1/2 CUP JULIENNED RED BELL PEPPER
1/4 POUND EXTRA FIRM TOFU, DRAINED AND CUT INTO 1-INCH CUBES
3 TABLESPOONS CORNSTARCH
1/2 CUP WATER

Heat the oil in a wok over moderate heat. Add the shallots, garlic, black mushrooms, and chili paste and stir until fragrant, about 30 seconds. Add the soy sauce, oyster sauce, and sugar and let sizzle for 2 minutes. Add the broth and bring to a boil. Add the zucchini and asparagus and cook until they begin to soften, 2 to 3 minutes. Add the broccoli and cook until hot, about 2 more minutes. Gently stir in the red bell pepper and tofu, making sure the tofu does not break apart. Bring to a boil again. In a small bowl, dissolve the cornstarch in the water and add only enough to the stir-fry, 1 tablespoon at a time, to thicken the sauce slightly. Remove from heat and serve immediately.

Packed in water and sold in plastic containers, tofu can be used as is, or it can be fried first. The latter technique produces a brown, chewy skin. Fried tofu can be used in almost every recipe.

To make fried tofu, fill a fry pan with 1/2 inch oil. Cut the tofu into the desired size and pat dry with paper towels. Fry the tofu, and using chopsticks or a spatula, turn so all the sides are nicely browned, about 3 to 5 minutes. Remove the tofu and drain on paper towels.

water spinach and cabbage in garlic-bean sauce

SERVES 4

Water spinach grows in Asia's numerous ponds, lakes, and rivers. Some times right in the heart of a city, farmers can be seen in the middle of a pond harvesting water spinach from canoes. Green, leafy, and crunchy due to its hollow stems, water spinach is enjoyed in stir-fries and soups. Sometimes it is shredded then submerged in cold water to become spinach "curls." Among some Vietnamese Northerners, the integrity of a salad depends on the fluffiness of these curls!

2 TABLESPOONS VEGETABLE OIL

1/2 YELLOW ONION, SLICED

4 CLOVES GARLIC, SLICED

2 FRESH THAI BIRD CHILIES (OPTIONAL)

1 1/2 TABLESPOONS BEAN SAUCE (SEE PAGE 22)

1 SMALL CARROT, PEELED AND JULIENNED

1 POUND WATER SPINACH, WASHED, TOUGH BOTTOM STEMS REMOVED, AND
     CUT INTO 3-INCH PIECES

1 CUP WHITE CABBAGE, CUT INTO 1/2-INCH SLICES

1 TEASPOON FISH SAUCE

1 TABLESPOON OYSTER SAUCE OR MUSHROOM SAUCE

Heat the oil in a large wok or skillet over high heat. Add the onion and garlic and brown slightly. Add the chilies and yellow beans and stir until fragrant, about 30 seconds. Add the carrot, water spinach, and cabbage. Add fish sauce and oyster sauce. Cover and cook until vegetables are just wilted, 2 to 3 minutes. If pan becomes dry, splash in a little water. Serve immediately.

warm vegetables on cool noodles

SERVES 4

Of all the vegetarian dishes I have cooked—and there are many—this is my all-time favorite. It's simple and straightforward, but the flavors are intense and lively. Make sure you have all the ingredients prepared before you start to cook. The actual cooking time for this dish is only minutes.

NOODLES

1/2 POUND DRIED RICE VERMICELLI, BOILED IN WATER FOR 4 TO 5 MINUTES, RINSED, AND DRAINED

2 CUPS BEAN SPROUTS

1/2 SMALL CUCUMBER, SEEDED AND JULIENNED

1/4 CUP FRESH MINT LEAVES, CUT IN HALF

3 ROMAINE LETTUCE LEAVES, SHREDDED

TOPPING

1 CUP JULIENNED CARROTS

2 CUPS BROCCOLI FLORETS, CUT INTO SMALL, THIN PIECES

2 TABLESPOONS VEGETABLE OIL

1 SMALL YELLOW ONION, SLICED

6 DRIED BLACK MUSHROOMS, SOAKED IN HOT WATER FOR 30 MINUTES, STEMMED, THEN THINLY SLICED

2 CUPS SHREDDED NAPA CABBAGE

1 MEDIUM RED BELL PEPPER, JULIENNED

3 TABLESPOONS SOY SAUCE

2 TEASPOONS SCALLION OIL (OPTIONAL, PAGE 48)

2 TEASPOONS CHOPPED ROASTED PEANUTS (OPTIONAL, PAGE 55)

ACCOMPANIMENT

1 CUP CILANTRO-LIME SOY SAUCE (PAGE 36)

In this recipe, it is extremely important to get the pan very hot before cooking. The onions, coupled with the black mushrooms, create a wonderful aromatic base for the dish. Remember that soy sauce added directly to a hot pan produces a stronger flavor than soy sauce added to vegetables.

After the rice vermicelli have cooled, gently toss with the bean sprouts, cucumber, mint, and lettuce until well blended. Set aside.

Bring water to a rolling boil in a medium pot. Using a sieve with a handle, blanch the carrots and broccoli until colors turn, about 10 seconds. Shock in ice water immediately. Drain and set aside.

Just before serving, heat the oil in a large wok or skillet over high heat. Wait for the pan to get very hot, almost smoking. Carefully add the onion (oil may splatter) and stir until it begins to soften, about 30 seconds. Add the mushrooms and sauté for 1 minute. Add the carrots, broccoli, napa cabbage, and red bell pepper and stir-fry for 2 to 3 more minutes. Vegetables should be very hot and sizzling. Push the vegetables to one side of the pan and add the soy sauce to the open area to create a distinctive fragrance. Then continue stirring vegetables for another minute and remove from heat.

To serve, place noodle mixture in individual soup or pasta bowls. Top with the stir-fried vegetables. Garnish with scallion oil and roasted peanuts. Invite each guest to drizzle 3 tablespoons of cilantro-lime soy sauce on the noodles and toss gently before eating.

Chapter eight

Never Taste the Same

rice and noodles

Toward the end of our stay in Bangkok, my father, who was the Vietnamese military attaché to Thailand, and my mother became quite involved in state functions. They played host to almost every dignitary visiting from Vietnam. Sometimes an entire delegation headed by the prime minister would visit, and my father would spend weeks arranging itineraries that included a meeting with King Bhumiphol Adulyadej Rama IX.

At the time, my sister Denise, my older brother Loc, and I were not really interested in our parents' activities as much as we were in their absences from home. You see, every time they left for a dinner or cocktail function, we would throw our own secret party at home. Loc, who was around 12 and yearning to drive, would jump into the family car to begin his version of a joyride. In a carport about 20 feet long, he would drive the family sedan, forward and backward, until our toddler brother, Fred, who was seated in the front seat, started to cry, or until the driver got car sick.

Then when Loc and Fred came back into the house, my sister Denise and I would be just finishing our sing-along games and rope jumping. And each time, like clockwork, we all decided it was time to eat our favorite meal together.

Together with Thong, our chocolate poodle, we all walked to the small, run-down restaurant at the corner. There, we bought one order of *rad na*, or rice noodles with pork, and a jumbo *o liang*, or Thai iced coffee. The owner, who was Chinese-Thai, made the best *rad na* we had ever tasted. After heating the oil in the wok to almost smoking, he threw in fresh garlic, chilies, and fermented yellow beans. Then he added pork and quickly stir-fried all. Before it was cooked all the way, he added blanched Asian broccoli and then flat rice noodles. After tossing for a few quick seconds, he neatly poured the entire dish on a banana leaf set on top of a sheet of newspaper. Then he wrapped it into a triangle-shaped bundle and tied it with a string for easy carrying. Without asking anything else, he then took the aluminum pitcher that we had brought from home and filled it with Thai iced coffee. After grabbing four drinking straws, we paid the man and ran home.

Sitting on the cool, marble tile floor of our front patio, we unwrapped our dinner and ate it right out of the banana leaf. We didn't give Fred any noodles because they were too spicy, but we did let him have a few sips of coffee. The flavors of the chilies and yellow beans burst out every time we took a bite of *rad na*. We devoured the meal quickly, fearing that whoever ate the slowest would get the least. Sometimes I drank the iced coffee so fast my head hurt.

When our parents came home, everything returned to normal. We made a deal with our nanny, *Chi Tu*, that if she never told on us, we would always behave and never create any problems for her. She must have taken that agreement seriously because my parents never knew anything about our secret activities until the day a dent appeared on the car. Loc's joyrides ended abruptly, but our noodle dinners continued for some time.

Today, decades later, my siblings and I often reflect on those days and find ourselves amazed at how much the *rad na* meant to us back then. Once in a while when we get together, we make the noodles, all in hopes of reliving our fond memories. Strange, but no matter how hard I try to cook this dish using the same ingredients, the noodles never taste the same.

flat noodles with chicken and chinese broccoli

SERVES 2 TO 3

Traditionally made with pork, this rad na *uses chicken and gets its distinctive flavor from the fermented yellow beans. In Bangkok, you can find this dish on practically any street corner and even in hotels. Imagine you are in the lush, tropical setting of a large hotel in the beautiful resort town of Phuket on the southern tip of Thailand. Instead of calling for room service and ordering bacon and eggs, how about asking for* rad na? *I've done it, and it was the best room service meal I ever had.*

It's important to use the

wide fettucine-style rice

noodles in this dish. You

can purchase either fresh

rice sheets and cut them

into 1-inch-wide noodles,

or the dried pre-cut kind.

If using fresh noodles,

omit the blanching but

decrease the stir-fry time

as fresh noodles are

more fragile and need

less cooking time.

$1/2$ POUND DRIED ($1/2$-INCH-WIDE) FLAT RICE NOODLES, BOILED UNTIL JUST
  DONE BUT STILL FIRM, ABOUT 3 MINUTES, RINSED WELL, AND DRAINED

2 PLUS 1 TEASPOONS SOY SAUCE

2 TABLESPOONS CORNSTARCH

$1/2$ CUP WATER

2 PLUS 1 TABLESPOONS VEGETABLE OIL

4 CLOVES GARLIC, THINLY SLICED

2 FRESH THAI BIRD OR ANY FRESH CHILIES, CHOPPED

1 TABLESPOON FERMENTED WHOLE SOYBEANS

$1/2$ POUND SKINLESS, BONELESS CHICKEN BREAST, CUT IN
  $1/4$-INCH-THICK SLICES

1 TABLESPOON OYSTER SAUCE

1 TEASPOON FISH SAUCE

1 TABLESPOON SUGAR

1 CUP HOMEMADE UNSALTED OR CANNED LOW-SODIUM CHICKEN STOCK

2 TEASPOONS WHITE VINEGAR

$1/2$ TO $2/3$ POUND CHINESE BROCCOLI, STEMMED, CUT INTO BITE-SIZE
  PIECES ON THE DIAGONAL, BLANCHED, AND SHOCKED IN ICE WATER
  (ABOUT 3 CUPS)

2 ROMA TOMATOES, CUT INTO THIN WEDGES

6 FRESH CILANTRO SPRIGS FOR GARNISH

WHITE PEPPER FOR GARNISH

THAI CHILI DIPPING SAUCE (PAGE 33)

In a mixing bowl, combine the noodles with the 2 teaspoons soy sauce and toss gently a few times. Set aside.

Using a small wire whisk or chop sticks, dissolve the cornstarch in the water and set aside.

Heat the 2 tablespoons oil in a large nonstick fry pan over moderate heat and tilt pan to completely coat the entire cooking surface. Add the noodles, and turning only once or twice, brown slightly on both sides, 3 to 5 minutes. Remove from heat and set aside.

In another fry pan, heat the 1 tablespoon oil over moderate heat. Wait for the pan to get very hot and add the garlic, chilies, and soybeans. Stir-fry until fragrant, about 1 minute. Add the chicken and toss to pick up the seasonings, 2 to 3 minutes. Add the oyster sauce, the 1 teaspoon soy sauce, fish sauce, sugar, chicken stock, and vinegar. Wait for sauce to boil, then add the broccoli. Stir in the cornstarch mixture, adding 1 tablespoon at a time until sauce slightly thickens. Add the tomatoes and cook until vegetables and chicken are done, about 3 more minutes. To serve, place the warm noodles on a plate and top with the stir-fry. Garnish with cilantro and a sprinkling of white pepper. Serve with Thai chili dipping sauce.

thai noodles with prawns (pad thai)

SERVES 4

A staple noodle dish of Thailand, pad thai *is a favorite among locals and foreigners alike. At crowded sections of Bangkok, one is likely to discover a* pad thai *hawker somewhere on a street corner. Though it consists of simple ingredients, this dish requires a great understanding of handling rice noodles and making the sauce. Traditionally,* pad thai *is made with only dried shrimp, eggs, and preserved turnips. At Lemon Grass, however, we omit the eggs and embellish the dish with prawns and broccoli.*

NOODLES

2/3 POUND DRIED RICE STICK NOODLES, PREFERABLY MEDIUM WIDTH

2 TABLESPOONS VEGETABLE OIL

1/2 TABLESPOON MINCED GARLIC

2 SHALLOTS, THINLY SLICED

2 TEASPOONS GROUND CHILI PASTE, OR TO TASTE

6 TABLESPOONS KETCHUP

4 TABLESPOONS SUGAR

2 TABLESPOONS FISH SAUCE

1/2 TEASPOON SALT

2/3 CUP HOMEMADE UNSALTED OR CANNED LOW-SODIUM CHICKEN STOCK

3 CUPS BEAN SPROUTS

3 GREEN ONIONS, SLICED INTO 1-INCH PIECES ON THE DIAGONAL

1/4 CUP CHOPPED ROASTED PEANUTS (OPTIONAL, PAGE 55)

TOPPING

1 TABLESPOON VEGETABLE OIL

1/2 SMALL YELLOW ONION, SLICED

1/2 TEASPOON MINCED GARLIC

1/2 POUND RAW MEDIUM PRAWNS, PEELED AND DEVEINED

2 CUPS BROCCOLI FLORETS, BLANCHED, SHOCKED IN ICE WATER,
    AND DRAINED

1/3 CUP HOMEMADE UNSALTED OR CANNED LOW-SODIUM CHICKEN STOCK

Thai cooks do not blanch the noodles. Instead, they soak the rice sticks and cook them directly in with the prawns. I prefer, however, to cook the noodles and the topping separately to control the presentation. I like to plate the noodles first and then top with an attractive arrangement of prawns and vegetables. This technique also requires far less oil and prevents the noodles from breaking.

GARNISHES

¼ CUP COARSELY CHOPPED, ROASTED UNSALTED PEANUTS (OPTIONAL)
FRESH CILANTRO FOR GARNISH
4 LEMON WEDGES
THAI CHILI DIPPING SAUCE (PAGE 33)

Bring 2 quarts of water to a rolling boil. Cook the noodles for 2 minutes, then rinse extremely well under cold running water. (This will ensure that the noodles are clean and free of the pungent dried rice flour odor). Drain the noodles in a colander and spread them out to dry for at least 20 minutes. The noodles will stick together, but don't be alarmed.

Meanwhile, heat the 2 tablespoons oil in a wok or large nonstick saucepan over moderate heat. Add the garlic, shallots, and chili paste and allow to sizzle until golden, about 30 seconds. Add the ketchup, sugar, fish sauce, and salt and reduce slightly, about 1 minute. Add the ⅔ cup chicken stock and reduce the heat. Stirring frequently, simmer for 3 to 5 minutes. Remove 2 tablespoons of the sauce and set aside.

Add the noodles to the wok and using chopsticks, gently separate the noodles. Turn often and sauté until noodles absorb all the sauce and are cooked until just tender, about 5 minutes. Add the bean sprouts, green onions, and peanuts and fold into the noodles. Remove from heat and set aside.

Heat the 1 tablespoon oil in another nonstick pan over moderate heat. Add the yellow onion and garlic and sauté until soft and aromatic, about 1 minute. Add the prawns. Toss in pan until they turn opaque, about 2 minutes. Add the broccoli, reserved sauce, and the ⅓ cup chicken stock. Cover and cook until vegetables are thoroughly hot, another 2 minutes.

To serve, portion noodles onto individual dinner plates and top with the prawns and broccoli stir-fry. Garnish with peanuts, cilantro, and lemon wedges. For extra flavor, sprinkle a little Thai chili dipping sauce on top.

warm beef on cool noodles

SERVES 4

A popular Vietnamese way to enjoy noodles is to prepare them almost like a salad. In this recipe, the noodles are cooked and served at room temperature (hence "cool") along with a lively combination of stir-fried beef, mint, and crunchy lettuce and cucumbers. Despite the lively flavors, this dish almost got taken off the menu of our restaurant. In the beginning years when many of our customers were unaware of the nuances of our cuisine, they would eat the meat topping first and then complain about the bland noodles on the bottom. These days, even die-hard meat and potato eaters will come in just for this dish, knowing full well the importance of tossing all the ingredients before eating.

SALAD
2 CUPS SHREDDED ROMAINE LETTUCE
2 CUPS BEAN SPROUTS
1 CUP JULIENNED CUCUMBERS
1/3 CUP CHOPPED FRESH MINT LEAVES
1/3 CUP CHOPPED FRESH THAI BASIL LEAVES

NOODLES
1/2 POUND DRIED RICE VERMICELLI, BOILED 4 TO 5 MINUTES, RINSED,
    AND DRAINED

TOPPING
1 POUND TOP SIRLOIN, THINLY SLICED ACROSS THE GRAIN ABOUT 1/4 INCH
    THICK AND 2 INCHES LONG
2 TABLESPOONS MINCED LEMON GRASS
1 TEASPOON FISH SAUCE
1 TEASPOON SOY SAUCE
1/2 TEASPOON SUGAR
2 TABLESPOONS VEGETABLE OIL
3 CLOVES GARLIC, SLICED
1/2 RED ONION, THINLY SLICED

All the components of this dish can made in advance with the exception of the beef, which must be stir-fried just before serving.

Mint is an important ingredient in this dish. If you're allergic to it, however, you may substitute other herbs, such as Thai basil or cilantro.

GARNISH
2 TABLESPOONS FRIED SHALLOTS (OPTIONAL, PAGE 45)
2 TABLESPOONS CHOPPED ROASTED PEANUTS (PAGE 55)
10 FRESH CILANTRO SPRIGS
VIETNAMESE DIPPING SAUCE (PAGE 32)

Combine all salad ingredients and toss gently. Place about a cup of the salad mixture in individual pasta bowls. Top each with about two cups of the noodles. Set the prepared noodle bowls aside.

Combine the beef, lemon grass, fish sauce, soy sauce, and sugar in a mixing bowl and set aside.

Heat the oil in a large nonstick fry pan over high heat. Add the garlic and onion and stir-fry for 30 seconds. Remove beef from marinade and stir-fry until just done, 3 to 4 minutes. Remove from heat.

Divide the beef topping among the bowls and garnish each with shallots, peanuts, and cilantro. Invite each guest to drizzle on 3 to 4 tablespoons of the Vietnamese dipping sauce. Have them toss the noodles several times with chopsticks to blend the ingredients.

pan-seared noodle pillow with prawns and chicken

SERVES 4

 This is one version of Hong-Kong style pan-seared noodles—crispy on the outside and soft on the inside. Although you can purchase very thin egg noodles in Asian grocery stores, I prefer the ⅛-inch-thick, Chinese-style fresh egg noodles found in the produce section of the supermarket. At the restaurant, we serve this dish with a number of different toppings. Sometimes I serve it with salmon, jumbo scallops, and prawns and other times, just with prawns and chicken. Use whatever you have in the refrigerator.

NOODLES

1 TEASPOON SALT

1 POUND FRESH CHINESE-STYLE EGG NOODLES

3 TABLESPOONS VEGETABLE OIL

TOPPING

2 TABLESPOONS VEGETABLE OIL

1 TABLESPOON MINCED FRESH GINGER

1 TEASPOON MINCED GARLIC

1 TEASPOON GROUND CHILI PASTE

½ POUND SKINLESS, BONELESS CHICKEN BREAST, CUT INTO
 ¼-INCH-THICK SLICES

6 TO 8 SMALL DRIED BLACK MUSHROOMS, SOAKED IN HOT WATER
 30 MINUTES, STEMMED, AND DRAINED

3 TABLESPOONS OYSTER SAUCE

1 TABLESPOON SOY SAUCE

⅔ CUP HOMEMADE UNSALTED OR CANNED LOW-SODIUM CHICKEN STOCK

¼ POUND RAW PRAWNS, PEELED AND DEVEINED

2 CUPS NAPA CABBAGE, CUT INTO BITE-SIZE PIECES

2 CUPS SNOW PEAS, TRIMMED, BLANCHED, SHOCKED IN ICE WATER,
 AND DRAINED

2 TOMATOES, CUT INTO THIN WEDGES

¼ CUP WATER

1 TABLESPOON CORNSTARCH

1 TABLESPOON RICE WINE OR DRY SHERRY (OPTIONAL)

FRESH CILANTRO SPRIGS FOR GARNISH

In a large pot, bring 2 quarts of water to a rolling bowl. Add the salt and noodles and cook briefly until just tender, about 2 minutes. Remove from heat and rinse under running water. Drain and set aside for 20 minutes.

Meanwhile, heat the 3 tablespoons oil in a large nonstick fry pan over moderate heat. Using your hands, form 4 round "pillows" with the noodles. Place the noodle pillows in the pan, and using a spatula, press gently to flatten slightly. Brown the noodles until nicely crisped, 3 to 5 minutes on each side. Drain them on paper towels and keep warm in the oven.

Just before serving, heat the 2 tablespoons oil in a wok or large fry pan. Let the pan get very hot. Add the ginger, garlic, and chili paste and stir until fragrant, about 30 seconds. Add the chicken and black mushrooms and stir-fry for 2 minutes. Add the oyster sauce, soy sauce, and chicken stock and cook until mixture boils. Add the prawns, napa cabbage, snow peas, and tomatoes. In a small bowl, whisk together the water and cornstarch. Add a tablespoon or so of this mixture to the sauce, just enough to thicken it slightly. Just before removing from heat, splash the pan with the rice wine.

To serve, place a noodle pillow in the center of each plate and top with the stir-fry and sauce. Garnish with cilantro.

thai fried rice with chicken and basil

SERVES 4

In Thailand, if you stop at a street food vendor and ask for a plate of kao pad, *chances are you'll be asked if you want a fried egg on top. While that may seem odd to Westerners, remember that many people in Asia cannot afford to eat meat, so eggs are considered a very desirable protein source. In this recipe, the red curry paste makes the fried rice distinctive and deliciously spicy.*

3 TABLESPOONS VEGETABLE OIL

3 CLOVES GARLIC, MINCED

1/2 TEASPOON RED CURRY PASTE (OPTIONAL)

1/2 POUND SKINLESS, BONELESS CHICKEN BREAST, CUBED

1/2 YELLOW ONION, CUBED

4 TO 5 CUPS COOKED RICE, PREFERABLY COLD OR ROOM TEMPERATURE

1/2 TABLESPOON FISH SAUCE

1 TABLESPOON OYSTER SAUCE

1 TEASPOON SOY SAUCE

1 TEASPOON SUGAR

2 RED RIPE TOMATOES, CUBED

1/2 CUP FROZEN PEAS

30 FRESH BASIL LEAVES

3 GREEN ONIONS, CHOPPED

THAI CHILI DIPPING SAUCE (PAGE 33)

Heat the oil in a wok or large nonstick fry pan to very hot. Add the garlic and curry paste and stir until fragrant, about 20 seconds. Add the chicken and onion and cook until chicken turns white, 3 to 4 minutes. Reduce heat to moderate. Splash in 2 table-spoons of water if the pan seems dry. Add the rice and, using a spatula, turn over often. Add the fish sauce, oyster sauce, soy sauce, and sugar and toss the rice so the seasonings are well mixed. Cook for 3 minutes, then add the tomatoes and frozen peas. Just before serving, stir in the basil and green onions. Remove from heat and serve with Thai chili dip-ping sauce.

curried rice with kaffir lime leaves

SERVES 4 TO 6

Sometimes, when plain rice just will not do, consider pairing your main dish with this aromatic curried rice. I particularly like serving this with grilled fish.

3 TABLESPOONS BUTTER
1 YELLOW ONION, CHOPPED
2 CUPS UNCOOKED JASMINE OR ANY LONG-GRAIN RICE
2 TABLESPOONS CURRY POWDER
1/2 TEASPOON GROUND TURMERIC
1/2 TABLESPOON SALT
2 1/2 CUPS BOILING WATER
2/3 CUP UNSWEETENED COCONUT MILK
4 KAFFIR LIME LEAVES, CUT INTO FINE SLIVERS, OR ZEST OF 1 LIME
2/3 CUP FROZEN PEAS, THAWED (OPTIONAL)

Heat the butter in a medium saucepan over moderate heat. Add the onion and sauté until slightly wilted. Add the rice, curry powder, turmeric, and salt. Toss for 2 to 3 minutes to evenly coat the rice, then add the boiling water and coconut milk. Bring to a boil. Using a wooden spoon or chopsticks, stir the rice a few times. Add the kaffir lime leaves. Cover and simmer over very low heat until liquid has evaporated and rice is tender, about 20 minutes. Turn off the heat. Stir in the peas and fluff the rice with a fork. (If rice seems dry, add 2 to 3 tablespoons boiling water and fluff again.) Let sit 5 minutes before serving.

chicken and rice in claypot

SERVES 4 TO 6

Called com tay cam, *this is an all-time favorite rice dish in Saigon. For authentic flavor and presentation, cook this dish in a large claypot, or use a Dutch oven. I prefer the latter since the rice cooks evenly and the larger container allows for easier mixing.*

2 CUPS UNCOOKED JASMINE OR ANY LONG-GRAIN RICE, RINSED
    AND DRAINED
3 TABLESPOONS VEGETABLE OIL
1/2 YELLOW ONION, SLICED
1 TABLESPOON MINCED GARLIC
2 TEASPOONS FIVE-SPICE POWDER
2 TABLESPOONS MINCED FRESH GINGER
8 CHICKEN THIGHS, BONED AND SKINNED AND CUT IN BITE-SIZE PIECES
8 DRIED BLACK MUSHROOMS, SOAKED IN HOT WATER 30 MINUTES,
    STEMMED, AND HALVED
3 TABLESPOONS SOY SAUCE
3 1/2 CUPS HOMEMADE UNSALTED OR CANNED LOW-SODIUM CHICKEN STOCK,
    BOILED JUST BEFORE USING
1 TEASPOON FISH SAUCE
1/4 TEASPOON SALT
1/2 CUP DRAINED CANNED STRAW MUSHROOMS
1/3 POUND GREEN BEANS, TRIMMED AND HALVED LENGTHWISE
2 CARROTS, PEELED AND CUT INTO 1/4-INCH ROUNDS
3 GREEN ONIONS, CUT INTO 1/2-INCH PIECES
FRESH CILANTRO SPRIGS FOR GARNISH
1 CUP CILANTRO-LIME SOY SAUCE (PAGE 36)

Brown the rice in a nonstick fry pan over low heat just so it turns opaque, about 5 minutes. Remove from heat and set aside.

Heat the oil in a Dutch oven over moderate heat. Add the yellow onion and garlic and stir-fry until fragrant, about 30 seconds. Add the five-spice powder and ginger and stir-fry for 1 minute. Add the chicken, black mushrooms, soy sauce, and sauté for 3 to 4 minutes. Add the browned rice, boiling chicken stock, fish sauce, and salt. When the broth comes to a boil, reduce heat to low. Stir in the mushrooms, beans, and carrots and cover. Cook until liquid has evaporated and rice is tender, about 15 more minutes. Stir in the green onions and fluff rice with fork

To serve, transfer to a large platter or individual plates and garnish with cilantro. Pass the cilantro-lime soy sauce on the side.

singapore noodles

SERVES 4

Delicately spiced, this noodle dish is always a favorite at our banquets and cater-
ing events. Slender, fluffy, and radiating bright yellow from the curry powder and turmeric
(hence the Malayan connection), these noodles are always the first to be gobbled up. Here
I've included prawns, but if you want to serve this as a side dish, simply omit them.

1/2 POUND DRIED RICE VERMICELLI, BOILED 2 1/2 MINUTES,
    RINSED, AND DRAINED
2 TABLESPOONS VEGETABLE OIL

SAUCE
3 TABLESPOONS UNSWEETENED COCONUT MILK
2 TEASPOONS SOY SAUCE, PREFERABLY LIGHT
1/2 TEASPOON SALT
2 TEASPOONS SUGAR
1 TABLESPOON CURRY POWDER
1/2 TEASPOON GROUND TURMERIC
1/4 CUP HOMEMADE UNSALTED OR CANNED LOW-SODIUM CHICKEN STOCK

STIR-FRY
2 TABLESPOONS VEGETABLE OIL
3 CLOVES GARLIC, MINCED
2 TEASPOONS MINCED FRESH GINGER
1/3 POUND RAW PRAWNS, PEELED AND DEVEINED
1 SMALL YELLOW ONION, SLICED
2 CUPS SHREDDED BABY BOK CHOY
1/2 POUND BEAN SPROUTS
3 GREEN ONIONS, CUT INTO 1-INCH PIECES
6 FRESH CILANTRO SPRIGS FOR GARNISH
1 CUP VIETNAMESE DIPPING SAUCE (PAGE 32)

Toss the cooked rice vermicelli with the 2 tablespoons oil to prevent sticking and set aside.

Combine the sauce ingredients in a small mixing bowl and set aside.

Heat the 2 tablespoons oil in a wok or large nonstick fry pan over moderate heat. Add the garlic and ginger and stir-fry for 30 seconds. Add the prawns and yellow onion. Toss around in the pan until prawns turn pink, about 2 minutes. Remove prawns (but not the oil or seasonings) and set aside on a plate.

Into the same pan, add the noodles. Reduce heat slightly. Using chopsticks or a kitchen fork, turn the noodles while adding the sauce. Cook until sauce evaporates, 3 to 5 minutes. Add the baby bok choy, bean sprouts, and green onions and the reserved prawns. Toss until vegetables are wilted and thoroughly hot, 2 to 3 more minutes. (If the pan seems dry, splash with 2 to 3 tablespoons water.) Remove from heat. Garnish with cilantro and serve with Vietnamese dipping sauce on the side.

chiang mai noodles

SERVES 4 TO 6

If you have a chance to visit Thailand, make a point to see Chiang Mai, a lovely city in the hilltop area of the north. If time permits, seek out a noodle shop specializing in this popular Burmese-influenced dish. A restaurant with good khao soi *is usually packed, but if you can squeeze yourself in, you may very well have discovered your new favorite noodle dish.*

2 TABLESPOONS VEGETABLE OIL

2 SHALLOTS, CHOPPED

3 CLOVES GARLIC, MINCED

1 TABLESPOON RED CURRY PASTE

2 TABLESPOONS CURRY POWDER

1/2 TEASPOON GROUND TURMERIC

1 POUND BEEF CHUCK OR STEW BEEF, CUBED

3 CUPS HOMEMADE UNSALTED OR CANNED LOW-SODIUM CHICKEN STOCK

3 CUPS UNSWEETENED COCONUT MILK

4 TABLESPOONS FISH SAUCE

2 TABLESPOONS SUGAR

2 TABLESPOONS FRESH LIME JUICE

1 POUND FRESH CHINESE-STYLE EGG NOODLES, PREFERABLY THE VERY
   THIN NOODLE "NESTS"

GARNISH

3 GREEN ONIONS, THINLY SLICED ON THE DIAGONAL

1/4 CUP CHINESE-STYLE PRESERVED CABBAGE (OPTIONAL)

10 FRESH CILANTRO SPRIGS, CHOPPED

1/2 LIME, CUT INTO 4 TO 6 THIN WEDGES

Heat the oil in a large saucepan over moderate heat. Add the shallots and garlic and stir for 20 seconds. Add the curry paste, curry powder, and turmeric and sauté for 2 to 3 minutes. Add the beef, chicken stock, coconut milk, fish sauce, sugar, and lime juice and simmer until meat is tender, 30 to 40 minutes.

While the meat is cooking, prepare the noodles. In a medium saucepan, bring water to a rolling boil. Shake the noodles loose and drop in the boiling water. Cook until just tender, 2 to 3 minutes. Rinse in cold water and drain.

To serve, place a handful of noodles in each serving bowl. Ladle the beef curry sauce on top and garnish with green onions, preserved cabbage, and cilantro. Invite guests to squeeze a little lime juice before eating.

warm prawns on cool noodles

SERVES 4

If my grandmother could taste this dish, I think she would like it better than her original recipe. When I first developed this for the restaurant, I wanted more flavor than what the mild tasting prawns could offer. So, I added black and white mushrooms along with a few carrots. Over the years as I watched and smelled this dish being cooked, I decided this is the only way to cook bun tom.

SALAD

2 CUPS SHREDDED ROMAINE LETTUCE

2 CUPS BEAN SPROUTS

1 CUP JULIENNED CUCUMBERS

10 FRESH CILANTRO LEAVES, CHOPPED

1/3 CUP CHOPPED FRESH MINT LEAVES

1/3 CUP CHOPPED FRESH THAI BASIL LEAVES

3 TABLESPOONS FRIED SHALLOTS (OPTIONAL, PAGE 45)

NOODLES

1/2 POUND DRIED RICE VERMICELLI, BOILED 4 TO 5 MINUTES, RINSED,
    AND DRAINED

TOPPING

3 TABLESPOONS VEGETABLE OIL

1 YELLOW ONION, THINLY SLICED

2 TEASPOONS MINCED GARLIC

2 TEASPOONS MINCED LEMON GRASS

1/2 TEASPOON GROUND CHILI PASTE

5 DRIED BLACK MUSHROOMS, SOAKED IN HOT WATER 30 MINUTES,
    STEMMED, AND THINLY SLICED

1 TABLESPOON SOY SAUCE

PINCH OF SALT

1 TEASPOON SUGAR

1/2 CUP JULIENNED CARROTS, BLANCHED AND SHOCKED IN ICE WATER

½ POUND RAW PRAWNS, PEELED AND DEVEINED

10 WHITE MUSHROOMS, SLICED ¼ INCH THICK

¼ CUP UNSALTED HOMEMADE OR CANNED LOW-SODIUM CHICKEN STOCK
    OR WATER

2 TABLESPOONS ROASTED PEANUTS FOR GARNISH (PAGE 55)

10 FRESH CILANTRO SPRIGS FOR GARNISH

1 CUP VIETNAMESE DIPPING SAUCE (PAGE 32)

Combine all the salad ingredients and toss gently. Place about a cup of the salad mixture in individual bowls. Top with about two cups of the noodles. Set aside.

Heat the oil in a wok or nonstick fry pan over moderate heat. Tilt the pan to evenly coat the entire surface. Wait for oil to get hot, then add the onion, garlic, and lemon grass. Stir-fry for about 10 seconds. Working very quickly, add the chili paste and black mushrooms. Add the soy sauce, salt, and sugar and stir a few times. Add the carrots and prawns and cook until both are almost cooked, 2 minutes. Add the white mushrooms and chicken stock. Cook until mushrooms begin to wilt, 2 to 3 minutes. Remove from heat.

To serve, place the prawns and vegetables on top of the noodles. Garnish with chopped peanuts and cilantro. Invite guests to add 3 to 4 tablespoons of Vietnamese dipping sauce to their noodles and toss gently before eating.

lemon grass stir-fried jasmine rice

SERVES 6

At Lemon Grass, we prepare a batch of this "house" rice before each meal to serve with our grilled dishes. Many of our employees love to eat this rice just by itself or with a sprinkling of Vietnamese dipping sauce.

3 TABLESPOONS BUTTER
3 TABLESPOONS CHOPPED YELLOW ONION
4 TABLESPOONS KETCHUP
1/2 TABLESPOON FISH SAUCE
1/2 TEASPOON SALT
2 TEASPOONS SUGAR
5 CUPS COOKED RICE, PREFERABLY JASMINE (PAGE 50)
1 CUP FROZEN PEAS, THAWED

Heat the butter in a wok or nonstick fry pan until bubbly hot. Add the onion and sauté until soft. Add the ketchup, fish sauce, salt, and sugar. Simmer until sauce is slightly reduced, about 2 minutes. Add the rice and, using a wooden spoon or spatula, stir-fry until rice is hot, 5 to 6 minutes. Add the peas and toss until hot. (This rice may be made in advance and reheated when needed.)

trong's cup of noodles

SERVES 2

Sometimes when friends and family ask Trong what it's like to be married to a chef, he jokingly (I hope) says it's wonderful except for the many late-night cups of noodles he's had to cook. You see, Trong knows that on Saturday nights when I come crawling home after cooking more than 200 meals, the best thing he can offer me is his cup of noodles. His simple noodle soup, embellished with colorful toppings, warms my soul and fills my belly in a special, gentle way.

1 TABLESPOON VEGETABLE OIL
¼ CUP THINLY SLICED YELLOW ONION
5 CUPS WATER
2 PACKAGES RAMEN NOODLES
1 CUP SHREDDED NAPA CABBAGE
½ CUP SLICED LEFTOVER ROAST CHICKEN OR BEEF
2 GREEN ONIONS, CHOPPED
5 FRESH THAI BASIL LEAVES, CHOPPED, FOR GARNISH
5 FRESH CILANTRO SPRIGS, CHOPPED, FOR GARNISH
2 FRESH THAI BIRD OR ANY CHILIES, CHOPPED, FOR GARNISH

Heat the oil in a pot over moderate heat. Add the onion and sauté until fragrant, about 1 minute. Add the water and bring to a boil. Add the seasoning packets that came with the noodles, or if you like, season with 1 tablespoon soy sauce and 1 teaspoon fish sauce. Add the noodles and cook until almost tender, about 2 minutes. Add the napa cabbage and remove from heat.

Just before serving, divide the noodles between 2 very large soup bowls. Top with the meat and green onions and pour boiling broth over the noodles. Garnish with basil, cilantro, and chilies and serve immediately with spoons *and* chopsticks.

Chapter nine

Perfect Black Skin

fish and shellfish

For me school was great, but sometimes no school was better. As a youngster I got to do special things when I missed school. My fondest memories are of tagging along with my Thai nanny, Chi Tu, to the open-air market where she shopped every day.

On one such day after breakfast, she quickly dressed me. Together we dashed out of the house, just in time to run down to the *klong*, or canal, and catch the 9 A.M. waterbus that would take us to the open-air markets on the other side of the river. Back then, Bangkok was the Venice of Asia, with narrow waterways connecting the entire city.

It was this market that made a life-long impression on me. Even as a child, I was amazed by the abundance of food and its remarkable variety and freshness, not to mention the tantalizing smells and incredible tastes. In Thailand, then as now, vendors displayed products sumptuously. Storefronts were filled from floor to ceiling with food, fruits, flowers, and housewares. Incredibly festive, the marketplace is the true heartbeat of any neighborhood.

Upon arriving at our local market, Chi Tu stopped at her favorite curry paste vendor first. On display were gigantic beehive-shaped mounds of red, green, and yellow curry pastes. After inspecting for quality and freshness, Chi Tu asked the vendor, who had hand-roasted and pounded spices for the previous twenty years, for some red curry paste. Using a small, flat wooden spatula, the vendor scooped out the paste and wrapped it in fresh banana leaves. Seeing that the kaffir lime leaves were freshly picked that morning, we grabbed some to use in that day's curry. In fact, everything looked so immaculately fresh at this stand that by the time we finished, a small crowd had gathered behind us.

I got particularly excited when Chi Tu said we were going to get some catfish. And it wasn't because I liked fish more than other foods. Somehow the fish section, which always seemed to be the busiest and most exciting area, had always interested me. As Chi Tu and I approached the fish section, the hustle and bustle got even louder. In the nearby river, baskets filled with live fish were held under water. Fish vendors hawked their specials, exciting potential customers who were frantically trying to pick out the best. Even though the offerings included a variety of shellfish, such as blood clams, stone crabs, and mussels, the most popular items were catfish, perch, pomfrets, eels, and other small catches. And everything was still alive and wiggling. As soon as Chi Tu and I found the catfish we liked, the one with the perfect black skin, healthy whiskers, and combative vigor when we touched it, the fishmonger killed and cleaned it right in front of our eyes.

While we were waiting, bystanders came up and asked how much we paid for the fine-looking catfish. We pretended not to hear and ignored their curiosity, thinking we already had our bargain so why jeopardize our friendship with the fishmonger.

As we headed back to the market's center to pick up vegetables and fruits, I kept wondering why the adults were so intense and captivated by the selling and buying of food. When the catfish was being cleaned, Chi Tu scrutinized every single move by the fishmonger, as if she were worried he might cheat and cut off a piece for himself. From every fishmonger to every customer and spectator, it seemed as if this business of haggling over food was more than a necessary chore. Somehow, from those times on, food seemed more alive to me. I began to feel it wasn't something you just passively ingested. Food makes us feel warm and content, but it also links our activities, thoughts, and spirits in a way nothing else can.

Funny, but I never learned any of that in school.

seafood paella

SERVES 6

    A popular dish at Lemon Grass, this paella, with its bright yellow rice and color-ful seafood and vegetables, is especially beautiful if served on an attractive platter. When entertaining, prepare the rice in advance and sauté the topping just before serving.

RICE
2 TABLESPOONS LIGHT OLIVE OIL
1 TEASPOON MINCED GARLIC
2 CUPS JASMINE OR ANY LONG-GRAIN RICE
$1/2$ TEASPOON SAFFRON THREADS, DISSOLVED IN $1/3$ CUP HOT WATER
$2^{1/2}$ CUPS UNSALTED HOMEMADE OR CANNED LOW-SODIUM CHICKEN STOCK
1 TEASPOON SALT
1 TEASPOON GROUND TURMERIC
1 CUP SLICED FRESH OYSTER, SHIITAKE, OR WHITE MUSHROOMS
3 TOMATOES, CUBED
3 GREEN ONIONS, CHOPPED

TOPPING
2 TABLESPOONS LIGHT OLIVE OIL
1 TABLESPOON MINCED GARLIC
$1^{1/2}$ TABLESPOONS MINCED FRESH GINGER
2 TABLESPOONS OYSTER SAUCE
1 DOZEN BLACK MUSSELS, DEBEARDED AND SCRUBBED CLEAN
$1/4$ POUND RAW MEDIUM PRAWNS, PEELED AND DEVEINED
$1/4$ POUND SEA OR BAY SCALLOPS
$1/2$ POUND SALMON FILLET, CUBED
$1/2$ CUP HOMEMADE UNSALTED OR CANNED LOW-SODIUM CHICKEN STOCK
2 CUPS SNOW PEAS, TRIMMED, BLANCHED, AND SHOCKED IN ICE WATER
$1/2$ CUP JULIENNED RED BELL PEPPER
2 TABLESPOONS DRY SHERRY
10 FRESH CILANTRO SPRIGS FOR GARNISH

This recipe works with just about any meat, or meat-and-fish combina-tion. You can even turn this into a vegetarian dish by omitting the seafood and using vegetable stock in place of chicken stock.

For an interesting pre-sentation, mound the rice onto a platter. Place the mussels around the edges of the rice in a crown-like fashion. Neatly arrange the other seafood on top of the rice.

To make the rice, heat the olive oil in a deep saucepan over moderate heat. Add the garlic and rice and stir gently until the grains turn white, about 3 minutes. (This technique gives the rice a nice, chewy texture.) Add the saffron liquid, chicken stock, salt, and turmeric and bring to a boil. Stir frequently but gently for about 2 minutes while the rice is boiling. Reduce the heat to very low, cover, and simmer for 20 minutes.

About 10 minutes before the rice is cooked, add the mushrooms, tomatoes, and green onions. Using chopsticks or thin wooden spoons, gently fold the vegetables into the rice. Quickly return lid to pan.

To make the topping, heat the olive oil in a large skillet or wok over moderate heat, just before serving. Brown the garlic and ginger until fragrant, about 1 minute. Add the oyster sauce and mussels. Toss for 2 minutes, then add the prawns, scallops, salmon, and chicken stock. Cook until mussels start to open and all the seafood is cooked, about 3 minutes. Add the snow peas and red bell pepper and cook until slightly soft, another 1 to 2 minutes. Just before removing from the heat, splash the pan with the sherry and give the ingredients a toss or two.

Transfer the rice to a large paella platter and top with the seafood and vegetables. Spoon just enough sauce left in the pan over the rice to make it moist, but not soggy. Garnish with cilantro sprigs.

gingered crab with szechuan peppercorns

SERVES 4

I first cooked this for a feature in ARTCulinaire, an international food magazine. Not only is it great to look at, but the flavors are wonderful. It's especially satisfying to suck on the crab joints, where the garlic and seasonings are hidden and waiting to be discovered.

3 TO 4 POUNDS LIVE DUNGENESS OR BLUE CRABS
3 TABLESPOONS VEGETABLE OIL
1 TABLESPOON BUTTER
1 TABLESPOON MINCED GARLIC
1 TABLESPOON MINCED FRESH GINGER
1 TEASPOON SZECHUAN PEPPERCORNS
1/2 TEASPOON CRACKED BLACK PEPPER
1 TABLESPOON KOSHER SALT
1/2 CUP HOMEMADE UNSALTED OR CANNED LOW-SODIUM CHICKEN STOCK
1/2 RED BELL PEPPER, JULIENNED
1 FRESH THAI BIRD OR JALAPEÑO CHILI, THINLY SLICED ON THE
    DIAGONAL (OPTIONAL)
3 GREEN ONIONS, CUT INTO 1-INCH PIECES ON THE DIAGONAL
10 FRESH CILANTRO SPRIGS FOR GARNISH

Bring a large pot of water to a rolling boil. Drop the crabs in and cook 6 to 8 minutes. (If using the smaller blue crabs, reduce the cooking time by half.) Remove the crabs and set aside to drain. To clean each crab, remove the top shell and discard the sets of feathery gills on the body. Using a small spoon, gently remove the roe and creamy tomalley, or liver, from the edges of the top shell and set aside in a small bowl. (Do not mistakenly remove the air sacs attached behind the eyes.) Next, remove the underbelly apron and discard. Rinse the crabs.

Next, snap off the legs and claws from each crab. Using a cleaver or heavy knife, cut the body into 2 or 4 pieces, about the size of 2 to 3 fingers. Using the flat side of the

If fresh crab is not available, substitute cooked whole crab.

Some Thais love crab roe so much that they "extend" it by adding beaten eggs. If you want to try this, beat one egg with two tablespoons water until fluffy and add to about 1/2 cup roe.

cleaver or a mallet, lightly crack the legs and claws so the seasonings can penetrate. Set aside in a bowl.

In a large wok or fry pan, heat the vegetable oil and butter over high heat. (You may have to cook the crab in two batches.) Wait until the oil almost smokes, then add the garlic, ginger, peppercorns, black pepper, salt, and the reserved crab roe. Quickly stir-fry until fragrant, about 20 seconds. Add the crab pieces and toss in the seasonings for about 3 minutes. Reduce the heat to low and add the chicken stock. Cover and cook for another 4 minutes. Uncover and add the red bell pepper, chili, and green onions.

Stir-fry until the red bell pepper starts to wilt and the sauce is slightly reduced, about 2 minutes. Remove from heat and garnish with cilantro. Serve immediately and provide lots of napkins.

grilled catfish with hoisin–peanut sauce

SERVES 4

When buying catfish, choose fillets that are pinkish-white over those with a milky color. They will have a slightly firmer texture and sweeter flavor. Also, smell the fish: If it has a musty odor, which is a common problem with this freshwater fish, pass it by.

In Asia, deep-fried whole catfish are used in this dish instead of grilled fillets.

I knew this dish was a big hit when customers—sometimes from as far away as New Zealand—arrived at the front door and asked if we were serving our famous grilled catfish. If we said no, they would turn around and leave. My father-in-law, Xuong Nguyen, a man who knows his catfish, claims my version is the best he's ever had. And that's a compliment. This recipe was featured by the U.S. National Catfish Institute during one of its promotional campaigns.

2 CLOVES GARLIC, FINELY MINCED
1/2 TEASPOON GROUND CHILI PASTE
1 TEASPOON VEGETABLE OIL
4 (8-OUNCE) SKINLESS, BONELESS FARM-RAISED CATFISH FILLETS
1 CUP HOISIN-PEANUT SAUCE (PAGE 35)

GARNISH
5 DRIED BLACK MUSHROOMS, SOAKED IN HOT WATER 30 MINUTES, DRAINED, AND THINLY SLICED
2 GREEN ONIONS, THINLY SLICED ON THE DIAGONAL
2 TABLESPOONS ROASTED PEANUTS (PAGE 55)

Combine the garlic, chili paste, and oil in a shallow dish. Add the catfish fillets and let marinate for 20 minutes. Meanwhile, preheat the broiler or a grill to high heat.

Just before serving, heat the hoisin-peanut sauce. (If sauce is too thick, thin it with a little stock or water.) Grill or broil the catfish fillets until just done, 5 to 6 minutes on each side.

Place the fish in the center of individual serving plates and carefully spoon the hoisin-peanut sauce on top. Do not cover the fish completely. Sprinkle with black mushrooms, green onions, and roasted peanuts. Serve with steamed vegetables and rice.

ginger clams and shrimp with basil

SERVES 4

If you like clams and shrimp, this is a great dish that's very simple to prepare. Make sure the clams are scrubbed well to remove all the grit. For more intense flavors, get the pan sizzling hot before adding the aromatics and seafood.

3 TABLESPOONS VEGETABLE OIL

2 TABLESPOONS MINCED FRESH GINGER

1/2 TABLESPOON MINCED GARLIC

1 TEASPOON GROUND CHILI PASTE, OR TO TASTE

2 POUNDS CLAMS, SCRUBBED CLEAN

2 TABLESPOONS OYSTER SAUCE

2 TABLESPOONS HOMEMADE UNSALTED CHICKEN STOCK OR WATER

1/4 POUND RAW MEDIUM SHRIMP, PEELED AND DEVEINED

3 CUPS BROCCOLI, BLANCHED AND SHOCKED IN ICE WATER

1/2 CUP THINLY SLICED RED BELL PEPPER

1/4 CUP FRESH THAI BASIL LEAVES

Heat the oil in a large fry pan or wok over high heat. Wait for the pan to get very hot, then add the ginger, garlic, and chili paste. Using a wooden spoon, stir the seasonings until fragrant, about 30 seconds. Add the clams and oyster sauce and stir continuously for 1 to 2 minutes. Add the chicken stock. When the liquid comes to a boil and the clams have just opened, add the shrimp and broccoli. Gently toss the ingredients, turning the shrimp and vegetables to make sure they cook fast and evenly, about 2 minutes. Add the red bell pepper and basil and cook for another minute. Remove from heat and serve immediately.

I was once asked why anise basil is called Thai basil when it is the Vietnamese who consume most of the supply in the U.S. It dawned on me then that perhaps we should stop naming uncommon herbs and vegetables based on the ethnicity of their first known users and instead call them by their botanical names. I think that makes better sense since exotic ingredients are becoming more easily available these days.

thai seafood curry with pumpkin and fresh basil

SERVES 4 TO 6

An example of the versatility of curries, this dish was created to include my favorite seafood combination. You can substitute the seafood ingredients with your personal favorites, but don't forget the lime leaves and fresh basil—they make the curry come to life!

3 CUPS UNSWEETENED COCONUT MILK

2 TABLESPOONS YELLOW CURRY PASTE

3 (2-INCH) PIECES LEMON GRASS STALK, BRUISED SLIGHTLY WITH THE
    BACK OF A KNIFE

3 TABLESPOONS FISH SAUCE

1/2 TEASPOON SALT

3 TABLESPOONS SUGAR

1/2 TEASPOON GROUND TURMERIC

1 POUND ASIAN PUMPKIN, PREFERABLY THE ORANGE-SKINNED KABOCHA
    VARIETY, OR BUTTERNUT SQUASH, PEELED AND CUT INTO LARGE CUBES

1 POUND BLACK OR GREEN MUSSELS OR CLAMS, DEBEARDED AND
    SCRUBBED CLEAN

1/2 POUND BONELESS, SKINLESS SALMON FILLET, CUT INTO 4 EQUAL PIECES

1/4 POUND RAW MEDIUM SHRIMP, PEELED AND DEVEINED

3 WHOLE KAFFIR LIME LEAVES, CUT IN THIRDS

2 RED RIPE TOMATOES, CUT INTO THIN WEDGES

1/2 CUP FROZEN PEAS

1 FRESH THAI BIRD OR ANY RED CHILI, THINLY SLICED (OPTIONAL)

1/2 CUP FRESH THAI BASIL LEAVES

FRESH THAI BASIL SPRIGS FOR GARNISH

Fill a medium pot with water and bring to a boil. Place all the seafood in a strainer and blanch until color is about to turn, about 15 seconds. Remove from heat and drain.

Heat a wok or large saucepan over moderate heat. Skim off the top creamy part of the coconut milk, about 1/2 cup, and add it to the pan. Add the curry paste and stir to dissolve. Let mixture sizzle and bubble for 2 to 3 minutes, then add the remaining coconut milk, lemon grass, fish sauce, salt, sugar, and turmeric. Increase the heat to high. Bring to a boil, add the pumpkin, and cook until slightly soft, 4 to 5 minutes.

Add the blanched mussels and cook 2 minutes, then add the salmon and shrimp. Cook until just done, another 3 to 4 minutes. Add the lime leaves, tomatoes, peas, chili, and basil leaves and remove from heat. Transfer to a tureen or large bowl and garnish with sprigs of Thai basil.

grilled ahi tuna with two sauces

SERVES 4

Fresh ahi tuna (also known as yellowfin) is plum-red, translucent, and has practically no smell. If you happen to see this high quality of ahi, buy it and cook it as soon as you get home, since it is quite perishable. If you like raw tuna, try it in the salad rolls.

This dish is an example of how I take traditional recipes and embellish them to create something new and different. In ca hap tuong, the fish is steamed in a black bean–ginger sauce. Here it is simply grilled and served with a similar sauce but also paired with a bright yellow curry sauce.

1 TABLESPOON MINCED LEMON GRASS

1 PLUS 1 TABLESPOONS VEGETABLE OIL

4 (6-OUNCE) AHI TUNA OR ANY FIRM WHITE FISH FILLETS

1 CUP BASIC CURRY SAUCE (PAGE 37)

1 CUP HOISIN-PEANUT SAUCE (PAGE 35)

2 CLOVES GARLIC, THINLY SLICED

2 CUPS BABY BOK CHOY, STALKS SEPARATED, CUT INTO THIRDS
    ON THE DIAGONAL

1 CUP CARROTS, JULIENNED, BLANCHED, AND SHOCKED IN ICE WATER

2 CUPS SNOW PEAS, TRIMMED, BLANCHED, AND SHOCKED IN ICE WATER

2 TABLESPOONS WATER

SALT TO TASTE

GARNISH

CHOPPED ROASTED PEANUTS (PAGE 55)

1 GREEN ONION, THINLY SLICED ON THE DIAGONAL

FRESH CILANTRO SPRIGS

Combine the lemon grass and 1 tablespoon oil in a mixing bowl. Place the tuna in this marinade and let sit for 20 minutes.

Meanwhile, preheat the broiler or a grill to moderate heat.

Just before serving, heat the basic curry sauce and the hoisin-peanut sauce until hot and set aside. (If the sauces are too thick, thin them with a little chicken stock or water.) In a nonstick fry pan, heat the second tablespoon of oil and garlic and allow to sizzle but not burn. Add the baby bok choy, carrots, and snow peas and sauté until just done,

mom's catfish in claypot

SERVES 2 TO 3

If you get invited to a traditional Vietnamese dinner, chances are you will probably be treated to this ca kho to. *It is so basic and popular that in many homes (mine included) it is served almost every other day and, more often than not, with a delightful bowl of Fisherman's Soup.*

3 TABLESPOONS VEGETABLE OIL
2 CLOVES GARLIC, MINCED
2 SHALLOTS, CHOPPED
1 POUND FRESH CATFISH FILLET, CUT IN THIRDS
4 TABLESPOONS CARAMEL SAUCE (SEE PAGE 52)
3 TABLESPOONS FISH SAUCE
3 TABLESPOONS UNSALTED CHICKEN STOCK OR WATER
2 GREEN ONIONS, THINLY SLICED
1/2 TEASPOON GROUND BLACK PEPPER

Heat the vegetable oil in a claypot or medium fry pan over moderate heat. Add the garlic and shallots. Stir until fragrant, about 2 to 3 minutes, and add the catfish pieces. Cook until they turn almost white, about 2 minutes. Add the caramel sauce and gently stir for 1 more minute until the fish absorbs the sauce. Add the fish sauce and chicken stock and reduce heat. Simmer uncovered until the sauce has slightly caramelized, 12 to 15 minutes. Remove from heat and serve right out of claypot. Garnish with green onions and black pepper.

shrimp and vegetables in sweet and sour sauce

SERVES 4

To me, no other sweet and sour dish is as delightful as this Vietnamese version calling for fresh pineapple, tomatoes, and cucumber. You may substitute chicken or any firm white fish for the shrimp.

3 TABLESPOONS VEGETABLE OIL

3 CLOVES GARLIC, MINCED

1 TEASPOON GROUND CHILI PASTE

1/3 POUND RAW MEDIUM SHRIMP, PEELED AND DEVEINED

1/2 SMALL YELLOW ONION, SLICED

1/2 CUP CUBED FRESH PINEAPPLE

1/2 CUCUMBER, SEEDED AND SLICED INTO 1/4-INCH-THICK PIECES

2 CELERY STALKS, SLICED ON THE DIAGONAL

2 RED RIPE TOMATOES, CUT INTO SMALL WEDGES

1 CUP BROCCOLI FLORETS, BLANCHED AND SHOCKED IN ICE WATER

1 TABLESPOON WHITE VINEGAR

3 TABLESPOONS HOMEMADE UNSALTED OR CANNED LOW-SODIUM
    CHICKEN STOCK

2 TEASPOONS FISH SAUCE

1 TEASPOON SOY SAUCE

2 TABLESPOONS SUGAR

1 TABLESPOON CORNSTARCH

1/3 CUP WATER

FRESH CILANTRO SPRIGS FOR GARNISH

Heat the oil in a wok or large skillet over moderate heat. Add the garlic and chili paste and brown slightly, about 1 minute. Add the shrimp and onion and stir-fry quickly for 2 minutes. Remove the shrimp and onion and set aside.

While the wok is still hot, add the pineapple, cucumber, celery, tomatoes, and broccoli and sauté lightly. Add the vinegar, chicken stock, fish sauce, soy sauce, and sugar and bring to a boil. Add the reserved shrimp and onion. In a small bowl, whisk together the cornstarch and water. Thicken the sauce slightly by stirring in 1 to 2 teaspoons of the cornstarch mixture. Remove from heat and serve immediately, with the cilantro garnish.

Chapter ten

Dream On

desserts

Two years ago, after a long day of playing tourist in Venice, Trong and I slumped into our chairs at a trattoria at San Marco plaza. We were wearied, having been on our feet for two weeks, and terribly hungry. We had eaten our way through Italy and loved every minute of it, but today, we were missing home. We had photographed every piazza, visited every museum, and seen enough glass-blowing for one trip. For now, we were just craving some of our good old food.

Sitting at the square where thousands of tourists were walking by, perhaps in the same predicament we were in, we wondered what it would be like to have a Lemon Grass Café right here in this magical city. It would probably have the same features as the café in downtown Sacramento. Gracing one side of the room, a shiny marble counter spanning 20 feet would frame a series of beautiful Italian-style display cases packed with different salads (including locally grown greens), as well as hot entrées such as Thai curries to pad Thai, and, of course, pastas. *Banh mi thit,* or Vietnamese sandwiches, would also be a must. Similar to the premade Italian focaccia sandwiches, *banh mi thit* are spread with very little sauce, stuffed with generous amounts of meat that peek out the sides, and stacked high on top of each other.

In an international setting such as Venice, our Lemon Grass Café would feature not only authentic signature items but a repertoire of exciting dishes inspired by its new environment. Perhaps at the beginning of the counter, where the espresso machine would be, another deli case would welcome customers with a variety of interesting pastries, from ginger-garlic focaccia to passion fruit tiramisù to coconut crème caramel.

Customers who entered the café would be welcomed by a lively space adorned with the vibrant colors that represent our cuisine. Like the juxtapositions in our cooking—the refreshing mint and herbs against the hot chilies and spices—the bold reds and golds and the wood textures of the interior would be offset by cool blues and marble textures. When hungry customers approached the counter, our friendly staff would ease their anxiety by quickly preparing their selections. Depending on their mood, customers could take their food home or dine at an outdoor table while watching the sun set over the Grand Canal.

As I ponder the future of Lemon Grass, and where this cookbook ought to lead, I feel that the message can't stop here. If ours is truly the best of Vietnamese and Thai cooking, it must be shared. If we have shared it in our backyard, perhaps we should go beyond. If the principles that I learned from the isolated kitchens of my grandmother and mother are so wonderful, then they should indeed have a place at our new global table.

I honestly do not know if I will ever cook in Venice, or in Maui, or in any of my other favorite spots around the world. But there's one thing I do know. I know that the successes of our Lemon Grass Restaurant and Lemon Grass Cafés all started out with just a simple dream.

So for now I will dream on about the day when I can take our cuisine across the oceans and share with others the same great food that I have shared with you here.

sticky rice and fresh mangoes

SERVES 4 TO 6

Think Thai dessert, and the first thing that comes to mind is kao new ma muang. *In the coastal town of Phuket, on the southern tip of Thailand, there is a night market near the town square that features nothing but mangoes when they are in season. After a big, sumptuous meal along the main beach drive, we would drive our rented jeep to this market and finish our day with this delightful dessert.*

If you prefer to steam sticky rice, which is a traditional method of preparation, place the soaked rice in a steamer lined with cheesecloth. Steam for about 30 minutes. Occasionally fluff the rice as it cooks and check its texture. Depending on its moisture level, you may need to sprinkle on a little hot water to help soften and cook the rice.

1¼ CUPS WATER
1 CUP THAI LONG-GRAIN STICKY RICE, SOAKED IN WARM WATER FOR 1 HOUR
    AND DRAINED
2 TABLESPOONS PLUS ¼ CUP SUGAR
⅔ CUP UNSWEETENED COCONUT MILK
¼ TEASPOON VANILLA EXTRACT
PINCH OF SALT
1 TABLESPOON CORNSTARCH
2 MEDIUM TO LARGE RIPE MANGOES, PEELED AND CUT INTO
    ATTRACTIVE SLICES
2 TABLESPOONS SESAME SEEDS, LIGHTLY TOASTED (OPTIONAL)

Bring the water to a boil in a small saucepan. Quickly stir in the soaked rice and add the 2 tablespoons sugar. Let boil for 2 minutes, then reduce the heat to very low. Cover and simmer only until water has evaporated and rice is tender, 8 to 10 minutes. Remove pan from heat and let sit for 20 minutes. Uncover and fluff rice with a fork or chopsticks. Set aside.

In another small saucepan, combine the coconut milk, vanilla, salt, and the ¼ cup sugar and bring to a boil. In a small bowl, mix the cornstarch with ⅓ cup water and stir until well dissolved. While the coconut sauce is simmering, slowly drizzle in the cornstarch mixture and stir until sauce is just thick enough to coat a spoon. Remove from heat and set aside.

To serve, place a small, neat mound of sticky rice, about ½ cup, in the center of each serving plate. Surround each mound of rice with mango slices. Drizzle 2 to 3 tablespoons of the coconut sauce over each mound and sprinkle with sesame seeds.

warm bananas with tapioca pearls

SERVES 4

In my grandmother's village, evenings often ended with a small bowl of warm banana stew. While people in bigger cities finished their meals with more cosmopolitan desserts such as gateaux, *or European-style cakes, or ice cream and espressos, village folks savored simpler things. After picking the bananas off a roadside tree, they poached them in fresh coconut milk with tapioca. A sprinkle of roasted peanuts finishes the dish.*

2 CUPS WATER

$1/2$ CUP SMALL TAPIOCA PEARLS (SEE GLOSSARY)

1 CUP UNSWEETENED COCONUT MILK

$2/3$ CUP SUGAR

$1/4$ TEASPOON SALT

$1/2$ TEASPOON VANILLA EXTRACT

5 RIPE BUT FIRM BANANAS, PEELED AND CUT INTO QUARTERS

2 TABLESPOONS ROASTED PEANUTS FOR GARNISH (PAGE 55)

Heat the water in a small pot over moderate heat. While waiting for it to boil, put the tapioca in a strainer and rinse under cold running water. Stirring often, add the tapioca to the boiling water. Simmer until tapioca is clear, 5 to 7 minutes. Gently stir the tapioca to prevent sticking. Fold in the coconut milk, sugar, salt, and vanilla. Add the bananas and cook only until they are thoroughly hot, 2 to 3 minutes. Sauce should be only thick enough to coat a spoon. If it appears too thick, add a little water or coconut milk. The mixture will be thicker once it cools.

Remove from heat and immediately transfer to individual dessert bowls. (It is hard to spoon out once it has set.) Let sit for about 15 minutes before eating. Garnish with peanuts.

saigon by night

The original version of this recipe calls for coffee ice cream. However, I find my embellished version with vanilla ice cream and hazelnut syrup much more satisfying.

SERVES 4

As a teenager, I liked to walk down Tu Do, *or Freedom Street, bypass all the nightclubs it was known for during the war, and visit a bubbly bistro called* Boda. *Always taking my usual spot near a window, I would order a* Café Liégeois, *or coffee ice cream with coffee. With a small, long spoon, I would slowly nibble on the ice cream while watching the world go by.*

This dessert was inspired by those moments, and by the fact that Capricorn Coffees, a San Francisco coffee roasting company Trong bought several years ago, makes such wonderful espresso that I wanted to sneak it onto our menu.

1 PINT GOOD-QUALITY VANILLA ICE CREAM
1 CUP FRESHLY MADE ESPRESSO, BROUGHT TO ROOM TEMPERATURE
1/2 CUP HAZELNUT SYRUP
1 CUP FRESHLY MADE WHIPPED CREAM OR COMMERCIAL WHIPPED CREAM
CHOCOLATE POWDER FOR GARNISH

To serve, put 1 scoop of the ice cream (about 1/2 cup) into each of four parfait glasses. Add 1/4 cup of the espresso to each and 2 tablespoons of the hazelnut syrup. Top each with 1/4 cup of the whipped cream and, if you like, sprinkle with chocolate powder.

sweet sticky rice pudding with black-eyed peas

SERVES 6 TO 8

In Vietnam and Thailand, desserts as we know them in the West rarely are served right after a meal. In fact, most sweet dishes are treated as snacks and enjoyed almost any time of day. One of the best things about living in Asia is that food vendors are everywhere, carrying their homemade delicacies right to your doorstep. As a child, I was spoiled by that service. I remember the time when my sister and I would wait for our favorite dessert lady to show up. She was a tiny person, yet every night, around ten o'clock, she arrived in our neighborhood with two steaming pots of desserts dangling from her shoulders. After situating them in front of our home, she dished up our favorite black-eyed pea dessert. Soft, sweet, and creamy, this pudding was a great way to end the night.

1/2 CUP DRIED BLACK-EYED PEAS, PICKED THROUGH AND RINSED
1/2 CUP THAI LONG-GRAIN STICKY RICE
2/3 CUP SUGAR
1/4 TEASPOON SALT
1 TEASPOON VANILLA EXTRACT
1 CUP UNSWEETENED COCONUT MILK
1/2 TEASPOON CONSTARCH

Place the black-eyed peas in a small saucepan with 4 cups of water and bring to a boil. Reduce heat to moderate and cook until peas are tender but not mushy, about 30 to 35 minutes. Rinse and set aside.

In another saucepan, bring 3 cups of water to a rolling boil. Add the rice and boil for 3 to 4 minutes. Reduce the heat to a simmer, and while stirring continuously, cook until the rice is soft but still keeps its shape, 25 to 30 minutes. Add the black-eyed peas, sugar, salt, and vanilla, stirring frequently but gently to prevent sticking. Cook for 5 more minutes, then remove from heat. The pudding will appear soupy at first, but will thicken when cooled.

Before serving, mix the coconut milk and constarch in a small saucepan and with a small whisk, stir to dissolve over low heat. Simmer until coconut milk mixture bubbles, then remove from heat. To serve, divide the rice pudding into attractive individual dessert bowls such as wide-mouthed sorbet glasses, and drizzle 1 to 2 tablespoons of the coconut milk sauce over each. Serve either warm or cold. (I prefer it cold.)

ginger twinkles

MAKES ABOUT 4 DOZEN

These wonderful, chewy cookies were created by Tony van Rees, the sous/pastry chef of Lemon Grass Café. Like the personality that he exudes, his cookies and pastries always win hearts and minds. From the day he first made these cookies, they were an instant hit. Because of their popularity, we have exported our cookie technology to La Bou, *our sister bakery/café company, and subsequently to Sacramento's* Arco Arena, *where they are fit even for basketball* Kings.

3 CUPS ALL-PURPOSE FLOUR
1/2 TEASPOON SALT
2 TEASPOONS BAKING SODA
2 TEASPOONS GROUND CINNAMON
4 TEASPOONS GROUND GINGER
8 OUNCES SWEET BUTTER, SOFTENED
1 PLUS 1/2 CUPS SUGAR
1/3 CUP DARK MOLASSES
1 LARGE EGG

Preheat oven to 325 degrees.

Sift the flour, salt, baking soda, cinnamon, and ginger into a mixing bowl and set aside.

Cream the butter, the 1 cup sugar, and the molasses in a mixer until fluffy, 3 to 4 minutes. While the mixer is running, add the egg and beat for 30 seconds. Decrease the mixer speed to low and add the dry ingredients. Mix until fully incorporated. Shape the dough into logs 2 inches in diameter and wrap in plastic wrap. Refrigerate for 30 minutes.

Just before baking, unwrap the dough and cut into 1/2-inch slices. Place the 1/2 cup sugar on a large plate. Drop the cookies into the sugar and coat evenly. Place the cookies on a nonstick baking sheet about 2 inches apart. Bake until golden brown and firm around the edges but still soft inside, 12 to 15 minutes. Let cool for 5 minutes before removing the cookies.

bananas flambé

SERVES 4

Traditionally, this recipe calls for the bananas to be dipped in batter, then deep-fried. At Lemon Grass, we simply sauté the bananas in a little butter and then flambé them tableside. Once the dancing flames and popping cinnamon dust have died down, the bananas are served with vanilla ice cream and toasted coconut flakes. On Saturday nights, our servers know that once the first order goes out, many more soon will follow. Please be very careful when igniting the brandy.

2 TABLESPOONS SWEET BUTTER

3 RIPE BUT FIRM BANANAS, PEELED AND CUT IN HALF

1 PINT GOOD-QUALITY VANILLA ICE CREAM

3 TABLESPOONS SUGAR

3 1/2 TABLESPOONS BRANDY OR COGNAC

GROUND CINNAMON FOR SPRINKLING

1/2 CUP UNSWEETENED COCONUT FLAKES, PAN-ROASTED OVER MODERATE HEAT UNTIL GOLDEN (OPTIONAL)

In a sauté pan, preferably copper and clean of any savory flavors, melt the butter over moderate heat. Add the bananas and increase the heat slightly to create a nice brown skin. (If butter begins to burn, reduce the heat.) Cook the bananas 2 to 3 minutes on each side until browned.

Meanwhile, have someone help dish out the ice cream into four dessert bowls.

Just before serving, heat the bananas in the pan until hot, about 1 minute. Sprinkle the sugar on top. Working very carefully, move the pan to an unused burner and drizzle the brandy around the pan. (Brandy should sizzle immediately upon contact.) Using a barbecue lighter or a long match stick, ignite the alcohol. Tilt the pan in a circular motion so the alcohol can burn off completely. When the flame dies out, sprinkle some cinnamon on top and, using a spoon, cut the bananas into bite-size pieces. Spoon equal portions of bananas and sauce onto each ice cream bowl. Garnish with toasted coconut flakes. Serve immediately while bananas are still warm.

chunky ginger ice cream

MAKES 1 QUART

When in doubt about what to serve for dessert, think ginger ice cream! Most chefs, myself in particular, love ice cream because it is simple to serve, and it complements almost every meal. In this recipe, the fresh ginger gives a sharp bite and the candied ginger an interesting texture. Since presentation is always important at the restaurant, we serve this dessert with a Grand Marnier–ginger sauce. But it's great even without it.

2 CUPS MILK

2 CUPS HEAVY CREAM

1 CUP SUGAR

1 TABLESPOON MINCED FRESH GINGER

1/4 TEASPOON SALT

4 LARGE EGG YOLKS

1/3 CUP CHOPPED CANDIED GINGER

1 TEASPOON VANILLA EXTRACT

1 TEASPOON FRESH LEMON JUICE

SAUCE (OPTIONAL)

1 CUP SUGAR

1 CUP WATER

3 TABLESPOONS GRAND MARNIER

2 TABLESPOONS CHOPPED CANDIED GINGER

1 TEASPOON FRESH LEMON JUICE

FRESH MINT SPRIGS FOR GARNISH

Combine the milk, heavy cream, sugar, fresh ginger, and salt and heat to just a simmer. Stir to dissolve the sugar. Remove from heat.

Beat the egg yolks until fluffy and pale yellow. Stirring constantly, add the egg yolks to the milk mixture and simmer until mixture slightly thickens and coats the back of a spoon, 5 to 7 minutes. Do not let the mixture boil.

Remove from heat and pour into a clean container. Let cool completely before adding the candied ginger, vanilla, and lemon juice. Stir well. Transfer to an ice cream maker and freeze according to manufacturer's instructions.

To make the sauce, combine the sugar and water in a small saucepan. Bring to a boil. Wait for syrup to develop bubbles, then continue stirring and cooking until syrup turns almost brown, like the color of iced tea. Immediately remove from heat and continue stirring to prevent the sugar along the edges from burning. (Sugar burns quickly.) Carefully stir in the Grand Marnier, candied ginger, and lemon juice. Return to heat and simmer for 1 minute to cook off the alcohol. If sauce seems too thick, add 1 to 2 tablespoons hot water. Transfer to a jar for storage. Sauce should remain syrupy.

To serve, scoop out ginger ice cream into dessert bowls. Drizzle with Grand Marnier–ginger sauce and garnish with sprigs of mint.

peach scones with passion fruit glaze

MAKES 1 DOZEN

At an international food show in Cologne, Germany, one year, I saw a line of purées and syrups made from tropical fruits, such as guava, carambola, mangosteen, and passion fruit. I got so excited, thinking about using the fruits that I grew up with in our baked goods. So for the opening of the first Lemon Grass Café, we created this unique scone. Since then, it has remained our most popular pastry.

2 1/2 CUPS ALL-PURPOSE FLOUR
1/3 CUP SUGAR
1/2 TEASPOON SALT
1 TABLESPOON BAKING POWDER
1 1/2 STICK SWEET BUTTER, CHILLED AND CUBED
1 2/3 CUPS CHOPPED FRESH OR FROZEN PEACHES
1 CUP COLD MILK
3/4 CUP POWDERED SUGAR, SIFTED
1/2 CUP PASSION FRUIT SYRUP

Preheat oven to 375 degrees. Grease a cookie sheet.

Sift all the dry ingredients together and place in the bowl of an electric mixer. (You may also mix by hand.) Turn the mixer to slow speed and add the cubed butter. Mix until mixture resembles a coarse meal, about 3 minutes. Add the peaches and milk and mix just until ingredients are incorporated, 5 to 10 seconds. Do not overmix, or the dough will get tough.

Using a small ice cream scoop or spoon, scoop balls of dough about 2 inches in diameter and place 3 inches apart on prepared cookie sheet.

Bake until the tops of the scones are firm but not hard and the edges are golden, 15 to 20 minutes.

Five minutes before the scones are done, beat the powdered sugar and passion fruit syrup in a small saucepan until sugar is completely dissolved. Warm the glaze over low heat and drizzle onto the scones as soon as they come out of the oven.

ginger pear tart

SERVES 10

Several years ago, a young, soft-spoken man came to the restaurant with a box full of cake and tart samples hoping to become our dessert purveyor. Well, it didn't take too many samples to convince me that practically everything that came out of Michael Bennett's oven is first-class, especially this pear tart. I asked Michael to "Asianize" his recipe by adding ginger to it. Together with a cup of mango tea, this tart makes a grand finale to a Lemon Grass meal.

If you can't find almond meal, make some out of almond slices. Toast 1¹/₃ cups almond slices lightly in a pan, then grind them as finely as possible in a food processor.

6 TABLESPOONS SWEET BUTTER, BROUGHT TO ROOM TEMPERATURE
6 TABLESPOONS SUGAR
2 LARGE EGGS, BROUGHT TO ROOM TEMPERATURE
2 TABLESPOONS MINCED FRESH GINGER
2 TABLESPOONS CHOPPED CANDIED GINGER
1 CUP ALMOND MEAL
1 READY-MADE (9-INCH) TART CRUST, BAKED AS PER INSTRUCTIONS BUT
    REMOVED ABOUT 15 MINUTES BEFORE DONE
4 MEDIUM FRESH OR CANNED PEARS, PEELED, CORED, AND HALVED
¹/₂ CUP APRICOT JELLY
2 TABLESPOONS HOT WATER

In a mixer, cream the butter and sugar on medium speed until white, about 3 minutes. Add the eggs, 1 at a time, beating 2 to 3 minutes in between and scraping the bowl. Adjust the mixer to low speed and add the fresh and candied ginger and beat for 30 seconds. Add the almond meal and beat for 30 more seconds.

Preheat oven to 350 degrees.

Fill the tart crust with the almond custard. Smooth the top with a spatula. Place 7 of the pear halves on top of the custard with the narrow ends toward the center and cut side down. Place the last pear half in the middle. Bake the tart until the filling is nicely browned around the border and light brown in the center, 30 to 40 minutes. The center should be firm. Cool at least 1 hour.

Combine the apricot jelly and hot water and heat until well blended. If glaze is too thick, thin with a little hot water. Using a soft pastry brush, glaze the top of the tart. Let sit for 30 minutes before serving.

grand marnier crème caramel

SERVES 6

My father, who has a very sweet tooth, loves his crème caramel, or flan, soft, velvety and without any air pockets (the Vietnamese call them freckles). In Saigon, flan usually is steamed because few households have ovens. And to prevent the common mistake of boiling the milk, and therefore causing holes in the custard, one must keep a very close eye on the temperature.

CARAMEL
1 1/2 CUPS SUGAR
1 CUP WATER

CUSTARD
3 EGGS
3 EGG YOLKS
1 CUP MILK
2 CUPS HALF-AND-HALF
2/3 CUP SUGAR
1/4 TEASPOON SALT
3 TABLESPOONS GRAND MARNIER
1 1/2 TEASPOONS VANILLA EXTRACT
BLACKBERRIES, STRAWBERRIES, OR RASPBERRIES FOR GARNISH

Preheat oven to 325 degrees.

To make the caramel, place the sugar and water in a small saucepan and bring to a boil. Stirring often, cook until the sugar mixture is thickened and brown, like the color of iced tea, 15 to 20 minutes. (If the caramel is darker than this, discard and start again. Burnt caramel is very bitter.) If the sauce seems too thick, add 2 tablespoons hot water. Carefully remove from heat. Using a spoon, pour about 1 tablespoon of the caramel into each of six 5-ounce ramekins. (Work fast before the caramel cools and becomes hard.) Tilt

Whenever I make this dish for my father, I bake the custard in a Bundt pan. To serve, I invert the pan onto a fancy platter and fill the middle hole with lots of fresh raspberries and blackberries. If you want to try making this crème caramel in a Bundt pan or soufflé dish, add 2 to 3 more eggs and bake it longer, about 15 minutes. The additional eggs make the custard more firm and less likely to collapse when unmolding and cutting.

the ramekin in a circular motion so the bottom is completely covered with caramel. Set aside.

To make the custard, beat the eggs and egg yolks in a mixing bowl and set aside.

In a heavy-bottomed saucepan, heat the milk, half-and-half, sugar, and salt over moderate heat. While stirring continuously, scald until the sugar dissolves. Remove from heat and add the Grand Marnier and vanilla. While whisking continuously, gradually add the milk mixture to the beaten eggs.

Strain the custard through a fine sieve into a bowl. Ladle the custard into the ramekins. Place the ramekins in a large baking dish. Pour warm water into the dish to halfway up the sides of the ramekins. Carefully place the dish in the oven.

Bake until the tops of the custards are firm to the touch, but still slightly soft in the center, 40 to 50 minutes. Let cool to room temperature before refrigerating. Chill for at least 1 hour.

To serve, run a small knife around the edge of each ramekin and unmold onto individual serving plates. Spoon some caramel sauce from the ramekins on top. Garnish with blackberries, strawberries, or raspberries.

lemon mousse cake

SERVES 12

When we entertain guests from Thailand at the restaurant, I always serve lemon mousse cake for dessert. Although there is nothing Thai about it, the delightful and refreshing taste of this dessert makes a Lemon Grass meal even more memorable. This recipe is rather involved, so have patience and make it ahead of time. The cake is easier to handle and cut if it sits overnight.

For best results, let the cake and mousse set over night before assembling them.

For a more attractive presentation, sprinkle fresh lemon zest on top of the icing.

CAKE
2 EGGS, BROUGHT TO ROOM TEMPERATURE
1 EGG YOLK, BROUGHT TO ROOM TEMPERATURE
1/3 CUP SUGAR
1/2 CUP CAKE FLOUR
1 1/4 TEASPOONS BAKING POWDER
3 TABLESPOONS BUTTER, MELTED

LEMON CURD
5 EGGS
1 EGG YOLK
1 CUP SUGAR
1 CUP FRESH LEMON JUICE
1/2 CUP SWEET BUTTER
ZEST OF 3 LEMONS, FINELY MINCED

MOUSSE
1/2 CUP LIGHT CORN SYRUP
1/4 CUP WATER
4 EGG WHITES, BROUGHT TO ROOM TEMPERATURE
1 1/2 TEASPOONS UNFLAVORED GELATIN
2 CUPS LEMON CURD (SEE ABOVE)
ZEST OF 1 LEMON, FINELY MINCED

ICING
2 CUPS HEAVY CREAM
3/4 CUP LEMON CURD (SEE ABOVE)

Preheat oven to 350 degrees. Grease, line, and flour a 9-inch springform pan.

To make the cake place the eggs, egg yolk, and sugar in saucepan and heat over low heat just long enough to dissolve the sugar, at about 110 degrees. Using a mixer or by hand, whip egg mixture until very light and thick. Sift together the flour and baking powder. Gently fold the melted butter and flour into the egg mixture. Pour the batter into prepared springform pan. Bake for 25 to 35 minutes, or until a toothpick inserted in the center of the cake comes out clean. Remove from oven. Let cool for 20 minutes, then remove and transfer to a plate. Cover and set aside.

To make the lemon curd, whip together the eggs, egg yolk, and sugar in a non-corrosive saucepan for 1 to 2 minutes. Stir in the remaining ingredients. Bring mixture to a simmer and stir constantly to prevent sticking. Cook for 5 to 7 minutes, until thick and bubbly. Remove from heat and strain through a fine sieve into a bowl. Place plastic wrap on the curd to prevent a skin from forming. Refrigerate for 2 hours.

To make the mousse, heat the corn syrup and the water in a small saucepan over moderate heat until large bubbles start to form, 5 to 7 minutes. Reduce the heat and keep warm. Whip the egg whites to stiff peaks. (Use an electric mixer if you have one. If not, get someone to whip the egg whites while you add the other ingredients.) While still whipping, carefully add the warm corn syrup in a thin stream. Make sure the syrup does not solidify on the bowl or beaters. Whip until cooled. In a small bowl, soften the gelatin in 2 table-spoons warm water. Stir to dissolve. Fold the gelatin, 2 cups lemon curd, and lemon zest into the whipped egg white mixture and set aside.

To assemble the cake, line the springform pan with plastic wrap and, leaving about 2 inches around the edges, pour in the mousse. Refrigerate overnight, or at least 3 hours.

Spread about 1/2 cup of the remaining lemon curd on the mousse. Place the cake on top and invert onto a flat serving platter. Carefully unmold the mousse by lifting the pan while holding down the edges of the plastic wrap. Remove and discard the plastic wrap. One hour before serving, whip the heavy cream until stiff, then stir in the lemon curd. Ice the cake and then chill and serve.

thai tea

SERVES 4 TO 6

In Thailand, where it's very hot and humid almost every day of the year, a glass of cold tea is both a thirst quencher and a sweet snack. Made from black tea mixed with anise and food coloring, Thai tea is prepared much like cowboy-style coffee. Just boil, strain, and drink!

$1/3$ CUP LOOSE THAI TEA
4 CUPS WATER
$2/3$ CUP SUGAR
ICE
$1/2$ CUP HALF-AND-HALF
FRESH MINT SPRIGS FOR GARNISH

Combine the tea, water, and sugar in a small saucepan and bring to a boil. Reduce the heat and simmer for 20 minutes. Remove from the heat and strain into a small pitcher. Allow to cool completely before serving. Tea will taste very sweet, but once ice is added, it will be more balanced. Refrigerate for 1 hour.

To serve, pack tall glasses with ice and pour in the chilled tea almost to the rim. Slowly pour about 2 tablespoons of the half-and-half over the ice in each glass, making sure to create an attractive, layered look. Garnish each with a sprig of mint.

thai coffee

SERVES 4 TO 6

One of my favorite drinks while growing up in Bangkok was o liang, *a strong sweet beverage made from coffee and roasted corn. It is usually served with lots of crushed ice and is a fine way to wash down a spicy noodle dish, such as* rad na *(page 180).*

$^1/_3$ CUP THAI COFFEE GROUNDS
4 CUPS WATER
$^2/_3$ CUP SUGAR
ICE, PREFERABLY CRUSHED

Combine the coffee, water, and sugar in a medium saucepan and bring to a boil. Reduce heat and simmer for 20 minutes. Remove from heat and strain into a small pitcher. Allow to cool completely before serving. Refrigerate for 1 hour.

To serve, pack tall glasses with ice and pour equal portions of the chilled coffee to the top.

vietnamese coffee

SERVES 2

In Vietnam, coffee shops are scattered practically everywhere, from the busiest urban centers to remote villages. Yet the ritual is always the same. The coffee made with individual drip filters, is enjoyed sip by sip, during a friendly conversation that could easily last a half day.

For this recipe, you will need two 6-ounce individual drip filters—the kind that sit on top of cups. Sorry, but Mr. Coffee and the like just will not do.

4 TABLESPOONS CONDENSED MILK
1/3 CUP DARK FRENCH ROAST OR A BLEND OF DARK FRENCH ROAST AND
    COLUMBIAN COFFEE, MEDIUM GRIND
2 CUPS BOILING WATER
ICE (OPTIONAL)

Pour 2 tablespoons of the condensed milk into two glass mugs, preferably Irish coffee–style ones. Make sure the milk doesn't stick to the sides. Put filters on top of mugs. Place 2 1/2 tablespoons of the coffee into each filter. When ready to serve, pour about 1 tablespoon of the boiling water over each coffee and wait 30 seconds for the coffee grounds to expand. Then fill each filter with equal portions of the remaining boiling water just once, and let the coffee slowly drip through. To serve, stir the condensed milk and coffee together. If you like it cold, add lots of ice.

lemon grass lemonade

MAKES ABOUT 1 QUART

When our bartender Dean Barnes first made this lemonade, we didn't think it would catch on as wildly as it did. This beverage is basically a good, strong lemonade sweetened by a lemon grass–infused syrup. It's one of our most popular nonalcoholic drinks, especially when the weather warms and the outdoor patio fills up.

1 CUP SUGAR

2 STALKS LEMON GRASS, CUT INTO $1/2$-INCH PIECES AND BRUISED LIGHTLY
    WITH THE BACK OF A KNIFE

3 CUPS WATER

JUICE OF 3 LEMONS

JUICE OF 2 LIMES

PINCH OF SALT

$1/2$ QUART ICE

GARNISH

1 LEMON, THINLY SLICED

2 STALKS LEMON GRASS, CUT INTO 2-INCH PIECES

Combine the sugar, lemon grass, and water in a small sauce pan and bring to a boil. Stir to dissolve the sugar and simmer for 20 minutes. Remove from heat and let sit for 1 hour before straining into a glass pitcher.

Before serving, add the lemon juice, lime juice, and salt to the syrup. Stir well and add the ice. Serve lemonade in tall glasses with lots of ice. Garnish with lemon slices and lemon grass pieces.

glossary

The following ingredients are also identified by their Vietnamese and Thai names respectively. Note that the latter are phonetic translations of a language whose alphabet is based on characters (unlike Vietnamese, which is romanized). For that reason, the phonetic spellings of Thai words can vary substantially from one source to another.

bamboo shoots *(mang, naw mai)*

A popular vegetable used extensively in soups, stir-fries, and salads, bamboo shoots are packed in water and sold in cans. Available in strips or slices, they should always be boiled before using to remove the tinny taste. Fresh bamboo shoots are sometimes available but hard to use since they need to be boiled for a considerable time before they become tender.

banana leaves *(la chuoi, bai tong)*

The aluminum foil, plastic wrap, and parchment paper of Asia, banana leaves are used to wrap sticky rice, desserts, and savory dishes. Foods steamed, grilled, and boiled in banana leaves take on an earthy, grassy flavor. Banana leaves are available frozen. To use, thaw and wipe dry before using. Be careful as the leaves break easily. Unused banana leaves should be returned to the freezer.

basil, holy *(rau que Thai, grapao)*

A cousin of Thai basil, this herb is available at Asian grocery stores and farmers' markets, usually during the summer. Sold in bunches, holy basil is green and has fuzzy stems and leaves. Spicy and a bit lemony, it is wonderful in stir-fries.

basil, Thai *(rau que, horopa)*

Also known as anise basil, this herb is used extensively in Southeast Asian cooking and fortunately is becoming more easily available in the United States. The Vietnamese love to tuck a few of these sweet licorice-tasting leaves into their salad rolls, while the Thais throw cupfuls into their stir-fries.

bean sauce *(tuong hot, tau jew)*

Made from either fermented soybeans or black beans, water, and salt, this sauce is sometimes labeled "salted soy beans" or "bean sauce." A tablespoon or two is all that is needed to give stir-fries a delightful complexity. Bean sauce is sold in cans and jars and is available in whole bean or puréed form. I prefer to buy the kind in clear glass jars as I can easily verify the product's quality.

bean thread noodles *(bun tau, woon sen)*

Also referred to as cellophane noodles and glass noodles, these stringy, semi-transparent strands are used in spring roll fillings, soups, and stir-fries. Wiry and very tough, they must be soaked in warm water for at least 15 minutes before cooking. Buy noodles that are individually portioned into small "nests" since most recipes call for small amounts. (The larger bundles are hard to handle, and the noodles are difficult to separate.)

bitter melon *(hu hoa, mah lah)*

This bitter, though quite savory, relative of the cucumber is used in soups and stir-fries. Similar in size and appearance to the cucumber but with bumps and ridges running from one end to the other, bitter melons may be thinly sliced and stir-fried, or stuffed and added to soups.

black mushrooms *(nam den, het haeng)*

Also known as shiitake, these dried mushrooms, traditionally grown on Japanese *shii* trees, are prized for their rich, meaty flavor and texture. Though available in different grades and prices, the most flavorful ones are those with deep fissures on the caps. To use, soften in hot water for 30 minutes. Remove and discard the rubbery stems. Black mushrooms can be added to soups, stews, stir-fries, and fillings.

cellophane noodles

See bean thread noodles.

chili paste, ground *(tuong ot toi, sos prik)*

Made with coarsely ground red chilies (with seeds and all), garlic, and vinegar, this versatile Vietnamese-style paste can be used as a table condiment or to season food. A stir-fry that starts with oil, ground chili paste, and garlic is on solid ground. Sold in small plastic jars, ground chili paste will keep almost indefinitely.

chili sauce *(tuong ot, sos sriracha)*

Similar to Tabasco, this fiery sauce is made from finely ground and seeded red chili peppers, vinegar, garlic, and sugar. Packaged in glass or plastic squeeze-bottles, this bright orange-red sauce is a favorite condiment to the Vietnamese *pho,* or beef noodle soup, and as a dipping sauce for seafood and grilled meats.

chili, Thai bird *(ot hiem, prik ki noo)*

Both the Thais and Vietnamese love this special variety of chili. Slender and tiny (about 1 inch long), Thai bird chilies are extremely hot and flavorful. Available green and red, they are wonderful when smashed and added to dipping sauces and stir-fries. You may use any hot chili, such as serrano or jalapeño, as a substitute.

cilantro *(ngo, pak chee)*

Distinctively aromatic, this soft, leafy herb is used extensively in Southeast Asian dishes. Once chopped, cilantro can be added to soups, stir-fries, and fillings. Interestingly, the Thais use every part of this herb, including the fragrant root, to season soups and salads.

coconut milk *(nuoc dua, nam gati)*

Used to give richness to soups, curries, stews, roasts, beverages, and desserts much in the same way milk and cream are used in the West, coconut milk is the juice extracted from grated coconut meat. Fortunately, in the United States, canned coconut milk imported from Thailand and elsewhere is readily available and of excellent quality. Once opened, canned coconut milk should be used as soon as possible as it is perishable.

curry paste *(cari Thai, kaeng phet)*

Intensely flavored by roasted spices and herbs, Thai curry pastes are used as a base for curries, soups, and stir-fries. Ready-made pastes are sold in small plastic tubs and in cans at Asian markets. The most common are green, red, and yellow curry pastes. To make curry paste from scratch, please refer to pages 38–41.

eggplant, Asian *(ca tim, ma khua)*

The three most common eggplants used in Southeast Asian cooking are Japanese, Chinese, and Thai. Both the long, thin lavender Chinese and the smaller dark purple Japanese varieties are sweet and delicious and can be used interchangeably. Unlike their Western relative, these eggplants do not need to be salted and rinsed before using. The small, marble-size Thai eggplant, on the other hand, is quite bitter. They should be rinsed in salted water and boiled briefly before being added to curries and stews.

fish sauce *(nuoc mam or nam pla)*

This is probably the single most important ingredient that gives Southeast Asian cooking its unique flavor. Made from fish or shrimp extract, salt, and water, this brownish, clear liquid is used to season food and make dipping sauces. (For more information, please see pages 20–21.)

five-spice powder *(ngu vi huong, dawg mai jeen)*

This fragrant brown powder is a blend of five or more spices, namely, ground star anise, fennel, cinnamon, ginger, clove, and Szechuan peppercorns. Lending a licorice, woodsy fragrance to food, this spice combination is great for marinades and especially for roast ducks, stews, and vegetarian dishes. The five-spice powder that is sold in cellophane bags at Asian grocery stores tends to be more fragrant than the powder found in supermarkets.

galanga *(gieng, kha)*

A rhizome similar to ginger in appearance and belonging to the same family, galanga has a more complex flavor than its cousin. Available fresh or frozen, it is generally

thinly sliced and used to season soups or curries. The Thais like to grind galanga and add to curry pastes. Galanga powder has little flavor and should be avoided.

ginger *(gung, king)*

Probably one of the most versatile ingredients in Asian cooking, ginger is used to liven up stir-fries, garnish sauce toppings, and even finish dessert sauces. Sliced, minced, or grated, it cuts the richness in meats and gives a refreshing lift to food. A fresh, young ginger root is firm and heavy and has a smooth, tender skin. I peel ginger only when the skin appears tough.

green papaya

See papaya, green.

ground chili paste

See chili paste, ground.

hoisin sauce *(tuong, sos hoisin)*

A versatile sauce made from soybean purée, sugar, and caramel sauce, this thick, smooth dark brown sauce is used primarily in dipping sauces, marinades, and stir-fries. When mixed with onions, garlic, chilies, vinegar, and crushed peanuts, hoisin sauce makes a delicious dipping sauce. This product is sold in cans or small jars. Refrigerate after opening.

holy basil

See basil, holy.

jasmine rice *(gao thom, kao)*

A naturally aromatic long-grain variety, this rice has a nutty, almost floral, scent when cooked. Mainly imported from Thailand, it is now available at large supermarkets. The closest substitute is Indian basmati rice. The general guideline for cooking jasmine rice is 1 part rice to 1½ parts water. (For more information, please see page 49.)

jicama *(cu san, munh kaew)*

This is probably one of the best-kept-secret vegetables in this country! In Vietnam, jicama is used extensively in stir-fries, salads, fillings, and soups. It resembles a large turnip and has a wonderful delicate taste with a pleasant, crunchy texture similar to a water chestnut. Fresh jicama is heavy, full of liquid, and free of blemishes. To use, peel and cut into desired shape and size.

kabocha squash *(bi vang, fak tong)*

Dull green on the outside but bright orange on the inside, this pumpkin-shaped squash is sometimes referred to as Japanese squash or Asian pumpkin. Once peeled of its thick skin, kabocha, with its distinctively tasty flesh, is used in curries, stews, soups, and desserts. You may use any winter squash or sweet potatoes as a substitute.

kaffir lime leaves *(chanh Thai, bai makroot)*

If it were not for kaffir limes, Thai cuisine as we know it would not exist! This citrus fruit resembles a lime but has very knobby and intensely fragrant skin. It has virtually no juice. In Thailand, the rind and the smooth, dark-green and figure eight–shaped leaves are used to flavor soups, salads, stir-fries, and curries. Although rather hard to find except in Thai or Lao grocery stores, kaffir lime leaves are available dried, frozen, and sometimes fresh. If you are lucky enough to locate them, stock up as they will keep for months in the freezer. There is really no substitue for kaffir lime leaves, although fresh lime zest is the closest thing.

lemon grass *(xa, takrai)*

A staple herb in Vietnamese and Thai cooking, lemon grass possesses a lovely citrusy, gingery character that does wonders to any food it touches. It has two main uses— to marinate foods and to infuse broths and curries. To use, discard the tough outer layers of this woody, fibrous stalk then slice very thin before mincing. (For more detailed information, please see pages 83–84.)

long beans *(dau dua, tua fak yao)*

Although used like green beans, these leggy (usually a foot long) beans are best when cooked a little longer. Sold in 1- and 2-pound bundles, these legumes come in dark-green, light green, and purple varieties. To use, cut into 2- to 3-inch pieces and add to stir-fries, soups, and curries.

luffa squash *(muop, fak)*

My favorite of the Asian squash family. This sweet, spongy, mild-tasting vegetable is wonderful in stir-fries and soups. Similar to a long cucumber but covered with ridges and dark green skin, luffa squash is generally harvested when it's about a foot long. To use, peel the skin, then slice and cook as you would zucchini.

mint *(rau thom, bai sara neh)*

An indispensable ingredient in the Vietnamese or Thai kitchen, mint can show up in almost any dish—from salads to soups to stir-fries. The Vietnamese prefer the mild spearmint variety and love to eat the leaves raw along with meat wrapped in rice paper. A small patch of mint in your backyard will keep you well-supplied year-round.

mung means *(dau xanh, tua kieu)*

The same beans used to grow bean sprouts, these beans are prized in Vietnamese cooking. Sold husked or unhusked, they generally are soaked in warm water before cooking. Mung beans are used to add texture to savory dishes such as Saigon Crepes and to sweet puddings and other desserts.

oyster sauce *(dau hao, nam man hoi)*

Made from oyster extract, caramel sauce, and soy sauce, this thick, brown sweet-salty sauce is used to enhance stir-fries, especially those with beef. Its velvety character is particularly useful in marinades because it seals in flavor and keeps meats moist and supple after cooking. Packaged in bottles, oyster sauce is also available MSG-free and in a vegetarian version.

palm sugar *(duong cot dua, nam tan beep)*

Used extensively in Thai cooking and especially in desserts, this delicious, robust sugar is made from the sap of the palmyra palm or coconut palm. Sold in blocks, this honey-colored sugar has an interesting flavor resembling a combination of maple syrup, brown sugar, and coconut. Palm sugar is a bit hard to find but worth the effort. Substitute brown sugar and a little maple syrup for palm sugar if unavailable.

pandan leaf (*la dua, bai toey hom)*

Also known as screw pine, this long, smooth pointed leaf is used to flavor rice and desserts. It is often bruised, then cooked in a syrup, which is strained before using. Very fragrant with grass and vanilla aromas, the juice of pandan leaves is bright green and turns every ingredient it touches that color. Pandan is available frozen and occasionally fresh.

papaya, green *(du du xanh, malah goh)*

When a Thai recipe calls for this ingredient, it refers to the unripe larger Asian variety, not the papaya generally found in supermarkets. Crunchy and a bit sour, green papaya is generally peeled, then shredded and used in salads.

peanuts *(dau phong, tua lisong)*

Peanuts are used extensively in both Vietnamese and Thai cuisines, particularly as garnishes. Once roasted, they are usually ground or chopped and sprinkled on barbecued meats and salads for added texture and flavor.

peppercorn *(tieu hot, prik thai)*

Both black and white peppercorns are used extensively in Thai cooking, especially in curry pastes. For a more intense flavor, lightly roast the peppercorns before using.

rice noodles *(banh pho, guaytiew sen lek)*

Made from rice flour, water, and salt, rice noodles (sometimes labeled "rice sticks") are flat noodles used in *pad thai, pho,* and other stir-fry and noodle soup dishes. They are generally sold in 1-pound bags and come in three different widths—large, medium, and small. The larger variety is preferred for stir-fry dishes. Rice noodles are more fragile and cook faster than wheat pasta, so timing is of the essence.

rice paddy herb *(ngo om)*

Used primarily as a souring agent in soups, this herb imparts a lemony, coriander-like flavor. It is sold in bunches of tiny sprigs with green, oval-shaped leaves about $1/4$ inch long. Store this highly perishable herb in a cup, with a little water to keep the cut ends wet, and refrigerate.

rice paper *(banh trang, pan miang yuan)*

Almost transparent and very brittle, rice paper wrappers are used to make Vietnamese-style spring rolls and salad rolls. Made from rice flour, water, and salt, they must be dipped in warm water before using. Rice papers are available in square, triangle, and round shapes and come in different sizes. (For more information, please see page 29.)

rice vermicelli *(bun, sen mee)*

These thin, round angel-hair type noodles are my favorite since they are very easy to cook and have a delightful mouth-feel. Sold in 1-pound packages, these noodles cook in less than 5 minutes and maintain their moist, supple character even when left at room temperature. Once cooked, they should be rinsed under cold running water to stop the cooking and then fluffed with your hand before the strands have a chance to stick together.

rice vinegar *(giam gao, nam som)*

Distilled white vinegar generally is used in Southeast Asian cooking, but I prefer the delicacy and sweetness of rice vinegar. In many restaurants, Thai chefs are fond of splashing their stir-fries with a little sweetened rice vinegar for added flavor.

saw leaf herb *(ngo gai)*

This herb is traditionally served with Vietnamese beef noodle soup and sweet and sour soup. The leaves are narrow, about 3 to 4 inches long, and serrated. When added to hot soups, they soften and give a subtle, floral, cilantro-like aroma. The leaves are usually sold in small bunches.

sesame oil *(dau me, mam nam nga)*

Made from roasted sesame seeds and graded similarly to olive oil (that is, first and second pressings), this rich, nutty oil generally is not used for cooking but instead to flavor salads, stir-fries, soups, rice, and dumplings. I prefer the Japanese-style sesame oil, either Kadoya or Marukan brand, to the Chinese-style.

sesame seeds *(hot me, nga)*

Easily available at any grocery store, white sesame seeds are best when lightly toasted in a dry pan. In Vietnamese cookery, toasted sesame seeds are sprinkled on sweet sticky rice and other desserts made with coconut milk.

shallots *(hanh huong, hom lek)*

Small, shiny, and pinkish, shallots are used in Southeast Asia almost like yellow onions are in the West. Considered more aromatic than its onion cousin, shallots are roasted, then pounded along with lemon grass, chili, and other spices to make curry pastes or marinades. The Vietnamese like to use fried shallots as tasty garnishes for soups and salads.

shrimp, dried *(tom kho, goong haeng)*

Pungent and salty, these tiny shrimp generally are soaked in water then added to soups, stir-fries, and just about any dish in which their intense seafood flavor is desired. In Thailand, ground dried shrimp is used to sprinkle on salad, rice, and soup dishes. Avoid the tiny, flaky shrimp as their flavor is not as great as the ones that are about the size of a penny.

shrimp paste *(mam tom Thai, kapi)*

Made from fermented dried shrimp and salt, this pungent paste is used to make curry pastes, sauces, and soups. Sold in small jars or blocks, shrimp paste should be used sparingly as the odor and taste can be overwhelming to an unaccustomed Western palate.

The only time you may need to have this ingredient is when you make homemade Thai curry pastes.

soy sauce *(nuoc tuong, nam siew)*

For simplicity, think of soy sauce in three general categories—light, dark, and sweet. The first two easily can be found at any grocery store. Japanese-style sauces contain more wheat and are generally lighter and sweeter than Chinese-style ones. Both, however, may be used interchangeably in the recipes in this book. When making dipping sauces, try the lighter versions. (For more information, please see page 30.)

spring roll wrappers *(banh trang mi, pan poh pia)*

Made with wheat flour, these Filipino-style *lumpia* wrappers are sturdy and easy to use. (I prefer them to rice paper for spring rolls since they turn out less oily.) Packaged in 1-pound packets and sold frozen in Asian grocery stores, these wrappers can be used for spring rolls, egg rolls, and dumplings. Reseal unused wrappers in the package and store in the freezer.

star anise *(hoi, poy kak bua)*

This beautiful eight-pointed spice pod lends a sweet licorice flavor to stews and soups, such as the Vietnamese *pho,* or beef noodle soup. For best results, I recommend adding this spice toward the latter part of cooking as its wonderful aroma seems to subside after prolonged simmering.

star fruit *(khe, ma fueng)*

Also called carambola, this beautiful, juicy star-shaped fruit has received much media attention in the food industry but still remains too exotic for most households, probably because of its limited availability and high price. In Southeast Asia, this aromatic yellow-green fruit is sold at street corners and can be picked from roadside trees. It's eaten as a fruit, and when sliced, served as part of a table salad.

sticky rice *(nep, kao new)*

In Southeast Asian cooking, glutinous long-grain rice generally is preferred over the short-grain variety used in Japanese cooking. An important staple, sticky rice is used interchangeably with regular rice in some some parts of Asia. It is also used in desserts and breakfast dishes.

straw mushrooms *(nam rom, het)*

Small and with oval-shaped caps, these grayish-black mushrooms are prized for their mild flavor and slightly crunchy texture. Available canned and in a variety of sizes, these mushrooms are used in soups and stir-fries. You can substitute fresh white mushrooms if straw mushrooms are unavailable.

sugar cane *(mia, oi)*

In Vietnam, sugar cane is often peeled and cut into 1-inch rounds, then skewered on a bundle of bamboo sticks. To enjoy, one pulls off a piece and chews it until all the juice is sucked out. The very fibrous and stringy meat is then discarded. Another way of using sugar cane is as a skewer onto which shrimp paste is molded and then grilled. Sugar cane is also pressed to make sugar cane juice or refined into sugar. In this country, sugar cane is easily available canned and sometimes fresh. If using as skewers, the canned type works wonderfully.

tamarind *(me, mak kam)*

The soft, mushy pulp of this sour fruit is used to flavor soups, salads, and stews. Tamarind usually is sold as a syrup or in blocks. In recent years, fresh tamarind pods have turned up at Asian grocery stores. Whether fresh or in paste form, tamarind must be mashed and strained before using. If tamarind isn't available, try simulating its flavor and color (which is similar to dried prunes and lime), by substituting lime juice and brown sugar and/or lime juice and cider vinegar. For directions on preparing tamarind juice, please see page 158.

tapioca pearls *(bot ban, sa ku)*

Made from the cassava root, these "pearls" are larger than the common granules found in supermarkets. To use, soak the whitish dried pearls in warm water for 15 minutes before cooking. (They cook best when added to *boiling* liquid.) Tapioca pearls are often used in sweet puddings. Packed in ¹/₂-pound plastic bags, tapioca pearls are available at most Asian markets.

Thai basil

See basil, Thai.

Thai bird chili

See chili, Thai bird.

Thai coffee *(o liang)*

More nutty and toasty than coffee-tasting, this is a blend of coffee and roasted corn. Brew it cowboy-style—that is, boil it in water for at least 15 minutes, then strain. Serve with sweetened condensed milk and ice, or just sugar and ice. It's available in 1-pound bags at most Asian grocery stores.

Thai tea *(tra Thai, cha thai)*

A blend of black tea, vanilla, cinnamon, and other spices along with food coloring, this popular drink usually is sweetened and served with lots of ice and a splash of milk or cream on top. This tea is sold in 1-pound bags in Asian markets. Brew as you would Thai coffee.

tofu (*dau hu, tau hoo*)

Also known as bean curd, tofu is made from soybean milk and is a very delicate ingredient, both in taste and texture. There are two main ways of preparing protein-rich tofu—use as is or pan-sear it to create a golden skin on the outside. The latter technique is desirable if you want a little more texture, especially for stir-fry dishes. Packed in water, tofu is are very perishable (check the expiration date on the tub), so use it soon after you bring it home.

tree ears *(nam meo, het hoo noo)*

Also known as wood ears, cloud ears, and black fungus, these thin black mushrooms have little flavor but a pleasing crunch. Sold dried in large and small sizes, they must be soaked in hot water for about 20 minutes before using. I prefer the tiny, thin flakes as they are more tender. Avoid the larger two-toned mushrooms as they can be tough and gritty, especially around the stems. Tree ears are generally used to add texture to stir-fries, soups, and meat fillings.

turmeric *(bot nghe, kamin)*

In Thailand, turmeric is easily available fresh. Like its ginger relative, this earthy tasting rhizome is peeled, ground, and added to curries and stews. Prized for its brilliant yellow tint, turmeric is used to make curry powders. Ground turmeric works fine since it is its color, not taste, that makes it important.

water chestnut *(cu nang, haew)*

This dark brown tuber has a delicate flavor and a delightful crunch. In Asia, it is peeled, then sliced and added to salads, stir-fries, and even desserts. Canned water chestnuts, which are easily available, have the same crunchy texture yet lack flavor.

water spinach *(rau muong, pak bung)*

Also called swamp cabbage and morning glory, this leafy green vegetable has crunchy hollow stems and arrowhead-shaped leaves. In Asia, it is generally grown in swamps and ponds. The Vietnamese like to make "curls" out of the stems to use in salads and soups; the Thais and Chinese love to stir-fry the leaves and chopped stems. Water spinach can be purchased at most Asian grocery stores with a produce department or at farmers' markets. If not available, substitute spinach or watercress.

index

A

Ahi tuna
  grilled, two sauces with, 212–213

B

Baby greens, with New York steak and sweet nectarines, 97
Bananas
  flambé, 239
  with tapioca pearls, 235
Bangkok beef with basil, 149
Basic curry sauce, 37
  grilled ahi tuna with, 212–213
Basil, *see also* Thai basil
  Bangkok beef with, 149
  ginger, clams, and shrimp with, 209
  in spaghetti-squash salad with poached shrimp, 88–89
  Thai fried rice and chicken with, 188
  Thai seafood curry and pumpkin with, 210–211
Bass, *see* Striped bass
Bead thread noodle
  and chicken soup, 117
Beans, *see* Black beans; Long beans; Yellow beans
Beef
  Bangkok, with basil, 149
  carpaccio, Vietnamese, 67
  curry, spicy red, 150
  lemon grass, with rice paper, 146–147
  noodle soup, Vietnamese, 110–111
  salad, grilled with pineapple, 46–47
  steak, New York, with baby greens and sweet nectarines, 97
  steak, Thai cowboy, with roasted tomato-chili sauce, 153
  warm, on cool noodles, 184–185
Beverages
  about, 16–17
  lemon grass lemonade, 251
  Thai coffee, 249
  Thai tea, 248
  Vietnamese coffee, 250
Black beans, steamed stripped bass with, 219
Black-eyed peas, sweet sticky rice pudding with, 237
Broccoli
  Chinese, chicken flat noodles with, 180–181
  in ginger sauce, spicy eggplant, 164
Broth, *see* Soups

C

Cabbage
  leaves, Thai mushroom salad with, 160–161
  salad, Mom's, 96
  and water spinach in garlic-bean sauce, 173
Cake, lemon mousse, 246–247
Canapés, grilled eggplant with ginger and scallion, 73
Caramel
  crème, with grand marnier, 244–245
  sauce, 52
Caramelized pork in claypot, 152
Catfish
  grilled, with hoisin-peanut sauce, 208
  Mom's, in claypot, 227
Cauliflower, in sweet and sour sauce, 168
Chiang mai noodles, 194–195
Chicken
  and bean thread noodle soup, 117
  and Chinese broccoli, flat noodles with, 180–181
  with coconut milk and galanga soup, 116
  ginger, and vegetable stir-fry, 140–141
  gooey ginger, 139
  grilled lemon grass, hot and spicy, 128–129, 134
  on pan-seared noodle pillow, 186–187
  rice and ginger soup, 122
  and rice in claypot, 190–191
  Saigon, 136–137

Chicken, *continued*
    satay, 66
    stir-fried, with Thai basil, 135
    stock, 22
    Thai fried rice and basil with, 188
    Thai green curry with, 130–131
    Thai-style roasted, with sticky rice, 142–143
    very crispy, 138
Chicken salad
    minty Thai, 85
    nutty Chinese, 102–103
Chili clams, 72
Chili sauce, *see* Tomato-chili sauce
Chowders, *see* Soups
Chunky ginger ice cream, 240–241
Cilantro-curry mayonnaise, 54
Cilantro-lime soy sauce, 36
Clams
    black mussels, garlic, and pasta with, 224
    chili, 72
    ginger, with shrimp and basil, 209
Claypot
    caramelized pork in, 152
    catfish in, 227
    chicken and rice in, 190–191
Coconut milk
    about, 23
    Thai chicken soup and galanga with, 116
Coffee
    Thai, 249
    Vietnamese, 250
Cognac- and garlic-marinated lamb chops
    with spicy peanut sauce, 148
Cookies, ginger twinkles, 238
Cooking techniques, 5–8, 10–14
    braising, 11
    deep-frying, 13–14
    grilling, 13
    pan frying, 13
    poaching, 12
    simmering, 11
    steaming, 11–12
    stir-frying, 11–12
Cornish hens, Vietnamese curries
    with, 144

Crab, gingered, with Szechuan peppercorns,
    206–207
Crab cake delights, 76–77
Crepes, sizzling Saigon, 70–71
Crispy spring rolls, 60–62
Cucumbers
    salad, spicy Thai, 46–47
    soup, 118–119
Curried rice salad, 98–99
Curried rice with kaffir lime leaves, 189
Curry
    basic sauce, 37
    and cilantro mayonnaise, 54
    spicy red beef, 150
    spicy vegetable, 166–167
    Thai green, with chicken, 130–131
    Thai jungle, 165
    Thai seafood, with pumpkin and fresh
        basil, 210–211
    Vietnamese, with Cornish hens, 144
Curry pastes
    green, 38–39
    red, 41
    yellow, 40
Custard, grand marnier crème caramel,
    244–245

D

Dipping sauces
    about, 21
    ginger-lime, 34
    Thai chili, 33
    Vietnamese, 32
Duck
    five-spice, 132–133
    roasted, in salad with watercress and
        mandarin orange, 92

E

Eggplant
    grilled canapés, with ginger and
        scallion, 73
    spicy, and broccoli in ginger sauce, 164

Equipment
    food processor, 9–10
    knives, 10
    mortar and pestle, 8
    rice cooker, 9
    wok, 9

F

Firecracker prawns, 68–69
Fish, *see* Seafood
Five-spice
    duck, 132–133
    powder, about, 24
    quail, 78
Flat noodles with chicken and Chinese
        broccoli, 180–181
French Vietnamese bouillabaisse, 220–221
Fresh mussels steamed with lemon
        grass, 226
Fried shallots, 45

G

Galanga
    about, 24
    Thai chicken soup and coconut milk
        with, 116
Garlic
    black mussels, clams and pasta with, 224
    broth, and lemon grass, salmon poached
        in, 225
    shrimp, with kaffir lime leaves, 218
Ginger
    about, 24
    chicken and vegetable stir-fry, 140–141
    chicken rice soup with, 122
    clams and shrimp with basil, 209
    crab with Szechuan peppercorns,
        206–207
    and grilled eggplant canapés with
        scallions, 73
    ice cream, 240–241
    and lime dipping sauce, 34
    noodle salad, 91

    pear tart, 243
    steamed stripped bass with, 219
    twinkles, 238
Ginger sauce
    broccoli in, spicy eggplant with, 164
Glazes, passion fruit, peach scones with, 242
Glossary, 253–266
Gooey ginger chicken, 139
Grand marnier crème caramel, 244–245
Green curry paste, 38–39
    about, 24
Green onions, *see also* Scallions
    and black beans and ginger, steamed
        stripped bass with, 219
Green papaya salad, 94–95
Greens, *see* Baby greens
Grilled dishes
    ahi tuna with two sauces, 212–213
    catfish with hoisin-peanut sauce, 208
    eggplant canapés with ginger and
        scallion, 73
    lemon grass chicken, 134
    lemon grass pork chops, 151
    prawns with spicy peanut sauce, 79
    salmon with Thai basil sauce, 222–223
    shrimp paste on sugar cane (hello Tom!),
        214–215
Ground chili paste, about, 23

H

Hoisin-peanut sauce, 35
    grilled ahi tuna with, 212–213
    grilled catfish with, 208
Hot and spicy chicken with lemon grass,
    128–129

I

Ice cream
    chunky ginger, 240–241
    Saigon by night, 236
Ingredients, about
    bean sauce, 22
    chicken stock, 22

Ingredients, *continued*
  chili paste, ground, 25
  coconut milk, 23
  curry paste, green, 24–25
  curry paste, red, 28
  curry paste, yellow, 31
  curry powder, Vietnamese-style, 31
  fish sauce, 23–24
  five-spice powder, 24
  galanga, 24
  ginger, 24
  hoisin sauce, 25
  jasmine rice, 26
  kaffir lime leaves, 26–27
  lemon grass, 27, 83–84
  oyster sauce, 27
  peanuts, 28
  rice noodles, 28–29
  rice paper, 29
  sesame oil, 29
  shallots, 29
  soy sauce, 30
  spring roll wrappers, 30
  star anise, 30
  tamarind, 30–31

J

Jasmine rice
  about, 26
  steamed, 50
  sticky, 51
  stir-fried lemon grass, 198

K

Kaffir lime leaves
  about, 26
  curried rice with, 189
  spicy garlic shrimp with, 218

L

Lamb chops, cognac- and garlic-marinated,
    with spicy peanut sauce, 148
Lemonade, lemon grass, 251
Lemon grass
  about, 27, 83–84
  beef with rice paper, 146–147
  fresh mussels steamed with, 226
  and garlic broth, salmon poached in, 225
  grilled chicken, 134
  grilled pork chops with, 151
  with hot and spicy chicken, 128–129
  lemonade, 251
  stir-fried jasmine rice, 198
Lemon Grass Restaurant, 5–7, 232–233
Lemon mousse cake, 246–247
Lime leaves
  kaffir, *see* Kaffir lime leaves
Limes, and ginger dipping sauce, 34
Long beans, Thai stir-fried, 169

M

Mandarin oranges, in watercress salad with
    roasted duck, 92
Mangoes, and sticky rice, 234
Markets, Bangkok open-air, 202–203
Mayonnaise, cilantro-curry, 54
Meat, *see* Beef; Lamb; Pork
Minty Thai chicken salad, 85
Mom's cabbage salad, 96
Mom's catfish in claypot, 227
Mushrooms
  oyster, pan-seared quail with, 145
  white, salad, with cabbage leaves,
      160–161
Mussels
  black, with clams, garlic, and
      pasta, 224
  steamed with lemon grass, 226

N

Nectarines, with New York steak and baby greens, 97
New York steak with baby greens and sweet nectarines, 97
Noodles
  Chiang mai, 194–195
  cool, on warm vegetables, 174–175
  cool, warm beef on, 184–185
  flat, with chicken and Chinese broccoli, 180–181
  pan-seared, with prawns and chicken, 186–187
  Singapore, 192–193
  Thai, with prawns (Pad Thai), 182–183
  Trong's cup of, 199
  vegetarian Pad Thai, 170–171
Nutty Chinese chicken salad, 102–103

O

Oils
  scallion, 48
  sesame, 28
Onions, see Green onions; Scallions
Oranges, see Mandarin oranges

P

Pad Thai, 182–183
Pad Thai, vegetarian, 170–171
Paella, seafood, 204–205
Pan-seared noodle pillow with prawns and chicken, 186–187
Pan-seared quail with oyster mushrooms, 145
Papayas, see Green papaya salad
Passion fruit glaze, peach scones with, 242
Pasta with black mussels, clams, and garlic, 224

Peach scones with passion fruit glaze, 242
Peanut-hoisin sauce, grilled catfish with, 208
Peanut(s)
  about, 28
  roasted, 55
  spicy, sauce, 44
Pears, and ginger tart, 243
Peas, see Black-eyed peas
Peppercorns, gingered crab with, 206–207
Pork
  caramelized, in claypot, 152
  grilled chops, with lemon grass, 151
Poultry, see Chicken; Cornish hens; Duck; Quail
Prawns
  and chicken, with pan-seared noodle pillow, 186–187
  firecracker, 68–69
  Thai noodles with, 182–183
  warm, on cool noodles, 196–197
Pumpkins
  Asian, Thai clam chowder with, 120–121
  Thai seafood curry and fresh basil with, 210–211

Q

Quail
  five-spice, 78
  pan-seared, with oyster mushrooms, 145

R

Red curry paste, 41
  about, 28
Rice, see also Jasmine rice; Sticky rice
  about, 14–15
  and chicken in claypot, 190–191
  curried, with kaffir lime leaves, 189
  fried, with chicken and basil, 188
  saffron, and seafood salad, 100–101

Rice noodles, about, 29
Rice paper
    about, 28–29
    lemon grass beef with, 146–147
    wrapped salad rolls, 63–65
Rice pudding, sweet sticky, with black-eyed
        peas, 237
Roasted duck salad with watercress and
        mandarin orange, 92
Roasted peanuts, 55
Roasted tomato-chili sauce, 43

S

Saffron rice, and seafood salad, 100–101
Saigon by night, 236
Saigon chicken, 136–137
Salad rolls, rice paper wrapped, 63–65
Salads
    cabbage, Mom's, 96
    caesar, Thai, 90
    calamari, Thai, 104–105
    cucumber, spicy Thai, 46–47
    curried rice, 98–99
    ginger noodle, 91
    green papaya, 94–95
    grilled beef, with pineapple, 93
    minty Thai chicken, 85
    mushroom with cabbage leaves, Thai,
        160–161
    nutty chicken, Chinese, 102–103
    roasted duck, with watercress and
        mandarin orange, 92
    seafood, Thai, 86–87
    spaghetti-squash, with poached shrimp
        and basil, 88–89
    table, 53
Salmon cakes, spicy, 74–75
Salmon poached in lemon grass-garlic
        broth, 225
Satay chicken, 66
Sauces, see also Dipping sauces
    about, 22

basic curry, 37
    caramel, 52
    chili, roasted tomato, 43
    chili, sweet Thai, 42
    cilantro-lime soy, 36
    hoisin-peanut, 35
    spicy peanut sauce, 44
Scallions, see also Green onions
    ginger and grilled eggplant canapés
        with, 73
    oil, 48
Scones, peach, passion fruit glaze with, 242
Seafood
    ahi tuna grilled, with two sauces,
        212–213
    black mussels, clams, and garlic with
        pasta, 224
    calamari salad, Thai, 104–105
    catfish
        in claypot, 227
        grilled with hoisin-peanut sauce, 208
    clams
        and black mussels and garlic with
            pasta, 224
        chili, 72
        and ginger and shrimp with basil, 209
    crab, gingered, with Szechuan pepper-
            corns, 206–207
    crab cake, spicy, 76–77
    curry with pumpkin and fresh basil, 210–211
    mussels steamed with lemon grass, 226
    paella, 204–205
    prawns
        firecracker, 68–69
        grilled, with spicy peanut sauce, 79
        on pan-seared noodle pillow, 186–187
        Thai noodles with, 182–183
    salmon
        grilled, with Thai basil sauce,
            222–223
        poached in lemon grass-garlic
            broth, 225
    salmon cake, spicy, 74–75

shrimp
> hot and sour soup, 112–113
> poached, spaghetti-squash and basil salad with, 88–89
> spicy garlic, with kaffir lime leaves, 218
> and vegetables in sweet and sour sauce, 228
shrimp paste grilled, on sugar cane, 214–215
striped bass with black beans, ginger, and green onions, 219
trout sot ngon, 216–217
Seafood salad
> saffron rice, with, 100–101
> Thai, 86–87
Sesame oil, 29
Shallots
> about, 29
> fried, 45
Shrimp
> ginger clams and basil with, 209
> spicy garlic, with kaffir lime leaves, 218
> and vegetables in sweet and sour sauce, 228
Shrimp paste
> grilled, on sugar cane, 214–215
Singapore noodles, 192–193
Sizzling Saigon Crepes, 70–71
Soups
> beef noodle, Vietnamese, 110–111
> bouillabaisse, 220–221
> chicken and bean thread noodle, 117
> chicken rice, with ginger, 122
> chicken with coconut milk and galanga, Thai, 116
> clam chowder with Asian pumpkin, Thai, 120–121
> cucumber, stuffed, 118–119
> fisherman's, vegetarian, 158–159
> fisherman's, Vietnamese, 114–115
> hot and sour shrimp, 112–113
Soy sauce
> about, 30
> cilantro-lime, 36

Spaghetti-squash salad with poached shrimp and basil, 88–89
Spicy dishes
> crab cake delights, 76–77
> garlic shrimp with kaffir lime leaves, 218
> red beef curry, 150
> salmon cakes, 74–75
> Thai cucumber salad, 46–47
> vegetable curry, 166–167
Spicy peanut sauce, 44
> cognac- and garlic-marinated lamb chops with, 148
> grilled prawns with, 79
Spring rolls
> crispy, 60–62
> vegetarian, 162–163
Spring roll wrappers, about, 30
Star anise, about, 30
Steamed jasmine rice, 50
Steamed striped bass with black beans, ginger, and green onions, 219
Sticky rice
> and fresh mangoes, 234
> jasmine, 51
> sweet, in pudding with black-eyed peas, 237
> Thai-style roasted chicken with, 142–143
Stir-fry
> about, 11–12
> jasmine rice with lemon grass, 198
> long beans, 169
> vegetable, and ginger chicken, 140–141
Striped bass, steamed, with black beans, ginger, and green onions, 219
Stuffed-cucumber soup, 118–119
Su co's delight, 172
Sugar cane, grilled shrimp paste on, 214–215
Sweet and sour sauce
> cauliflower in, 168
> shrimp and vegetables in, 228
> Vietnamese, 49

Sweet sticky rice pudding with black-eyed peas, 237
Sweet Thai chili sauce, 42

T

Table salad, 53
Tamarind, about, 30–31
Tapioca pearls, warm bananas with, 235
Tea, Thai, 248
Thai
    caesar salad, 90
    calamari salad, 104–105
    chicken soup with coconut milk and galanga, 116
    chili dipping sauce, 33
    clam chowder with Asian pumpkin, 120–121
    coffee, 249
    cowboy steak with roasted tomato-chili sauce, 153
    cuisine, about, 5–8
    fried rice with chicken and basil, 188
    green curry with chicken, 130–131
    jungle curry, 165
    mushroom salad with cabbage leaves, 160–161
    noodles with prawns, 182–183
    seafood curry with pumpkin and fresh basil, 210–211
    stir-fried long beans, 169
    style roasted chicken with sticky rice, 142–143
    tea, 248
Thai basil
    sauce, grilled salmon with, 222–223
    stir-fried chicken with, 135
Tomato-chili sauce, roasted, Thai cowboy steak with, 153
Trong's cup of noodles, 199
Trout sot ngon, 216–217
Tuna, *see* Ahi tuna

V

Vegetables
    and shrimp in sweet and sour sauce, 228
    spicy, curry, 166–167
    stir-fry, ginger chicken and, 140–141
    su co's delight, 172
    warm, on cool noodles, 174–175
Vegetarian
    cuisine, about, 156–157
    fisherman's soup, 158–159
    Pad Thai, 170–171
    spring rolls, 162–163
Velvety chicken rice soup with ginger, 122
Very crispy chicken, 138
Vietnamese
    beef carpaccio, 67
    beef noodle soup, 110–111
    coffee, 250
    cuisine, about, 5–8
    curry with Cornish hens, 144
    dipping sauce, 32
    fisherman's soup, 114–115
    sweet and sour sauce, 49

W

Warm bananas with tapioca pearls, 235
Warm beef on cool noodles, 184–185
Warm prawns on cool noodles, 196–197
Warm vegetables on cool noodles, 174–175
Watercress, roasted duck salad with, mandarin orange and, 92
Water spinach and cabbage in garlic-bean sauce, 173

Y

Yellow bean-garlic sauce, water spinach and cabbage in, 173
Yellow curry paste, 40
    about, 31
Yummy hot and sour shrimp soup, 112–113